Digital Citizenship
The Internet, Society, and Participation

Karen Mossberger, Caroline J. Tolbert, and
Ramona S. McNeal

The MIT Press
Cambridge, Massachusetts
London, England

For information about special quantity discounts, please e-mail ⟨special_sales@ mitpress.mit.edu⟩.

This book was set in Sabon on 3B2 by Asco Typesetters, Hong Kong.
Printed on recycled paper and bound in the United States of America.

Library of Congress Cataloging-in-Publication Data

Mossberger, Karen.
Digital citizenship : the internet, society, and participation / Karen Mossberger, Caroline J. Tolbert, and Ramona S. McNeal.
  p. cm.
Includes bibliographical references and index.
ISBN 978-0-262-13485-9 (hardcover : alk. paper)—ISBN 978-0-262-63353-6 (pbk. : alk. paper)
1. Information society. 2. Citizenship. I. Tolbert, Caroline J. II. McNeal, Ramona S. III. Title.
HM851.M669 2007
303.48'33—dc22   2007002797

10 9 8 7 6 5 4 3 2 1

We dedicate this book to our parents and children

James and Theresa Pavlik; Heather and Lauren Mossberger

Bert and Anne Tolbert; Jacqueline, Eveline, and Edward Dowling

Harry and Doris McNeal

Knowledge and information are passed from older generations as a resource for the young

Contents

Preface

This book builds on prior research that all of the authors have done on different aspects of Internet use and public policy. This technology is being used by individuals to improve their lives in many ways, but we have been most interested in policy-relevant issues such as its use for economic opportunity and political participation.

We see this work as distinctly different from our collective past efforts, however, as well as other prior research. First, we recognize the benefits that society might enjoy from Internet use, but we are most concerned with viewing the issue in terms of the opportunities and rights of citizenship, and whether individuals have the capacity to participate fully in society. Drawing on sociologist T. H. Marshall, we explore the ways in which the capabilities needed for membership in society have been altered in the information age. We develop a theoretically grounded argument moving beyond economic efficiency and the availability of new technology by turning to the work of Rogers Smith and Rodney Hero, who define three traditions of citizenship in the United States: liberalism, civic republicanism, and ascriptive hierarchy. We focus on political and economic participation because of their close association with citizenship in the U.S. context, and describe the individual and collective costs of exclusion from digital citizenship as well as the benefits of inclusion.

The second way in which this research differs from some of our previous efforts is that we are now able to examine the *impact* of the Internet, rather than attitudes and experiences. The uses of the Internet are burgeoning, and currently there is fragmentary evidence of how this matters for policy-relevant concerns such as civic engagement, voting, or economic advancement. More than half of U.S. Internet users go online at work, and online news and political Web sites have helped to shape events in the past several elections. We offer evidence of the benefits of

Internet use in the political and economic arenas; and conversely, the costs of exclusion from society online.

Digital citizenship requires educational competencies as well as technology access and skills; and problems such as poverty, illiteracy, and unequal educational opportunities prevent more people from full participation online and in society more generally. Technology inequality is part of the larger fabric of social inequality in the United States.

We would like to thank Clay Morgan at The MIT Press for his support and sage advice throughout this process, and especially for his patience during our cross-country moves and the attendant delays in finishing the manuscript. We are grateful for the help of The MIT Press staff, and the useful comments of the anonymous reviewers, who improved our original efforts immeasurably.

We appreciate the collaboration of our coauthors on several chapters: Kimberly Johns, PhD candidate at the University of Illinois at Chicago, on chapter 2; Jason McDonald, assistant professor at Kent State University, on chapter 3; and Bridgett King, PhD candidate at Kent State University, on chapter 5. Gena Miller of the University of Illinois at Chicago also contributed to the literature review on gender for chapter 5. We would like to thank Steven Rathgeb Smith (University of Washington) for alerting us to Marshall's work on citizenship, and Jeff Keefe (Rutgers University) for his ideas and advice on broadband. We also thank Stuart Shulman (University of Pittsburgh) and Jeffrey Seifert (Congressional Research Service), our discussants at the 2006 American Political Science Association meeting, for their helpful comments on chapter 2. We received useful feedback from our audiences at talks given at the University of Florida and the Sam Nunn Policy Forum at the Georgia Institute of Technology. On chapter 4, we extend a special thanks to Thomas Hensley and Stanley Wearden, both of Kent State University. John Logue of Kent State University and Mike Pagano of the University of Illinois at Chicago provided invaluable funding for research assistants, some of whom are listed as coauthors above. We thank Jan Winchell (Kent State University) and Daniel Bowen (University of Iowa) for their precision in helping us compile the Current Population Survey (CPS) data used in this study.

Finally, we thank our families and friends for their forbearance, and the numerous ways in which they encouraged and sustained us throughout this project.

Digital Citizenship

1
Defining Digital Citizenship

Citizenship is a status that is bestowed on those who are full members of a community.

—T. H. Marshall, "The Problem Stated with the Assistance of Alfred Marshall," 1949

"Digital citizenship" is the ability to participate in society online. What, however, does it mean to invoke the notion of citizenship in relation to the use of a technology? More than half a century ago, British sociologist T. H. Marshall defined citizenship as endowing all members of a political community with certain civil, political, and social rights of membership, including "the right to share to the full in the social heritage and to live the life of a civilized being according to the standards prevailing in the society" (1992, 8). Information technology, we argue, has assumed a secure place today in the civilized life and prevailing standards of U.S. society. In much the same way that education has promoted democracy and economic growth, the Internet has the potential to benefit society as a whole, and facilitate the membership and participation of individuals within society. We contend that digital citizenship encourages what has elsewhere been called social inclusion (Warschauer 2003).

We define "digital citizens" as those who use the Internet regularly and effectively—that is, on a daily basis. Previous research has defined a "digital divide" in terms of access to technology (Norris 2001; Bimber 2003) or the skills to use technology as well as access (Mossberger, Tolbert, and Stansbury 2003; Warschauer 2003; Van Dijk 2005). Daily Internet use implies sufficient technical competence and information literacy skills for effective use along with some regular means of access. In 2006, digital citizens accounted for a little under half of the U.S.

population. Twenty-seven percent of Americans still do not go online at all, and are completely excluded from participation in society online (Pew Internet and American Life Project 2006).

This book examines three aspects of participation in society online: the inclusion in prevailing forms of communication through regular and effective use; the impact of Internet use on the ability to participate as democratic citizens; and the effects of the Internet on the equality of opportunity in the marketplace. Digital citizens are those who use technology frequently, who use technology for political information to fulfill their civic duty, and who use technology at work for economic gain. To understand the potential and challenges for digital citizenship, we turn to Rogers Smith's three traditions of citizenship in U.S. history: Lockean liberalism (equality of opportunity), civic republicanism (politics), and ascriptive hierarchy (inequality). These traditions demonstrate how Internet use is integral to citizenship in an information age, and why political and economic uses of the Internet differ from other activities online. The ability to participate in the civic sphere and compete in the economic realm are both central to U.S. conceptions of citizenship as embracing political community and equality of opportunity.

The following pages present new evidence that Internet use does indeed have significant benefits for democratic participation and economic welfare. We find that Internet use increases the likelihood of voting and civic engagement; it also promotes higher incomes for African Americans and Latinos in particular. Our findings establish that patterns of exclusion endure even as Internet use has grown, and that they are linked to other inequities. Economist Amartya Sen (1993) has argued that poverty and inequality should be viewed not in terms of material possessions but in light of the capacities and functioning of the members of a society. The capacity to use the Internet includes access to technology at home and in other settings, and educational and technical skills. Drawing on Sen and our empirical findings, we view digital citizenship as representing capacity, belonging, and the potential for political and economic engagement in society in the information age.

The Role of Public Policy and the Internet

The Internet is a unique technology in its varied properties and wide range of uses. It is interactive, enabling point-to-point communication through e-mail, chat rooms, and instant messaging, but also supports broadcast capability through text, video, and visual images on Web sites (DiMaggio et al. 2001; Wellman 2001). It is a telephone, library, and soapbox; it is a storehouse of information and channel for communication (DiMaggio et al. 2001). These varied properties enable new forms of participation, which may either change or replicate existing social relations. Some observers have compared the Internet to the invention of the printing press, which stimulated the demand for greater literacy in society (Rainie 2005). Such a far-reaching technology clearly has policy implications, but how best do we understand these? There are two different frameworks that can be used to evaluate the need for public policy intervention. Welfare economics emphasizes collective benefits and spillover effects. Political theory addresses the rights of citizenship and issues of social justice. While the following chapters are based on the latter, we briefly consider the spillover effects of Internet use for society as a whole before discussing traditions of citizenship.

Collective Benefits and Externalities: The Economic Perspective

Information technology has many aspects of what economists call positive externalities, which are social benefits beyond those reaped by the individuals who use the technology. If information available online helps citizens to be more informed about politics and more inclined to participate, then society as a whole profits from broader and possibly more deliberative participation in democratic processes. If modern communication technologies offer new channels for contacting officials, discussing issues, and mobilizing, then the network externalities or the benefits of bringing people together online exceed the satisfaction gained by the individual participants.

There is already evidence of spillover economic benefits as a result of readily accessible information and communication online. Technology use in industries throughout the economy has resulted in productivity gains (McGuckin and Van Ark 2001). If technology skills contribute to the development of human capital throughout the economy, including in economically underdeveloped urban and rural areas then the U.S. economy benefits. Inequality in technology use can be justified as a public policy issue if there are market failures that produce underinvestment and inhibit society's potential to capture the full benefits of the technology. This is one reason why the Internet is more than just another commodity, and why its diffusion throughout society is a matter of public concern. Expanded technology use represents positive external-ities for society that may justify a public policy response.

Our concern here, however, is based less on the logic of spillover ben-efits and the positive externalities of Internet use. Instead, we examine whether and how the Internet is integral for economic opportunity and political participation, and whether on that basis, all Americans should have the ability to use the Internet, if they so choose. This implies a con-cern for *equality*, not just a utilitarian calculation of market efficiency based on the relative costs and benefits. For this, we turn to political theory and an analysis of multiple traditions of citizenship to place the issue of digital inequality within the larger context of social equity in the United States.

From Spillover Effects to Citizenship

As mentioned earlier, Smith argues that there are multiple and contend-ing U.S. traditions regarding citizenship: liberalism, republicanism, and ascriptive hierarchy. These traditions frame our understanding of the issues related to digital citizenship. Economic opportunity is a central concern of the liberal tradition, whereas political participation is critical in the republican tradition. Smith's discussion of ascriptive hierarchy explains the persistence of disparities based on race and ethnicity in U.S. society, including digital inequalities.

Liberalism and Economic Opportunity

Lockean liberalism (originating in the philosophy of John Locke) has been called the American creed by philosopher Louis Hartz (1955). It is an individualist perspective; that values individual rights, individual ef-fort, personal liberty, and the free market (Hartz 1955, 4). Citizenship, within this framework, endows members of society with the right to pur-sue their own vision of the good life and be free from unreasonable gov-ernment interference, such as restrictions on free speech. In this sense, individualism has a negative view of liberty.

Yet overlapping and sometimes conflicting with this tradition of indi-vidualism in liberal thought is egalitarianism. The very basis of liberal citizenship is the prior belief that Americans are "born equal," in the words of Alexis de Tocqueville (Hartz 1955, 66). Comparing the development of political rights in the United States and western Europe, this belief in political equality resulted in the relatively early extension of suffrage, or the right to vote, at least to nonproperty-holding white men. The U.S. liberal tradition, though, has clearly defined economic as well as political implications.

In the economic sphere, U.S. public policy emphasizes the equality of opportunity rather than the equality of outcomes. As chapter 2 shows, U.S. citizens are willing to tolerate a greater income inequality than citizens of most other industrialized countries, and are more likely to stress individual merit as the key to success. Hartz refers to the "Horatio Alger" myth; others have called this "the American dream," and have demonstrated that the poor and the excluded often cherish most fervently the conviction that everyone has the chance to prosper (Hochschild 1995). Some scholars have described this belief in the equality of opportunity "the most distinctive and compelling element of our national ideology" (Rae et al. 1981, 64).

Implicit in the liberal tradition, however, is the expectation that the competition is fair. Government support for education stands in stark contrast to other social policy in the United States, in part because of the belief that education can provide a level playing field—the equality of opportunity, if not the equality of result. For this reason, Jennifer Hochschild and Nathan Scovronick (2000, 209) have perceptively called public education the U.S. version of the "welfare state." In the information age, digital citizenship may rival formal education in its importance for economic opportunity.

The information and communication capabilities of computers and the Internet have permeated the U.S. economy. Indeed, the impact of technology is visible in nearly every corner of the labor market, far beyond "high-tech" industries, and technology promises to increase throughout a range of occupations and industries (McGuckin and Van Ark 2001). For workers who are lower paid and less educated, computer and Internet skills may be one factor needed for mobility into better-paying jobs, with greater job security, health insurance benefits, and full-time hours. For those who are seeking new or better jobs, Web sites have become a tool for finding job openings and researching employers. Economic opportunity based on the traditions of liberalism may justify public policy to expand technology access, beyond market arguments for improved efficiency.

Republicanism and Democratic Citizenship

A second political tradition in the United States is that of civic republicanism. Rooted in the practices of the New England town meeting as well as the ideology of the American Revolution, the republican ideal promotes the widespread participation of the citizenry (Bellah et al. 1985, 30–31, 253–256; Abbott 1991, chapter 2; Skocpol 1992, 19). Yet the basis of participation is a duty toward the community rather than the individual rights of liberalism—republican virtue that promotes the common good. Virtuous citizens must consider the needs of the whole rather than self-interest, and should be enlightened and informed in order to make good decisions on behalf of the community. For Thomas Jefferson, public education offered the means of developing the skills and commitment needed for a republican polity.

This differs from the liberal vision, where education serves to enhance individual equality of opportunity. Public education began to flourish at the same time as the expansion of the suffrage during the Jacksonian period of the 1830s, when property ownership was no longer required for the right to vote. According to Theda Skocpol, "The purpose of widespread basic education, the early school reformers declared, was not to help individuals get ahead but to educate a virtuous American citizenry to serve as the democratic backbone of the Republic" (1992, 19).

More recent proposals for participatory or "strong" democracy blend the republican values of civic virtue with liberal norms advocating political equality (Barber 1984, 118; Bowler, Donovan, and Tolbert 1998). To the extent that information technology enhances information capacity and mobilizes civic participation, it may be defended in terms of republican traditions of citizenship. What economists call the positive externalities of technology might also be seen as contributing to the larger public interest. In republican thought, "the virtuous citizen was one who understood that personal welfare is dependent on the general welfare and could be expected to act accordingly," to enhance the well-being of the community (Bellah et al. 1985, 254).

The growth of e-government and the explosion of political information on the Web mean that the Internet has already become an important resource for civic and political information, through Web sites hosted by government, community organizations, interest groups, political campaigns, and news organizations, among others (Norris, Fletcher, and Holden 2001; Larsen and Rainie 2002; West 2004). Previous research has found that online news may have a mobilizing potential, increasing political participation (Bimber 2003; Krueger 2002, 2003; Tolbert and McNeal 2003; Shah, Kwak, and Holbert 2001; Graf and Darr 2004). Citizens who have used government Web sites report more positive attitudes about government at all levels, and even greater trust in government in some cases (Tolbert and Mossberger 2006; Welch, Hinnant, and Moon 2005).

In the following chapters we show technology use can facilitate civic participation, improving community engagement and democracy. Expanded technology access and use may also be justified on the grounds of promoting civic republicanism.

Ascriptive Hierarchy and Inclusion

Smith (1993) makes the argument that there is a third tradition in U.S. society, which he refers to as ascriptive hierarchy. This tradition has at times excluded large segments of the population from full citizenship based on ascriptive characteristics such as race, gender, or ethnicity. Historically, the slaveholding antebellum society of the South resembled feudalism more than liberal capitalism, and had an ideology that justified slavery and social stratification. African Americans first gained the right of citizenship only with the passage of the Fifteenth Amendment—a right that was still frequently denied in practice over more than a century of legalized discrimination comprised of white primaries, poll taxes, Jim Crow laws, and lynchings. The popularity of social Darwinism for many years is another manifestation of beliefs in ascriptive hierarchy that have flourished in the United States. Smith (1993) points to these not as a departure from U.S. ideals but as evidence of a more systematic and coherent tradition that legitimizes the exclusion of some groups from citizenship.

In the current context, those who formally possess the political, civic, and social rights of citizenship have often been deprived of inclusion as well. Rodney Hero (1992, 189) has called this "two-tiered pluralism," in which some citizens enjoy formal legal equality, but in practice suffer discrimination and diminished opportunities. Smith (1993) contends that while there has been great progress toward liberal ideals such as equal opportunity, the long and persistent traditions of ascriptive hierarchy have made the struggle an arduous one where tentative gains are threatened by potential reversals. Donald Kinder and Lynn Moss Sanders (1996) show that many white Americans have more egalitarian attitudes toward African Americans and other people of color today, but they assume that the gains of the civil rights era have eliminated discrimination. There is less recognition of the role played by institutional barriers, such as the persistence of neighborhood racial segregation, and concentrated poverty within these segregated communities.

These enduring inequalities have shaped society online. The term digital divide has been used to describe systematic disparities in access to computers and the Internet, affecting Americans who are low income, less educated, older, African American, and Latino. Studies that have used appropriate statistical methods, such as multivariate regression, have demonstrated that income, education, age, race, and ethnicity all matter for having Internet connections at home (Mossberger, Tolbert, and Stansbury 2003) or using the Internet in any place (Katz and Rice 2002).[1] These disparities have continued over time, with the exception of gender. The gender divide in Internet access has nearly closed (Katz and Rice 2002; Mossberger, Tolbert, and Stansbury 2003, chapter 2), although men continue to be more intensive users of the Internet than women (Fallows 2005). There is also a parallel skills divide, which affects the same groups and may be even more critical for limiting Internet use. The ability to use the Internet entails technical skills using hardware and software, but also literacy along with the ability to use and evaluate complex information (Mossberger, Tolbert, and Stansbury 2003).

In the following pages, we discuss more recent gaps in high-speed/broadband Internet access and their impact on skills, and show that segregation and poverty play an important role in limiting technology access and skill as well. Chapter 5 reveals persistent disparities in daily Internet use, or digital citizenship, for Latinos and African Americans, the poor and less educated. Technology inequalities that overlap with existing societal inequalities based on race or ethnicity are consistent with Smith's notion of ascriptive hierarchy. Government policy to expand technology use may be justified in removing barriers to participation online for racial and ethnic minorities, consistent with civil rights legislation.

Together, these multiple traditions offer a framework for understanding digital citizenship as an integral part of inclusion in the larger society, rather than simply providing entertainment, convenience, or even economic efficiency. Because the use of the Internet is now widespread in the United States, this new medium is affecting the way in which people engage in the public sphere and their individual economic pursuits. Like education, the Internet has the ability to provide information, skills, and networks that enable political and economic participation. Broadening access and skills supports the equality of opportunity and membership in the political community. Smith's notion of ascriptive hierarchy connects exclusion from society online with the more general fabric of discrimination and inequality. Although we find in subsequent chapters that poverty and class are also needed to fully explain digital exclusion, what we show is that inequality online does not stand apart from other inequities. We find that disparities online deepen existing inequalities and hinder full participation in society.

Digital Citizens as Frequent Participants Online

The issue of the digital divide first gained prominence in the middle of the 1990s after reports issued by the National Telecommunications and Information Administration depicted systematic inequities in home access to computers (U.S. Department of Commerce 1995).[2] The rapid growth in Internet use has meant that the Internet has become a part of daily life for an increasing number of Americans of all backgrounds. In 1997 only 18.6 percent of Americans had Internet access at home (U.S. Department of Commerce 1999). By the fifth NTIA report, *A Nation Online*, the population of Internet users constituted a majority of Americans for the first time, but there remained persistent gaps in Internet use based on race, ethnicity, age, income, and education (U.S. Department of Commerce 2002). Early work on technology inequality defined the digital divide in either/or terms—whether or not individuals have computer and Internet access at home. Recent research depicts churning in the Internet population, a more complex continuum of use, and the need for skills as well as access (Katz and Rice 2002; Lenhart 2003; Hargittai and Shafer 2006). For these reasons, we argue that the frequency of use, especially daily use, more accurately measures digital citizenship than home access or simply having used the Internet at some point. Those who have Internet connections at home may still lack the ability to find and evaluate information online, for example, because of a lack of familiarity with search strategies or even limited literacy. Infrequent use at a public library may not sufficiently develop the skills needed for the workforce or provide sufficient time to find needed information.

How Should We Measure Use?

The Pew Internet and American Life Project has surveyed Americans about their use of the Internet since March 2000. At first glance, Pew surveys show that Internet use has grown appreciably, with 73 percent of the population in February–April 2006 reporting that they have gone online "at least occasionally" in some place—home, work, school, the homes of others, or at public access sites (http://www.pewinternet.org/trends/Internet_Activities_7.19.06.htm).[3] But if we examine the proportion of Americans who use the Internet on a daily basis, this segment has grown more slowly and is much smaller—48 percent in 2006.

As of January 2005, new wording in Pew surveys asked whether respondents had ever used the Internet "at least occasionally," totaling the responses for this question with the results for a separate and similar question about the use of e-mail "at least occasionally." A respondent who had used the Internet once is counted as online using this measure. There is some utility in knowing the percentage of Americans who have had *any* experience at all with the Internet, but this does not represent the percentage able to use the Internet effectively. The question wording before January 2005 asked whether respondents ever used the Internet or e-mail. The addition of the phrase "at least occasionally" may have prompted some respondents who were infrequent users to answer in the affirmative, although this is difficult to assess.

Box 1.1 below depicts trends in the percentage of Americans using the Internet from 2000 to 2005, based on the questions that Pew has used to define the Internet population in the right-hand column. On the left, we show what the growth of the Internet over the same period looks like focusing only on those for whom the Internet is a part of their everyday lives.

Box 1.1
Daily and Occasional Internet Use, 2000–2006

	% of Americans Used Yesterday	% of Americans Occasional Use
Feb.–Apr. 2006	48	73
Feb. 2005	40	67
Feb. 2004	35	63
Feb. 2003	39	64
Jan. 2002	36	61
Feb. 2001	31	53
Mar. 2000	29	48

For 2005: "Did you happen to use the Internet yesterday?" was used for half the sample, and half the sample was asked the question below, used prior to January 2005. The new wording was used in 2006.

Prior to 2005: "Did you happen to go online or check your e-mail yesterday?"

For 2005 and 2006: "Do you use the Internet, at least occasionally? Do you send or receive e-mail, at least occasionally?"

Prior to 2005: "Do you ever go online to access the Internet or the World Wide Web, or to send or receive e-mail?"

Source: Major Moments Survey, Pew Internet and American Life Project (see February–March 2005 questionnaire/topline, which includes results from previous years; see questionnaire for May–June 2005, which accompanies the Fox 2005 report, *Digital Divisions*). Questionnaire does not include daily use or frequency of use. All data available at ⟨http://www.pewinternet.org⟩.

Measured by any amount of use, the percentage of Americans online has grown by about half since 2000. Using a question about whether individuals had used the Internet yesterday, we can see that there has indeed been growth in frequent use, from just under 30 percent of Americans in 2000 to about 48 percent in 2006.[4] This is a significant achievement, demonstrating the growing relevance of the Internet in daily life. Still, only two-thirds of those counted as Internet users went online daily as of 2006 (Madden 2006). As chapter 5 will show, variations in the frequency of use are not random but are patterned along the lines of social inequalities such as race and class.

We believe it is crucial to address the issue of how to measure Internet use, and how this influences public policy. As political scientist Deborah Stone (2002, 176) has noted, counting is not a neutral act, for it involves the way that we define issues and policy priorities. Pew reports such as "Digital Divisions" (Fox 2005) present a more nuanced picture, and acknowledge that their measures include Americans who have casual or irregular connections to the Internet. But policymakers, the media, and even some scholars see the rising numbers and assume that the gap in Internet use is vanishing, and that it is time to divert attention and resources in another direction.

The debate over how to measure Internet use has colored government reports and administration positions as well in the past few years. Earlier reports and academic studies of the digital divide focused on home access to computers and the Internet with the assumption that it provides the most frequent opportunities for use (U.S. Department of Commerce 1995, 2002; Norris 2001). The fifth NTIA report, *A Nation Online*, was the first government report to measure Internet use at any location, rather than home access, leading to an expansion of the population officially counted as online (U.S. Department of Commerce 2002). As discussed above, the 2005 Pew survey enlarged this definition even further, by including those who only occasionally have used the Internet in any venue.

Frequency is a more appropriate way to measure Internet use than either home connections or occasional use. Daily Internet use *is* most likely to occur at home, as box 1.2 shows. But a small minority of those who go online daily—20 percent or less—have used the Internet primarily at work. And as we demonstrate in chapter 2, use at work can be important for economic opportunity. Access is merely a means to an end; it is the ability to use information technology that is the ultimate goal. Digital citizens use the Internet every day for a wide range of activities; the Internet becomes integrated into their daily routines and they are more likely to acquire the skill to use the technology.

A Continuum of Access and Skill

A final reason for relying on the frequency of use as a key measure is that there is a continuum of capacities online in terms of both access to technology and the skills to use it. A useful way of thinking about informa-

Box 1.2
Where Frequent Users Go Online

	% of Those Going Online Yesterday Used the Internet at...		
	Home	Work	Both
Feb. 2005	54	17	25
Feb. 2004	55	19	23
Feb. 2003	53	20	24
Jan. 2002	61	16	20
Feb. 2001	59	17	21
Mar. 2000	56	21	20

For 2005: "Did you happen to use the Internet yesterday?" was used for half the sample, and half the sample was asked the question below, used prior to January 2005.

Prior to 2005: "Did you happen to go online or check your e-mail yesterday?" was asked before place of use.

Source: Major Moments Survey, Pew Internet and American Life Project (see February–March 2005 questionnaire/topline), which includes results from previous years, available at ⟨http://www.pewinternet.org⟩.

tion technology has been offered by Paul DiMaggio and colleagues, who define the digital divide more broadly as "inequalities in access to the Internet, extent of use, knowledge of search strategies, quality of technical connections and social support, ability to evaluate the quality of information, and diversity of uses" (2001, 310).

According to the Pew Internet and American Life Project, Americans can be characterized as highly wired, tenuously connected, or truly disconnected. The "highly wired" (Fox 2005, 12) have high-speed broadband connections, which are associated with more frequent use and a greater range of online activities. In 2006, this amounted to 42 percent of Americans—close to the proportion who are daily users (Madden 2006).

There is other evidence demonstrating that occasional use is an insufficient measure of participation online. In an earlier study, James Katz and Ronald Rice (2002) identified about 10 percent of the U.S. population as

Internet dropouts. These former users often cited the lack of an Internet connection, a broken computer, changes in circumstances that made time for going online more difficult, frustration with the medium, or a decline in interest in the Web (Katz and Rice 2002, 75). Internet dropouts tend to be younger, lower income, and less educated than current Internet users. Like other nonusers, they have less income to devote to paying for Internet connections, and may have some skill deficits that make the Internet more frustrating and less relevant. Novices are most likely to express frustration with finding information on the Internet. Compared to experienced users, they travel the Internet aimlessly and often have negative reactions to their experience online in the absence of social support (DiMaggio et al. 2001).

Mark Warschauer (2003, 111–119) identifies a number of literacies associated with computer and Internet use, which he argues are necessary for social inclusion in the information age. Skills vary widely, including information literacy (the ability to find, evaluate, and use information online) and technical competence. The poor, the less educated, older individuals, African Americans, and Latinos are significantly less likely to report being able to find information online, controlling for other factors. These same groups are also the least likely to have the technical competence to use hardware and software. In 2001, 37 percent of the population said they needed help navigating the Internet. This may include some who can use the computer, but have difficulties searching for information (Mossberger, Tolbert, and Stansbury 2003, 45). One study of a hundred randomly recruited participants observed their ability to search online for information on jobs, political candidates, tax forms, and other topics. Fully 15 percent failed to complete three or more of the tasks, despite being given all the time they needed to find the information (Hargittai and Shafer 2006).

Increasing technology skill is clearly an educational issue for some as well as a matter of technical training or exposure to technology. The Internet is a reading-intensive medium, and many Web sites have challenging content. The average government Web site, for example, requires an eleventh-grade level of reading comprehension, even though about half of the U.S. population reads at an eighth-grade level or lower (West 2005, 54). A widely cited national study of literacy conducted in the early 1990s concluded that between 21 and 23 percent of Americans function at the lowest level of literacy, barely able to do more than sign a form or read the most simple and brief of instructions. Another 20 percent have difficulty reading a few pages of text and comprehending them (Kaestle et al. 2001). Limited literacy may pose a substantial barrier to the further diffusion of Internet use or the effectiveness of some who do go online.

The importance of education is demonstrated by what Paul DiMaggio and Coral Celeste (2004) call the "deepening" of Internet use. The authors found that educational attainment is related to the amount of time that people spend online, and that it is a stronger predictor of Internet involvement in nonentertainment activities than variables such as race, ethnicity, or income. Controlling for other factors, education, years online, and youth are significantly associated with using the Internet to enhance human capital (visiting Web sites involving school, work, health, finances, or science) or social capital (visiting sites related to news, government, or politics). These findings are especially relevant for understanding the link between educational competencies and digital citizenship.

As the motivation to go online and physical access to the Internet become more widespread, disparities still remain in the frequency of use and digital skills, according to Jan Van Dijk (2005, 73). It is not only those who are "truly off-line" who are likely disadvantaged in terms of the ability to use technology effectively—to find information or have appropriate job skills. Those who drop out or have a tenuous connection to the Internet through others, or via infrequent use at public access sites, may also be among those left behind. These issues will be analyzed in more depth in chapter 5, where we examine the patterns and causes of inequality.

As subsequent chapters will show, the development of the Internet and the migration of more Americans online over the past decade represent significant social changes with many potential benefits. But in contrast to those who claim that the digital divide is disappearing over time, we see a substantial minority (up to half of the U.S. population) lagging behind in a society that is largely online and using technology in an expanding variety of pursuits.

Approach and Methods

This book examines information technology use by analyzing data from recent national opinion surveys conducted by the Pew Internet and American Life Project, the Pew Research Center for the People and the Press, the American National Election Studies (NES), and the U.S. Census Bureau/CPS. Individual chapters describe in greater detail the sources of the data and the methods used to analyze the data. A summary of methods is provided within each chapter, but with more technical details contained in separate sections in each chapter, so those wishing to skip this discussion may do so.

Many studies on the social impact of the Internet and the digital divide have relied on descriptive statistics, case studies, or other methods of analysis that lack multivariate controls to untangle the overlapping influences. These can be useful for understanding trends, as the summaries of the Pew surveys in this chapter showed. In the rest of the book, we use a number of multivariate methods that allow us to explore the causes of trends, including the relative importance of overlapping influences such as income and education. Understanding the role of the Internet in fostering civic and political participation also requires the use of methods that can better untangle cause and effect. A common problem in previous studies is that individuals who use online political information may be more interested in politics, younger, or different in some other ways due to self-selection. In the chapters on civic engagement and political participation, two-stage causal models are used to isolate cause and effect as well as remedy selection bias (or endogeneity problems). We also rely on a variety of advanced statistical methods.

For those who are familiar with multivariate methods, these include logistic regression (for binary outcome variables), ordinal logistic regression (for ordinal outcome variables), multinomial probit (for nominal outcome variables), Poisson regression (for count outcome variables), and calculations of the standard errors that correct for problems that can lead to biased estimates using robust standard errors. Depending on the coding of the dependent variables, these methods are used in models in various chapters. In our analysis of the large-sample CPS data, we use "subsample" analyses, predicting technology access or the frequency of Internet use for subsamples of the population, such as African Americans,

Latinos, the poor, or the less educated. These fine-grained analyses allow us to isolate the factors that encourage technology use for disadvantaged groups more accurately than standard statistical methods, and also provide controls for endogeneity and selection bias concerns.

Despite the advanced methods underlying the findings, we present the results in a format accessible to readers without a background in statistics. We will use "what matters" tables that list statistically significant factors along with probability simulations (or predicted values) that are as easy to understand as simple percentages, but that are based on the regression coefficients, and so show the relative size of the impact on outcomes. All multivariate regression tables will be included in an appendix for those who wish to examine our data and results in greater detail.

The Plan of the Book

Chapters 2 through 4 assess the benefits of inclusion in society online—how the Internet matters for economic advancement, civic engagement, and political participation. This constitutes the empirical evidence for digital citizenship as part of the liberal and republican traditions. In chapters 5 and 6, we analyze patterns of exclusion from society online and the extent to which they resemble ascriptive hierarchy. The conclusion evaluates digital citizenship and the costs of exclusion in light of the prior evidence and Smith's framework.

Chapter 2 examines the growing income inequality in the new economy and asks what role Internet use might play in economic opportunity, especially for less-educated workers, who are more likely to lack technology skills. Most research examining the effects of information technology use on wages predates the Internet and the widespread diffusion of technology in the workplace, and there is little national evidence on the impact of technology use for less-educated workers. Using the 2003 CPS as well as 2002 and 2005 Pew national opinion data, we examine the impact of Internet use at work on wages for all workers, and also for lower-skilled workers with a high school education or less. If technology use does indeed lead to increased economic opportunity, public policy based on expanding skills and the equality of opportunity is justified in the tradition of liberal individualism.

Few published studies have explored the effect of the Internet on civic engagement, which is essential to the republican tradition of citizenship. Those studies that do exist use older data or fail to analyze the impact of Internet use on varying forms of engagement simultaneously (Jennings and Zeitner 2003; Uslander 2004; Price and Cappella 2001; Kim et al. 2004; Shah, Kwak, and Holbert 2001). Does Internet use lead to a more informed, engaged, and politically interested electorate, contributing to civic republicanism? Drawing on recent research, we hypothesize in chapter 3 that the Internet may be a new stimulus for political knowledge, interest, and discussion.

Chapter 4 takes a further step, asking whether varied uses of the Internet increase political participation. Just as Jefferson and others have championed education for its potential to enhance civic and political knowledge, interest, and participation, public policy to expand technology access may be justified on similar grounds. While earlier research has found that the use of the Internet increases voting and political participation (Bimber 2003; Tolbert and McNeal 2003), no published research has explored the influence of varying forms of Internet use (e-mail, chat rooms, and online news) on political participation. We also compare the effects of the Internet to other media.

Chapter 5 offers new evidence to define digital citizenship (daily Internet use) using the 2003 large-sample CPS conducted by the U.S. Census Bureau. Using multivariate statistical methods (logistic and ordered logistic regression) and a sample population of over one hundred thousand U.S. adults, we present models for home Internet access and use. Most important, we determine the factors leading to digital citizenship or daily Internet use. Given the large sample sizes, we are able to conduct subsample analyses predicting access and use for the poor, the less educated (high school degree or less), racial minorities (African Americans and Latinos), and older and younger samples of the population. Our analysis of younger respondents, in particular, suggests implications for the future.

A new dimension of technology inequality is broadband or high-speed access, which is examined in chapter 6. Broadband users are those with digital subscriber lines (DSL), cable modems, wireless connections, or fiber (T-1) connections, and as of 2006, 42 percent of Americans had high-speed access (Horrigan 2006). We analyze patterns of broadband adoption and ask whether broadband use may encourage skill development and the migration of daily tasks online. Although broadband access has now become more widespread, there are marked disparities in rural areas, and other gaps in broadband access and use are clearly related to social factors rather than infrastructure.

Chapter 7 ties together the previous evidence by discussing the costs and causes of exclusion from digital citizenship. The conclusion also presents a claim for policy attention to technology, and recommends federal and subnational policy to create universal access and equal educational opportunity.

2

The Benefits of Society Online: Economic Opportunity

with Kimberly Johns

There is strong evidence that the Internet has played a major role in the productivity revival experienced by the U.S. since the early 1990s....[Yet] there is increasing concern that unequal access to Internet services is contributing to widening inequalities in income, wealth, and power.
—Charles Ferguson, Brookings Institution, 2002

The development of Web browsers and commercial applications for the Internet contributed to what has been characterized by some economists as the "Roaring Nineties," which produced robust economic growth (Krueger and Solow 2001). When viewed over the longer term, however, technology has also reshaped the terrain of the U.S. job market and contributed to widening inequality. In order to understand the role of information technology for economic opportunity, we ask whether computer and Internet use on the job benefits U.S. workers by raising wages beyond what they would otherwise receive, given their other qualifications and characteristics. There has been some prior evidence indicating that this is so, along with some debates over this research. Our findings update earlier studies on the benefits that individuals receive from technology use at work, as most research predates the Internet and the visible productivity gains from technology in the 1990s.

A more pointed question, though, is whether or not public policy should encourage the acquisition of digital skills among those who are least likely to have them—low-income workers, the least educated, and the unemployed. Information technology use on the job is most prevalent in occupations requiring higher education levels, such as professional and managerial jobs (U.S. Department of Commerce 2002). Do technology skills matter for less-educated Americans in terms of their economic well-being? If so, those who are already disadvantaged in the job market because of discrimination and lesser skills may have this disadvantage compounded. Part of our analysis in this chapter highlights the benefits of information technology use for less-educated workers. Prior research on the benefits of technology use among less-educated employees—those who have a high school diploma or less—is based on employer surveys in several cities. Using national data on actual earnings, we find that technology is in many ways even more important for income among these individuals. We offer new and comprehensive evidence that technology skills are critical for wages, among disadvantaged workers as well as all workers. This provides a strong case for digital citizenship as a societal concern.

While all of the advanced industrialized countries experienced rapid increases in income inequality during the 1980s and 1990s, this inequality has grown most extensively in the United States (Morgan and Kim 2006; Jacobs and Skocpol 2005; Friedman 2003). This is not merely the result of an expansion of wealth at the top of the income distribution but of the declining fortunes of many Americans as well. Compared to other industrialized nations, the United States has substantially more poverty, whether calculated in relative terms in distance from the median income or in absolute terms based on cross-national standard-of-living measures (Smeeding and Rainwater 2001). For some Americans, especially those at the bottom of the wage distribution, there has been a decline in real wages during this same period (Krueger 2003).

In the liberal tradition, the equality of opportunity is a more important value than the equality of outcomes. If workers are rewarded differentially for the choices they make based on their interests, natural talents, or the amount of effort they are willing to devote to economic success, then income inequality is fair in the view of most Americans. But such inequality is sanctioned by public opinion only if there are equal opportunities to succeed.[1] As the following section will show, widening income inequality in the United States is at least partially caused by changes in skills. The consequences of technology disparities are unequal chances to participate in the economy and prosper.

We review prior research on the importance of technology for economic opportunity and then present new findings based on multiple sources. First, we examine the comprehensive, large-sample CPS. The most recent CPS that includes questions about information technology use was conducted in 2003, and its large size yields representative samples even for smaller subgroups in the population, such as minorities or less-educated employees. We supplement these analyses with data drawn from the Pew Internet and American Life Project in 2002 and 2005. In contrast to the CPS, the Pew opinion surveys contain information about the frequency of technology use at work. We have argued that the frequency of use is a proxy for skill, and so this should provide a more nuanced test of the role of technology use in the labor market.

Beyond Amazon and Silicon Valley

The Internet has had highly visible impacts on business and the economy as well as more subtle but far-reaching effects. There is evidence that information technology has increased productivity and growth, while checking inflation rates (Welfens and Jungmittag 2003). Productivity gains during the 1990s were attributed to industries that produce technology *or* those outside the information technology industry that use it intensively (Stiroh 2001). Information technology has continued as a "major driver" of growth well beyond the 1990s, according to the U.S. Department of Commerce (Gallagher 2005). Computer use and higher productivity reduced the inflation rate by 0.3 to 0.4 percentage points in the period between 1987 and 1998—that is, goods and services in the economy were cheaper because of the increased efficiency with which they were produced (Crepon and Heckel 2002). Some scholars argue that information technology will lead to long-term deflationary trends, reducing the costs of doing business in every industry (Tapscott, Ticoll, and Lowy 2000). Lower costs combined with greater productivity also produce increases in real wages for individuals (Tanaka 2004).

Throughout the 1980s and the early 1990s, economists puzzled over the absence of any discernible productivity gains from the widespread application of computer technology—a mystery that Robert Solow termed the "productivity paradox" (Blinder 2000). This paradox disappeared by the late 1990s, as it became clear that information technology was powering growth and productivity (Mishel, Bernstein, and Schmitt 2001, 19–20; Barrington 2000). The appearance of Web browsers in the early 1990s and the growing popularity of the Internet were not the only factors enhancing the use of information technology by businesses and consumers during the 1990s. Better and cheaper hardware and software increased the utility of computers in many other ways (Atkinson 2004). But the Internet provided a newfound ability to network operations, communicate with suppliers and consumers instantly, and market products on the Web.

Perhaps the most obvious development was the emergence of e-commerce, conducted on Web sites from Amazon.com to zworld.com (which sells computer keyboards).[2] But e-commerce is still dwarfed by old-fashioned commerce, as it accounts for only 3 percent of the total adjusted sales (U.S. Department of Commerce 2007). Technology can also have an impact because of investment and use throughout the economy, in manufacturing, retail, banking, transportation, health care, and other sectors. The need for high-tech applications varies across industries, but the demands for technology innovation and proficiency reach well beyond Silicon Valley. Almost two-thirds of the growth in investment can be attributed to information technology (Welfens and Jungmittag 2003, 15), and this investment continued to expand in 2004 and 2005 (Gallagher 2005). The emergence of broadband is predicted to accelerate the adoption of Internet strategies by firms (OECD 2003).

The integration of Internet applications throughout the economy is fueling economic growth and has the broadest implications for understanding the role of technology skills in the workforce. The gains in productivity that first appeared in the 1990s are likely to continue, albeit at a slower pace (Litan and Rivlin 2002). Experts predict that it is the "old economy" sectors that will account for future growth, and that this will be "not from new activities, but from faster, more efficient conduct of existing ones—faster, cheaper handling of information needed in ordinary business transactions such as ordering, billing, and getting information to employees, suppliers, and customers" (Litan and Rivlin 2002, 6). Delta Airlines, for example, has cut the time for loading planes in half and reduced the number of workers by half with the introduction of Internet terminals at gates to direct baggage handling, cleaning, and fueling. Federated Department Stores uses the Internet to disseminate information from the floor throughout the company, and has decreased inventory costs and improved pricing decisions (Sommers and Carlson 2003).

Whether increases in productivity and growth will persist over the long term depends on how that technology continues to be used, with sustained innovation, investment in capital, the reorganization of work processes, and worker training (Bresnahan 1999; Autor, Katz, and Krueger 1998; Allen 2001; Arnal, Ok, and Torres 2003). The increased use of the Internet has changed work processes and required more training as part of the reorganization of work practices (Arnal, Ok, and Torres 2003; OECD 2003). Technology creates a need for the continuous updating of employee skills through human resource development (Wentling, Waight, and King 2002, 11). This contributes to the stock of human capital in the economy.

Information Technology and Economic Change

At the same time that the economy as a whole has clearly benefited from the introduction of new technologies, less-skilled workers have borne the costs of economic change. Information technology has been a contributing factor in rising income inequality over past decades (Autor, Katz, and Krueger 1998; Acemoglu 2002). Other explanations for greater wage inequality and the simultaneous decline in real wages for less-educated workers include trade, globalization, the weakening of unions, and changes in the supply of skilled workers; but a consistent theme is the role of technological change and rising skill demands (for reviews, see Katz 2000; Acemoglu 2002).

Declining wages for less-educated workers are in part due to shifts toward more knowledge-intensive industries and away from manufacturing. This creates a demand for higher levels of education as well as technology use. Knowledge-intensive (and information technology–intensive) industries such as telecommunications, finance, business, and insurance comprise more of the economic activity of the United States than ever before. In 2003, these knowledge-intensive industries accounted for 25 percent of the value added in the United States (OECD 2005b). Information is increasingly important in the economy and leads to competitive advantage (Wentling, Waight, and King 2002, 15).

There have been changes within industries as well. Information technology has had contradictory effects, raising the skills needed for some jobs and spurring the development of new occupations, while lowering the skills and compensation for other jobs, or eliminating them entirely

(Autor, Levy, and Murnane 2003; Capelli 1996). Frank Levy and Richard Murnane (1996) explain that work can be categorized as consisting of routine tasks that computers can perform at practical costs or as exceptional tasks that entail a higher cost when performed through computers rather than human labor. Innovations such as online banking have eliminated some routine tasks performed by bank clerks, for example. But such Internet applications have also created new occupations or increased the demand for some existing job categories. More highly skilled technicians, systems analysts, security specialists, Web designers, and others are needed to implement online banking.

The overall effect of technological change has been to raise the level of skill in the workforce. The demand for college graduates has increased *within* industries and is not just a reflection of a shift away from manufacturing. Occupations with higher average pay and higher educational requirements expanded more rapidly between 1984 and 1993 in those sectors that adopted computer technology at a faster rate (Autor, Katz, and Krueger 1998; see also Dunne, Haltiwanger, and Troske 1997). Economists view the spread of computers as not only an increase in the demand for computer users and technicians but more broadly as part of a technological change that has altered the organization of work and thereby affected the need for workers with various skills (Autor, Katz, and Krueger 1998). In a review of research from member countries of the Organization for Economic Cooperation and Development, Young-Hwa Kim (2002) concluded that there has been a general effect of "up-skilling" since the 1980s, and that there is a positive relationship between this upskilling of the workforce and the use of information technology in the economy.

In their study of wages and skills, David Brauer and Susan Hickok (1995) found that technological change is the most important factor driving the rising wage inequality between low-skilled and high-skilled workers. Because highly educated workers are more likely to employ computers, the growth in computer use alone accounts for as much as 40 percent of the increase in the return to education, or the "wage premium" enjoyed by more educated workers (Brauer and Hickok 1995). Using CPS data from 1979 and 1989, the authors found that technological change had reduced the total of wages paid by industry for all skill levels, except for college graduates. This suggests a significant displacement of low-skilled or less-educated workers (Brauer and Hickok 1995).

Subsequent to the time period discussed by the Brauer and Hickok study, the Internet has decentralized the distribution of work within organizations and across space, and this leads to pressures eliminating jobs for lower-skilled workers as well. Outsourcing, facilitated by the Internet, is most detrimental for less-educated workers. Networking allows job functions to more easily move to distant locations to capture the lowest prices for labor. Less-educated workers are less likely to relocate than college-educated workers (Bound and Holzer 2000). From the perspective of the economy as a whole, relocation and/or outsourcing may lower costs. Yet the brunt of the impact may be shouldered by individual workers who have lost their jobs and find that there are relatively fewer opportunities available for low-skilled workers (Autor 2001).

This description depicts a complex set of changes in which higher levels of skill include educational attainment as well as computer competencies. Technological change has also emphasized the importance of building "human capital" through education, training, and skills development. The remainder of this chapter will explore the effects of computer and Internet use on wages, reviewing existing research and presenting new analysis.

Impacts for Individual Workers

A growing percentage of workers at differing educational levels use computers and the Internet at the workplace. Frequencies from the most recent (2003) CPS data used in the multivariate analysis for this chapter indicate that 72 percent of Americans who are employed and have more than a high school education use computers at work, and 58 percent of employed Americans with more than a high school education use the Internet on the job. This compares with 35 percent of workers with a high school education or less who use computers at the workplace, and 21 percent of less educated employees who use the Internet at work. There is about a 37 percent point gap between high- and low-skilled workers for both computer and Internet use. Still, more than a third of less educated workers use computers at work, and more than a fifth go online at their jobs.

What influence do information technology use and skills have on individual economic opportunity? Some existing studies indicate that technology use at work increases wages, but this is subject to some debate, and there are real gaps in the research in this area. Yet it is one of the most important questions to ask if we want to justify expanding technology access.

Wage growth in occupations in the 1980s and early 1990s was associated with computer use (Card, Kramarz, and Lemieux 1996; Autor, Katz, and Krueger 1998). Prior research (predating the Internet) indicates that individual workers enjoy higher wages in return for computer use, beyond what their education and occupation would predict. In a widely cited study of 1980s' CPS data, Alan Krueger (1993) estimated the premium for computer use to be wages that were 14 percent higher in 1984 and 16.5 percent higher in 1989 than for similarly situated workers who did not use computers. He explained these findings as the result of greater productivity for workers with technology skills. David Autor, Lawrence Katz, and Alan Krueger (1998) found a similar premium for the early 1990s. Other studies showing increased wages for technology use at work include research on Canada (Reilly 1995; Morissette and Drolet 1998), Australia (Miller and Mulvey 1997), the Netherlands (Oosterbeek 1997), and the United Kingdom (Arabsheibani, Emami, and Marin 2004) as well as for older workers in the United States (Friedberg 2001). Most of these studies indicated that the wage premium attributable to technology use ranged between 10 and 15 percent (Arabsheibani, Emami, and Marin 2004), but there are some exceptions. The studies cited above examined data from earlier time periods when there was little Internet use outside some scientific and academic circles.

The pioneering study by Krueger (1993) was criticized by John DiNardo and Jörn-Steffen Pischke (1997), who used their analysis of German data to argue that workers using pencils or sitting down on the job enjoy higher wages as well. Although Krueger controlled for observable differences such as educational attainment and occupation, there may be unobservable factors other than computer use that contribute to higher wages in certain occupations (for example, more talented workers being assigned to jobs using computers). In fact, one study using panel data indicated that French workers who were among the first to employ computers and other new technologies on the job tended to be the most qualified workers, and that controlling for this, the wage premium for computer use was approximately 2 percent rather than 15 percent (Entorf, Gollac, and Kramarz 1999). The French research contained some unique data that would be difficult to replicate. Yet the French study also focused on employees who were in the vanguard of the early diffusion of a technology. During a period of widespread use, unobserved individual differences among workers may be less of a threat to validity. One group of scholars responded to the "unobserved variables" critique of Krueger's work by using two-stage models (Heckman's regression) to control for endogeneity in their study of British computer use, and they found a wage premium comparable to Krueger's study over the same period in Britain (Arabsheibani, Emami, and Marin 2004).

Another criticism is that technology use represents only one part of the rising skill requirements in the workforce. Timothy Bresnahan (1999) concludes that cognitive abilities and people skills account for more of the return to increases in education and skills than information technology use, although he does find some positive effects for technology use as well. While we are most concerned here with the impact of technology skills, we acknowledge that they may be just one part of the changing skill set demanded in the new economy.

This highlights the need to better understand whether technology use significantly increases the wages of less-educated workers. Phil Moss and Chris Tilly (2001) conclude from a review of the literature that skill needs are indeed rising for jobs at all levels, not just managerial or professional jobs. According to a telephone survey of employers in four cities, the needed competencies include computer skills as well as other "hard" skills such as reading, writing, and math, and "soft" or social skills (Holzer 1996; Moss and Tilly 2001). Forty percent of the employers who were surveyed mentioned some increase in the level of skills needed for jobs requiring a high school diploma or less, and computer use was cited by about 70 percent of these employers as the reason for the rising requirements. Across occupations, computer use was mentioned as a reason for increasing skills in 92 percent of the clerical occupations that had experienced an increase, 63 percent of the customer service jobs with rising skills, and 48 percent of the blue-collar jobs with changing skills (Moss and Tilly 2001, 55). In a separate set of face-to-face interviews with employers, "the most common skill change reported" was the requirement for computer skills, but the need for other hard and soft skills was also commonly cited as accompanying these changes (Moss and Tilly 2001, 63–64).

The multicity survey cited by Moss and Tilly in the preceding paragraph was also analyzed by Harry Holzer (1996). Between 1992 and 1994, employers were randomly sampled in four cities: Boston, Detroit, Atlanta, and Los Angeles. Holzer (1996, 116–117) found that computer skill requirements were a significant determinant of wages for noncollege jobs across all racial, ethnic, and gender groups, but that white females were the most heavily rewarded for computer use at work. Those who were the least likely to experience higher wages for computer use were African American and Latino males (Holzer 1996, 125, 127–128). Other factors that were significant across the models for all workers were requirements for reading and writing, a high school diploma, vocational training, and experience (Holzer 1996, 116–117). The dependent variable in this study was the log of the weekly starting wage of the last person hired in each of the firms responding to the survey. While suggestive, these data are neither as comprehensive nor as precise as the national CPS, which is based on the current wages of individual respondents. Additionally, there may have been considerable change since the early 1990s. With the emergence of the Internet and the more widespread use of information technology in the workforce, a more recent assessment of the impact of technology is needed.

There is some initial research on Internet use in the United States. Ernest Goss and Joseph Phillips (2002) found that in the manufacturing sector, Internet users were paid more highly—a wage premium of 13.5 percent. Controlling for other factors influencing pay, Internet use was still a significant predictor of higher wages. This study was based on the 1998 CPS and was limited to one economic sector. The work by Goss and Phillips (2002), and earlier research on computers by Krueger and his colleagues, all indicate that Internet use at work might have similar effects across the economy.

Using more recent and complete data, we test whether the income gap due to Internet use is significant beyond the manufacturing sector. Does the frequency of use matter, given that we have defined digital citizenship as regular and effective use? We are also interested in how information technology affects workers in different occupations. Are the benefits of technology concentrated primarily in high-level managerial and professional jobs, or are they spread to a greater extent throughout the workforce? To better understand the consequences of digital citizenship, it is also important to investigate differences in the benefits of technology use for less-educated workers and minorities. Women, African Americans, and Latinos are even more likely than others to view information technology as an avenue for increasing economic opportunities in the United States (Mossberger, Tolbert, and Stansbury 2003). Can Internet skills confer some advantages in the job market that might offset, to some extent, other inequities? There is currently a lack of recent national research that directly evaluates the effects of the Internet on the wages of U.S. workers.

In the next section, we use the 2003 CPS to test the impact of information technology use at work for employee earnings, first using a general sample, and then examining a subsample of only less-educated workers (with a high school diploma or less). The sample of less-educated workers has two advantages. First, it allows us to test whether technology use at work is consequential for this group, which is also most likely to experience digital inequality. Second, analyzing the subsample permits us to better isolate the effects of Internet use from education—the endogeneity problem, when education leads to both better-paying jobs and a greater likelihood of Internet use. Next, we supplement this analysis with survey data collected by the Pew Internet and American Life Project in 2002 and 2005 to examine the significance of the frequency of Internet use at work for income. This is important, given our emphasis on the frequency of use for digital citizenship.

Approach

We explore the impact of Internet use at work using the 2003 CPS, which is the most recent survey conducted by the U.S. Census Bureau that includes a supplement on information technology use. The large-sample survey not only provides accurate estimates of the population as a whole but also information on weekly earnings that is not found in most other sources. The CPS does not, however, include data on the frequency of computer or Internet use at work. Additionally, we examine the effects of frequent use and online training using national opinion data collected in 2002 and 2005 by the Pew Internet and American Life Project: *The May 2002 Workplace Email Survey* and *The Internet and American Life Major Moments Survey, February–March 2005*. These surveys feature questions about Internet use at work, job training activities, and income. The Princeton Survey Research Associates conducted the random national telephone surveys for Pew, and the U.S. Census Bureau collected the data for the CPS. Our primary hypothesis is that Internet use at work leads to higher incomes for employees, controlling for other factors, including education, occupation, and age. The following section provides a detailed explanation of our methods and variable coding for all three surveys. For those who are less interested in methods, you may skip to the findings in the section ("Results") that follows.

Discussion of Methods and Variable Coding

Data and Methods: 2003 CPS

In order to explore the impact of technology access at work on wages, we turn to the 2003 CPS March Supplement on information technology conducted by the U.S. Census Bureau. The national random sample survey includes over 103,000 respondents. This sample (a hundred times larger than a typical national opinion survey) provides accurate estimates of the population as a whole, with detailed questions about occupations and employment as well as technology use. This unique data set allows a rigorous empirical test of whether computer and Internet use at work leads to increased income, especially among subpopulations, such as those with a limited education. We estimate multivariate regression models to predict weekly earnings for the population as a whole and less-educated Americans.

We begin by filtering our sample population for only employed workers in the labor force. Of the 103,000 respondents in the sample, 62 percent (or 64,259) are employed at work and 2 percent (or 2,193) are employed/absent from the job. These individuals are included in the analysis. The remaining respondents in the sample are unemployed due to a layoff (.34 percent), unemployed but looking for a position (3 percent), not in the labor force due to retirement (17 percent), not in the labor force because of a disability (4.5 percent), or not in the labor force for some other reason (11 percent). These respondents were excluded from the analysis. Additionally, we include a binary variable in our models coded 1 if the respondent is employed full-time, and 0 if the respondent is employed part-time. We expect full-time workers will earn more than those in the labor force part-time.

The primary dependent (or outcome) variable measures weekly earnings of the respondent in dollars. A limitation of these data is missing values for the variable measuring income. Of the 103,000 respondents, 90 percent had missing values on the weekly earnings question, because the CPS rotates the percentage of panel respondents who are asked about earnings. Because of missing data on the dependent variable, our models included 14,851 cases/individuals. This sample is still almost fifteen times larger than a typical thousand-person survey, and is still randomly selected. As a follow-up analysis, we measure the annual household income of the respondent as the dependent variable. Unlike weekly earnings, almost all respondents in the survey answered questions about annual household income yielding a full sample of a hundred thousand cases.

Three questions are used as the primary explanatory (independent) variables, each measuring technology use at work. The respondents were asked if they used a computer at work, engaged in "computer use at work for internet or e-mail," and had used the Internet this year to take courses. The latter question was included to find out whether Internet use for increasing skills had any effect on wages. Affirmative responses to each question were coded 1 (yes) and 0 (no). These three binary variables serve as our explanatory variables, and separate our sample among those who use technology on the job and those who do not. Separate regression models are estimated for the three types of technology use on the job.

Beyond technology use at work, many other factors are known predictors of income and earnings, especially occupation. An advantage of the CPS data beyond standard surveys is detailed employment information. We use the eleven industry and occupation job categories measuring a respondent's primary occupation.[3] A series of binary (1/0) variables was created for each occupation, with production as the reference (left-out category).[4] We expect that management and professional occupations will have the highest earnings. As an additional control, we include a binary variable measuring whether the respondent is employed in the job sector that the U.S. Census defines as the "information industry," which includes technology/computing jobs as well as publishing. We would expect those employed in the information industry to have a higher probability of using computers and the Internet at work.

Our models also include standard demographic controls given known earnings gaps based on gender, race, age, and education. We expect that white males who are older with a higher education will earn more than minority females who are younger with a lower education. By including these demographic variables in the models, we control or hold constant the effect of demographic factors on earnings. A binary variable measures gender, with females coded 1 and males 0. Compared to standard surveys, our national data include large and representative samples of African Americans and Latinos. Of the 103,000 total sample, 10 percent (or 10,113) reported being of Hispanic origin, and almost 10 percent (or 9,920) reported being black.[5] Additionally, almost 5 percent (or 5,037) were Asian American. Three binary variables measure whether the respondent is an African American (coded 1), Latino (coded 1), or Asian American (coded 1), with white non-Hispanic as the reference group. Age is measured in years. It serves as a proxy for experience; we presume that older employees have greater job experience and will earn more. The educational attainment of the respondent is measured on a 5-point ordinal scale ranging from 1 (less than a high school degree) to 5 (a bachelor's degree or higher). Geography/location is measured with binary variables for urban and suburban residents, with rural residents and those who did not identify their location as the reference group (coded as 0). Private sector and federal government jobs tend to pay more than local governments and nonprofits. We use a series of binary variables to measure the job sector (federal government, private, or local government), with state government and nonprofit sectors as the reference category coded 0. Including a different grouping of binary variables for the job sector does not change the substantive findings reported here.

Data and Methods: 2002 and 2005 Pew Surveys

As a robustness check, we also examine the 2002 and 2005 Pew surveys with multivariate regression used to model the effects of the frequency of

Internet use and other factors on the respondent's personal income. The dependent variable is an 8-point ordinal scale, where 1 indicates that the family income in the previous year ranged from $0 to $10,000, and 8 signifies a family income of $100,000 or higher. We use two alternative measures of Internet use at work. Internet use at work is measured with a binary variable, where yes responses are coded 1, and no responses are coded 0. This coding is comparable to the coding used in the above CPS analysis.

Because we have emphasized the importance of the frequency of Internet use as a preferable way to measure skills and digital citizenship, we measure the use of technology at work on an ordinal scale. In the 2002 survey question, the wording was: "Counting all of your online sessions, how much time did you spend using the Internet yesterday [at work]?" The responses were coded on an 8-point scale from 1 (less than fifteen minutes) to 6 (two to three hours) to 8 (four or more hours). For the 2005 survey, the question wording was: "In general, how often do you use the Internet from work—several times a day, about once a day, three to five days a week, one to two days a week, once every few weeks, or less often?" The responses were coded on a 6-point scale, with 6 equal to several times a day, and 1 equal to "less often." These detailed questions on the frequency of Internet use at work create a measure of skills associated with access and their impact on employee income.

The models also include a number of demographic and socioeconomic factors that are known to influence income, which are coded to be similar across the two years of the national opinion data and comparable with the analysis of the CPS data. These variables include education measured on a 7-point scale, ranging from an eighth-grade education or less coded 1 to postgraduate work coded 7 as well as age measured in years. Gender is measured using a binary variable coded 1 for males and 0 for females. We expect males to earn higher incomes than females. To control for race and ethnicity, dummy variables were included for African Americans, Asian Americans, and Latinos, each coded 1, with non-Hispanic whites as the reference group (coded 0). Because of differences in metropolitan and rural labor markets, two dummy variables were included to measure the respondent's geographic location, with residents of suburban and urban areas coded 1, and residents of rural areas coded 0.

Like the CPS data, the 2002 Pew survey included a question on the occupation of the respondent. A series of dummy variables measure the job category of the respondent, including professional, manager or executive, clerical or office worker, business owner (with two or more employees), and sales (either store clerk or manufacturer's representative). Variables for the respondents who named each one of these job categories are coded 1, and 0 for the respondents who did not name this as their job type. The reference group is composed of service workers, skilled trades, semiskilled labor and laborers, all coded 0. Unique in this survey is a series of binary variables that measure employer type and size. These variables include large corporations, medium-size companies, small businesses, schools or other educational institutions, and other (including nonprofits). The employees of these organizations are coded 1, and if the individual did not work for this type of organization they are coded 0. The reference group is government workers, including federal, state, and local government employees.

Finally, the models control for economic conditions in the respondent's state that affect employment opportunities. State unemployment rates in 2002 and 2005 are from the Economic Census. The models also include a measure of the number of information technology jobs in the respondent's state from the State New Economy Index conducted in 2002 (Progressive Policy Institute 2002). States with a larger share of workers trained and skilled in the use of information technology are expected to foster higher incomes than states with a smaller share. The Progressive Policy Institute explains that this measure includes workers in a variety of industries. The variable used in this analysis measures the

Results: Appendix Tables

Table 2.A.1 (CPS, general population, technology use at work, earnings)
Table 2.A.2 (CPS, less-educated population, technology use at work, earnings)
Table 2.A.3 (Pew, general population, frequency of technology use at work, income)
Table 2.A.4 (CPS, general population, technology use at work, household income)
Table 2.A.5 (CPS, general population, technology use at work, household income)

number of information technology jobs in the information technology sectors and then subtracts this number from the total number of workers in information technology occupations in a state. This creates a more accurate measure of the extent to which traditional industries employ information technology professionals. Nevertheless, states with high scores are high-tech locations such as Colorado, Washington, and Massachusetts. Low-scoring states tend to have economies based on natural resources or traditional manufacturing.

Results, CPS: Information Technology Use for All Workers

Since the dependent variables in tables 2.A.1 and 2.A.2 are weekly earnings in dollars, ordinary least squares regression is reported, with robust standard errors to control for heteroskedasticity. Column 1 (table 2.A.1) tests whether computer use at work is associated with increased weekly earnings for the *general population*, holding other factors constant, while column 2 includes an identical set of control variables, but swaps computer use at work for Internet/e-mail use at work. Finally, column 3 includes a variable measuring whether the respondent took courses online. Across the three models in table 2.A.1 (total population sample) we see strong and consistent evidence that technology use at work is related to higher wages, even after controlling for a battery of factors known to increase earnings, including education, age, and occupation.

The substantive magnitude of the effects of technology use at work on economic opportunity is substantial Average weekly earnings are $692.35 (standard deviation $519.32), which equals roughly $2,768 a month or $33,000 a year before taxes. Holding other demographic, occupational, economic, and job sector factors constant, an individual who uses the computer at work is predicted to earn $101 more per week than the same individual who does not use the computer at work (column 1). This is a 14.5 percent boost in earnings based on technology use at work, and is consistent with Krueger's earlier (1993) findings of a 14 to 16.5 percent wage premium for computer use.

Internet/e-mail use at work creates a larger boost in wages, all else being equal (see column 2) Weekly earnings are $118.27 higher for those individuals using the Internet at work than those employed individuals who do not use the Internet on the job—a 17 percent boost in weekly earnings, all else being equal. Even taking courses online appears to increase weekly earnings by a predicted $39 a week over those who have not taken online courses (see column 3). This is strong and consistent evidence that technology use at work may increase wages for the U.S. population.

Many of the control variables are in the expected direction, lending validity to our findings. Females earn on average approximately $200 less per week than their male counterparts, while older individuals earn more than the young. Racial and ethnic minorities (African Americans, Latinos, and Asians Americans) earn less than whites. Employees with bachelor's degrees gain a bonus of approximately $350 per week, in comparison with those who only have high school diplomas. The effect of Internet use is therefore around one-third of the impact of having a four-year college degree rather than high school only—a considerable amount, given the literature on the increasing returns to education. Geographic location matters as well, with suburban residents (who have more employment opportunities) earning roughly $100 more per week than their rural counterparts, all else being equal, while urban residents earn roughly $50 more per week than rural residents. Occupation also matters significantly for wages, with those in management and professional occupations earning considerably more than the reference category (production). Sales and construction occupations also earn more than our baseline occupation (production). As predicted, federal government and private sector employees earn between $200 and $100 more per week, respectively, than those working in nonprofits or state government. As expected, full-time workers earn almost $400 more per week than those who work only part-time.

So far the analysis provides fairly robust evidence that technology use at work is associated with increased economic opportunity among the employed segment of the U.S. population, and that the substantive size of the effect rivals that of increased education, place (suburban/rural/urban), occupation, or job sector (working in the private sector or for the federal government). The models in table 2.A.1 are robust, accounting for 41 percent of the variation in weekly earnings among the sample of fifteen thousand respondents.

Results, CPS: Information Technology Use for Less-Educated Workers

The more important question, for our purposes, is whether technology use at work can increase the wages of the less-educated employees. Table 2.A.2 replicates the models in table 2.A.1, but includes only those respondents in the CPS survey with a high school degree or less. Box 2.1 below is drawn from the analyses reported in tables 2.A.1 and 2.A.2, and it compares the average dollar amounts attributable to computer and Internet use for the general population and less-educated workers with the effects of demographic and other variables. The models control for a wide range of occupations, as shown in tables 2.A.1 and 2.A.2, but for simplicity of comparison, we have listed only selected occupations that involve a high degree of Internet use: management and secretarial workers.

Technology use on the job is associated with even greater proportionate wage increases for less-educated employees   Within this segment of the population, technology use at work was less common than for those with education beyond a high school degree. Yet we see that technology use continues to have a positive and statistically significant effect in increasing weekly earnings. Less-educated workers who use the computer at work are predicted to earn $90 more per week than the same less-educated worker who does not use the computer on the job, all else being equal. Again, Internet use at work leads to even larger economic gains—a $111 increase in weekly earnings. These dollar figure increases are comparable to those for the population as a whole, but because average weekly earnings are significantly lower for this population, these increases account for a larger percentage change.

The control variables largely mirror the U.S. population as a whole, but with some notable exceptions that we would expect among less-educated workers. While women and racial minorities continue to earn less than males and whites (although the gender and racial gaps are smaller among the less educated), urban residents are now statistically no different than rural residents in earnings, while those in suburbs continue to earn roughly $50 more per week, all else being equal. Among the less educated, the trades earn higher wages (construction, repair, and transportation), while those in service, sales, and secretarial positions

Box 2.1
What Matters for Weekly Earnings, CPS 2003

The variables reported are all statistically significant with a 95 percent confidence interval for predicting weekly earnings. The dollar amounts are based on regression coefficients in table 2.A.1 and 2.A.2, and represent the independent effect of each variable, holding other factors constant.

	Weekly Earnings	
Variable	Model 1: Computer Use	Model 2: Internet Use
General Population (Table 2.A.1)	+$101.60	+$118.27
Education (difference, 4 yrs. college vs. h.s. diploma)	+$354.72	+$343.72
Age (per year)	+$4.86	+$4.83
Female	−$208.36	−$205.22
Latino	−$52.30	−$55.38
Asian American	−$51.92	−$52.99
African American	−$65.70	−$64.12
Urban	+$49.90	+$48.55
Suburban	+$99.37	+$98.33
*Management vs. Production	+$319.29	+$311.82
*Secretarial vs. Production	−$40.81	−$37.82
Federal Government vs. State/Nonprofits	+$189.68	+$195.96
Private Sector vs. State/Nonprofits	+$88.76	+$97.14
Full-time	+$379.59	+$373.93
Less-Educated Workers (Table 2.A.2)	+$89.76	+$111.33
Age (per year)	+$2.92	+$2.92
Female	−$133.73	−$133.78
Latino	−$72.15	−$74.13
Asian American	−$46.45	−$50.98
African American	−$27.07	−$26.89
Suburban	+$44.68	+$44.86
*Management vs. Production	+$223.69	+$219.24
*Secretarial vs. Production	−$26.02	−$23.96
Federal Government vs. State/Nonprofits	+$76.71	+$76.71
Full-time	+$290.63	+$289.01

* *Selected Occupational Categories*: See tables 2.A.1 and 2.A.2 for other categories where the difference between the occupation and the reference category (production) is statistically significant.

Box 2.2
Wage Premium for Internet Use for Less-Educated Workers

The figures below are the expected percentage difference that Internet use at work makes for wages, controlling for other factors. Predicted values estimated from table 2.A.1.

	Wage Premium/Internet Use at Work
African American Men	18.36%
African American Women	17.31%
Latinos	16.99%
Latinas	16.11%
White Men	14.77%
White Women	13.56%

---

earn considerably less than the baseline (production) occupations. Full-time workers earn almost $300 dollars more per week than part-time employees among the less-educated population.

In order to compare the magnitude of information technology's impact for different groups of workers, expected wage premiums are estimated based on the regression coefficients in table 2.A.1 varying race, ethnicity, and gender, with all other variables set at their modal or mean values. These categories are associated with Smith's definition of ascriptive hierarchy.

Information technology use at the workplace matters even more for minorities   Among less-educated workers who use the Internet in their jobs, African Americans and Latinos enjoy a higher premium for Internet use than similarly situated whites, even though Internet use does not begin to compensate for otherwise-lower wages. African American men with a high school education or less earn 18.36 percent more than similarly situated African American men who do not use the Internet at work, while African American women gain a bonus of 17.31 percent. For less-educated Latino workers, the wage premium is 16.99 percent for men and 16.11 percent for women. Among less-educated white workers, the Internet increases earnings 14.77 percent for men and 13.56 percent for women. This demonstrates that information technology use at work is indeed related to economic opportunity for less-educated workers, and that the effects are slightly greater for minorities.

In contrast to Holzer (1996), women do not enjoy the greatest advantage from technology use, at least not in terms of the percentage gain in wages. Differences based on gender, however, are slight. This shows that the Internet can be a mechanism for leveling the playing field among less-educated workers, who have generally fared poorly in the new economy. For minorities, digital skills are even more important for economic gain.

Online courses increase weekly earnings, according to the 2003 CPS— particularly for less-educated workers Additionally, the 2003 CPS includes a question about taking an online course, which allows us to estimate changes in employee earnings as well as the significance of online education (see column 3 in tables 2.A.1 and 2.A.2). The research on upskilling in the workforce as a result of technological change suggests that Internet use in the workplace encourages individuals to learn new skills as jobs and work processes are reorganized (requirements may be increased for mobility within a firm or an occupation), and this in turn increases wages. It is reasonable to expect Internet use at work to stimulate further training or education. Higher incomes for workers may also be the result of continued human capital development.

How substantive is the magnitude of the effects of distance learning or online job training on economic opportunity? For the general population, table 2.A.1 (column 3) indicates that even taking courses online appears to increase weekly earnings by a predicted $39 a week over those who have not taken online courses. In contrast, less-educated workers who have taken online courses (see table 2.A.2, column 3) enjoy a larger gain in income than the general population, with less-educated employees experiencing a $63 per week increase in earnings from online courses. Again, this suggests that Internet use can have a greater marginal effect for certain groups such as the less educated.

Results, Pew: The Frequency of Use and Income

A further test of the effects of Internet use at work is to ask whether or not the frequency of use affects income, based on 2002 and 2005 survey data from the Pew Internet and American Life Project (table 2.A.3). The Pew survey does not report individual earnings, and so household income is the best available alternative outcome measure. The variables are described in the previous "Data and Methods" section in this chapter, and are shown in table 2.A.3. The results for the 2002 and 2005 Pew surveys are reported using a dependent variable that is measured on an ordinal 8-point scale, where 1 indicates that the family income in the previous year ranged from $0 to $10,000, and 8 signifies a family income of $100,000 or higher. Higher scores are associated with higher personal income. Since the dependent variable is ordinal and there are enough categories that it approaches a continuous variable, the model is estimated using Ordinary Least Squares (OLS) regression.

Frequent use at work is related to higher incomes for workers As shown in columns 2 and 4 in table 2.A.3, income increases with the frequency of computer and Internet use at the workplace in both 2002 and 2005. Income increases as information technology use becomes more central in accomplishing job-related tasks, thereby enhancing productivity. This further supports the case that information technology use is important for economic opportunity (and perhaps for mobility into more technology-intensive and higher-paying jobs). More frequent use may suggest a higher level of skill and a greater range of activities using the Internet. Frequent use may be accompanied by other types of expertise or skill. But controlling for occupational differences, education, and other factors, the frequency of use is significantly related to higher income.

Additional Support: Other Models Using Income

To further test the impact of Internet use at work, we conducted several other analyses that measure effects on income. The CPS data only asked weekly earnings for a limited sample of respondents, but included annual household income for the full sample of 103,000 individuals. We replicate the models presented in tables 2.A.1 and 2.A.2, where the dependent variable is annual household income, rather than weekly earnings in tables 2.A.4 (general population) and 2.A.5 (low-educated sample). In the 2003 CPS, annual household income is measured on a 16-point scale from $2,500 to $150,000. Both computer and Internet use at work are related to higher household income in the 2003 CPS, holding constant the same factors used in the CPS analysis of weekly earnings. As expected, the magnitude of the effect on household income is somewhat smaller, as this may include multiple wage earners and other sources of income. Across the models in tables 2.A.4 and 2.A.5, we see strong and consistent evidence that technology use at work is related to increased family household income, even after controlling for a number of factors known to increase earnings.

Second, we replicated the Pew 2002 and 2005 income analysis based on the binary variables of whether or not the respondent used computers or the Internet at work, rather than the frequency of Internet use at work (table 2.A.3, columns 1 and 3). This provides a check on the validity of the income findings for the frequency models reported above. Income may include earnings from multiple household members, so it is a less precise outcome measure of the impact of Internet use than the individual wages used in the first CPS analysis (tables 2.A.1 and 2.A.2).

The Pew 2005 survey lacked the occupational and employer information included in the 2002 Pew survey, but allowed us to assess whether the impact of Internet use has diminished over time, as suggested by Goss and Phillips (2002), given the recent data. The results for both years were similar to those obtained from the CPS analysis discussed above, and so this increases our confidence in the finding that technology use at work boosts wages and income. Those respondents who use the Internet at work have significantly higher incomes than those who did not in 2002, even when controlling for individual level demographics, state economic conditions, occupation, the size of a business, and geography. The 2005 data indicate that Internet use continues to lead to higher incomes. In fact, Internet use at work may have greater economic payoffs over time. This is suggested by the unstandardized regression coefficient for 2005 in table 2.A.3, which is nearly double the one for 2002. Without similar control variables, though, it is difficult to evaluate whether the wage premium for Internet use has indeed grown between 2002 and 2005.

Summary of Results

Just as computer use at work produced a wage premium in earlier studies, Internet use at work is also clearly associated with economic gains, whether they are measured in terms of weekly earnings or annual household income. This pattern emerges in both the large-sample CPS and the smaller-sample Pew surveys, using a number of controls in both studies. It appears in 2002, 2003, and 2005. Both use at work and the frequency of use are related to higher wages or incomes. The consistent results across models increase our confidence that computer and Internet use are important contributors to economic opportunity in the digital economy.

Digital Citizenship and Economic Opportunity

Together, our findings indicate that technology use at work advances the economic prospects for individuals. We update older research (such as Krueger 1993) and show that the development of the Internet has in fact lifted the fortunes of some. Those who use the Internet on the job are more likely to have higher weekly earnings and incomes. The frequency of Internet use at work implies differing levels of capabilities online, and we find that as the frequency of use rises, so does income. As Krueger has indicated, this suggests that higher levels of skill (and productivity) are rewarded in the marketplace. Our findings are consistent across years and surveys, in 2002, 2003, and 2005.

Perhaps most notable, however, is the magnified effect of Internet use for workers who are lower paid and often disadvantaged: less-educated workers, African Americans, and Latinos. It would be reasonable to expect that the payoff for Internet skills is most concentrated in high-paying, knowledge-intensive jobs, where Internet use is most pervasive. Instead, the potential gains are relatively greater precisely for those groups in society that are also most likely to lack regular Internet access and effective skills. No prior research has demonstrated the benefits of digital skills for less-educated workers, using national data and evidence based on individual earnings.

The use of the Internet for distance learning is also associated with higher incomes and weekly earnings, especially for less-educated workers. The literature on skill-biased technological change suggests that Internet use may be just one dimension of the more general human capital development encouraged by technology diffusion.

Our findings provide powerful evidence that digital citizenship matters for economic participation and technology disparities are not a trivial concern for future equality of opportunity. The growth of income inequality through the development of the new economy is in part the result of fundamental technological change that has increased the need for information technology skills as well as education. A higher premium is also placed on education and cognitive skills, with the adoption of technology-intensive practices within manufacturing and other "old economy sectors," and with the shift toward more knowledge-intensive industries such as finance. Yet even among less-educated workers, technology skills garner higher wages.

The skills needed to adapt to these changes are not evenly distributed, as our analysis of digital inequality in chapter 5 will show. They are bound together with existing inequalities, such as disparities in educational opportunities in low-income communities (see chapter 5; Mossberger, Tolbert, and Gilbert 2006). The liberal tradition of citizenship in the United States has produced a prevailing view that social justice requires equal chances, if not equal results. Firmly within this tradition, Krueger (2003) advocates education and training as a form of "redistribution" to narrow the inequalities of the new economy. In the context of the information age, equal justice requires that everyone in the United States has the ability to develop the digital and educational skills to participate fully in the economy.

3

The Benefits of Society Online: Civic Engagement

with Jason McDonald

Political knowledge and interest in public affairs are critical preconditions for more active forms of involvement. If you don't know the rules of the game and the players and don't care about the outcome, you're unlikely to try playing yourself.
—Robert Putnam, *Bowling Alone*, 2000

In America there cannot be enough of knowledge, for all knowledge benefits both those who possess it and those who do not.
—Alexis de Tocqueville, *Democracy in America*, 1835

Does the Internet provide greater access to political knowledge, enabling democratic participation? Does it enhance political interest and discussion? What are the possible benefits of digital citizenship for inclusion and the polity?

The republican vision of the founders was based on the development of civic virtue among the citizenry. In this view, it is the duty of citizens to be informed participants in the exercise of democracy. French observer Alexis de Tocqueville (1835) reflected this perspective in his comments on the benefits of knowledge for democratic participation and the enhancement of the political community as a whole.

Today, the republican tradition informs debates over civic engagement and political participation in the United States (Hero 2007; Putnam 2000; Smith 1993). The next chapter will examine whether or how the Internet facilitates political participation. Here we explore the effects of the Internet on civic engagement, which provides the motivation and capacity for political participation.

Civic engagement is at the heart of republican virtue, for it offers the foundation for long-term political participation. There are prominent debates about the effects of the Internet on civic engagement and "social capital," or the capacity to participate as a member of the larger political community (see Putnam 2000). Many of these controversies are based on preliminary findings during an early stage of the development of the Internet. The medium has great potential for providing opportunities for information, discussion, and mobilization of interest, and yet there is little research on the Internet's effect on civic engagement (Shah, Kwak, and Holbert 2001; Jennings and Zeitner 2003; Uslander 2004; Price and Cappella 2001; Kim et al. 2004).

The contribution of this chapter is to provide evidence across several elections, examining the relationship between Internet use and civic engagement. We define civic engagement as a multifaceted concept, consisting of political interest, political discussion, and political knowledge. This chapter draws on previously unexamined survey data from the national elections in 2000 and 2002 as well as from the 2004 primary elections. We use two-stage causal models to control for endogeneity or selection bias in who uses the Internet for political news. Increased education, for example, is related to news media consumption, but also to political interest and political knowledge, and two-stage models allow us to draw more valid conclusions about the impact of the Internet than a single-stage model. Two-stage causal models isolate the effects of the Internet on civic engagement, controlling for selection bias in the online population. In other words, they allow us to understand the real contribution of Internet use for civic engagement, over and above other factors.

In a separate analysis, we devote special attention to civic engagement among younger Americans. Because young people are most likely to go online regularly for a variety of activities, the Internet may have its greatest impact on civic engagement among the young. Past survey research showed that younger Americans are more likely to express interest in politics and government on the Web (Mossberger, Tolbert, and Stansbury 2003).

We hypothesize that consuming political information online helps citizens obtain higher levels of political knowledge, become more interested in politics, and deliberate with their fellow citizens about politics more frequently. If the consumption of online political information stimulates interest, increases political sophistication, and fuels discussion, it may partially counteract a three-decade trend of declining engagement (Abramson and Aldrich 1982; Putnam 2000; Verba, Schlozman, and Brady 1995). While the causes of this decline in civic engagement and participation are complex, and not easily remedied by any single solution, the Internet may be a tool for enhancing citizenship in the information age.

Debates over Civic Engagement, Social Capital, and the Internet

Some existing research has established a positive link between Internet use and participation, including voter turnout (Krueger 2002; Bimber 2003; Tolbert and McNeal 2003; Graf and Darr 2004), campaign contributions (Bimber 2001, 2003; Graf and Darr 2004), and citizen-initiated contact with government (Thomas and Streib 2003; Bimber 1999). Civic engagement may help to explain the emerging findings on political participation, if the link between Internet use and participation is paralleled by heightened engagement. By facilitating civic engagement, Internet use may represent a more fundamental transformation, altering citizen orientations toward politics and society, and motivating individuals to participate over the long term.

There are conflicting accounts of the impact of the Internet on civic engagement in particular and social capital more generally. Early research suggests that the use of the Internet for political information has little effect on declining civic engagement and that in certain respects it may even exacerbate this grim trend (e.g., Davis and Owen 1998; Putnam 2000; Margolis and Resnick 2000).

One explanation for this is that the Internet reflects politics as usual. As Michael Margolis and David Resnick conclude,

Paradoxically, one of the hardest things to predict is whether the Internet will improve the quality of democracy by creating a more informed citizenry. We say paradoxically, because it seems obvious that because the Internet provides instant and almost cost-free information, it should enable the ordinary citizen to be fully informed about all relevant policy areas.... We remain skeptical.... To be sure, the Net is now and will continue to be a boon to those who already have an active and sustained interest in public affairs, but there is little evidence that the Internet by itself will increase the attentive public. (2000, 212)

Many of the initial studies on this topic found that once researchers controlled for levels of educational attainment, Internet users were indistinguishable from nonusers on civic engagement measures (Bimber 1999; Putnam 2000; Pew 1998; Aspden and Katz 1997). While the poor and less educated are less likely to use online political information, including e-government (Mossberger, Tolbert, and Stansbury 2003; Thomas and Streib 2003), they are also less likely to vote or participate overall (Verba, Schlozman, and Brady 1995; Campbell et al. 1960; Wolfinger and Rosenstone 1980). Existing disparities are simply replicated in cyberspace.

A darker interpretation is that the Internet may actually diminish the social connections that cement individual commitment to the larger society, including civic engagement. In his landmark book *Bowling Alone*, Robert Putnam finds that "respondents who say that they rely primarily on the Internet for news are *less* likely than other Americans to volunteer, to spend time with friends, to trust one another" (2000, 479). Based on his analysis of the DDB Needham Life Style surveys from 1996 to 1998, Putnam found that online news consumers volunteered, trusted, and spent time with friends at lower rates than other Americans. Putnam (2000, 221) is therefore skeptical that online communication could foster increased engagement, and believes that it is likely to have a detrimental effect.

Building on Putnam's findings, scholars have considered why the consumption of political information online may diminish civic engagement. One explanation notes that computer discussions may depersonalize communication and psychologically weaken social cues (Nie and Erbring 2000). Eye contact, gestures, nods, body language, seating arrangements or even hesitation are omitted in online discourse. Hence, computer-mediated communication masks the nonverbal communication of face-to-face encounters, which otherwise enhance trust (Putnam 2000, 176). The absence of social cues in computer-mediated communication may make the Internet better at fostering participation than civic engagement.

Cass Sunstein (2001) argues that the Internet may limit the scope of information and discussion to those who hold similar views, reducing exposure to, and tolerance of, other groups and ideas. Such "cyberbalkanization" occurs when individuals purposefully communicate only with others who share their beliefs, screening out information that challenges their predispositions (Putnam 2000, 178). Real-world interactions as well as print and broadcast media often force individuals to confront diversity, according to Sunstein, but the virtual world may be more homogeneous, quashing debate and deliberation.

All of these findings rely on data collected immediately after the initial explosion of Internet usage during the late 1990s, and may misrepresent the current impact of the Internet on political and civic life. Not only is Internet use more widespread but creative new methods of online organizing emphasize political community rather than isolation. One vivid example is the spontaneous rise of "meetups" arranged online during the 2004 election. Meetings were publicized on Web sites such as meetup .com and gathered like-minded individuals in a physical location for the purpose of coordinating their efforts on behalf of a candidate. Internet meetups enabled people to connect with others in their communities, and resulted in face-to-face interactions that often would not have occurred otherwise.

In recent years, the Internet has become an integral part of campaigns and politics. Salient news stories often break first online, and are then circulated through listservs, e-mails, and finally the Web sites of news organizations. Candidates now advertise and raise substantial sums of money online. Indeed, the presidential primary campaigns of John McCain in 2000 and Howard Dean in 2004 were credible largely due to online fund-raising. By 2004, Web sites were a central tool in presidential campaigns, as evidenced by John Kerry's constant encouragement to voters to visit his Web site for information on policy proposals and Vice President Dick Cheney's admonition to voters to visit an online clearinghouse for factual information during his debate with John Edwards. Given this evolution, we must reassess the relationship between Internet use and civic engagement.

Later research does provide some evidence of the beneficial effects of Internet use on engagement (Jennings and Zeitner 2003; Uslander 2004; Price and Cappella 2001; Kim et al. 2004). Kent Jennings and Vicki Zeitner (2003), for instance, use panel surveys over a fifteen-year period (from 1982 and 1997) to explore the impact of the Internet on civic engagement. They find that Internet use magnified civic engagement, but also that those who were civically engaged before the Internet were more likely to adopt the new technology. Similarly, Yong-Chan Kim and colleagues (2004) find frequent Internet users involved in more political and civic activities related to the tragedies of 9/11 than non-Internet users, or infrequent users. In an experimental design where the participants took part in a series of online political discussions during the 2000 election, members of the experimental group were more politically interested and knowledgeable, reported increased social trust, and were more likely to vote than those in the control group, who did not participate in the online discussions (Price and Cappella 2001). The impact of the Internet on social trust is unclear, however. Drawing on national Pew survey data, Uslander (2004) found that Internet users were no more trusting of strangers than were nonusers.

Why Would Online News Enhance Engagement?
Beyond this preliminary research, there are good reasons to believe that the consumption of online political information facilitates engagement. There is evidence that the cyberbalkanization argument is overdrawn. Contrary to this hypothesis, Internet users have greater overall exposure to political arguments, including those that challenge their candidate preferences and policy positions. Controlling for education and other influences on political knowledge, Internet use encourages exposure to diverse political views (Horrigan, Garrett, and Resnick 2004).

Although Putnam and others have depicted the Internet as a fairly impoverished form of communication, there are characteristics of interaction online that may encourage civic engagement. The Internet's interactivity, diversity, flexibility, speed, convenience, low cost, and information capacity potentially allow the public to become more knowledgeable about politics and government—a first step toward greater participation (Norris 2001). Interpersonal and small group communications are also possible online, in contrast to the passive consumption of news offered by other media. There may also be unique advantages to online political discussions that are important for civic engagement. Research has shown that online discussions are more frank and egalitarian than face-to-face meetings. Women, for example, are less likely to be interrupted in cyberspace discussions (Sproul and Kiesler 1991; Putnam 2000, 173). Online communication has also been found to be more heterogeneous with regard to physical factors such as race, gender, and age (Rheingold 2000).

How Online News Differs

Differences between the information available online and through more traditional media may have some impact on civic engagement. Research has shown that the content of online news tends to be more diverse and ideologically extreme than mainstream media, such as television and newsprint (Pew 2004a). Examples from the Left include truthout.org, the largest Internet news service in the world, or from the Right, freerepublic.com. Much of the in-depth news online is only partially covered by mainstream media outlets or never receives airing via the mainstream media. Instances are so numerous it has become common knowledge, with scholars such as Robert McChesney (1999) arguing that waves of media mergers and acquisitions have created a television media monopoly that no longer provides citizens with the information they need to participate in a democracy. Evidence of this is that credibility ratings for the major broadcast and cable television outlets have fallen in recent years, due in large part to increased cynicism toward the media on the part of conservatives (Pew 2004b). From 1996 to 2002, CNN was viewed as the most believable broadcast or cable outlet, but its ratings have fallen gradually over time. Today, only 32 percent of those able to rate CNN say "they can believe all or most of what they see" on the cable network. This is down from 37 percent in 2002, 39 percent in 2000, and a high of 42 percent in 1998. Ratings of the major broadcast networks have declined as well, with NBC News, ABC News, and CBS News rated about equally in terms of believability by the public. Only a quarter of U.S. viewers find the network channels highly credible, down from roughly one-third in the mid-1990s (Pew 2004b).

Competing with traditional media, online news has become increasingly important. The population of online news users has grown dramatically in the last decade with 29 percent of Americans regularly going online for news in 2004 (Pew 2004b). Given this growth, we may now be approaching a critical tipping point in which the use of online news may affect elections and engagement.

As mentioned above, the diversity and partisan nature of news online has led to concerns about the dangers of limiting the scope of discourse (Sunstein 2001). But the flip side of this argument is that Internet sources may be more emotional, richer, and more likely to mobilize involvement in the political process. As a result, online news may facilitate the use of the likability heuristic, by which people make informational inferences on the basis of their likes and dislikes (Sniderman, Brody, and Tetlock 1991). If Internet news sources differ from traditional ones, as the research suggests, what is the impact on citizen behavior?

Media Effects on Political Knowledge, Discourse, and Interest

The consumption of political information from media sources enhances civic engagement by increasing citizens' knowledge about politics (Delli Carpini and Keeter 1996; Tan 1980; Brians and Wattenberg 1996). Television advertising increases the levels of knowledge among voters (Freedman, Franz, and Goldstein 2004; Brians and Wattenberg 1996), especially those with low levels of information (Freedman, Franz, and Goldstein 2004).[1] With regard to the specific mechanisms through which individuals accrue knowledge, Jack McLeod and Daniel McDonald (1985) find that viewing television news and reading newspapers increases individuals' political knowledge and efficacy, while Craig Brians and Martin Wattenberg (1996) find that citizens learn about candidates from campaign ads. More specifically, voters acquire information on candidate traits (Weaver 1996) and issue positions (Chaffee and Kanihan 1997; Weaver and Drew 1993) through the consumption of news. Campaign spending increases voter knowledge about candidates (Coleman and Manna 2000; Coleman 2001) through the political communication it purchases. Voter awareness about the importance of issues in Senate elections is enhanced by the degree to which the issues are discussed by candidates and the media (Kahn and Kenney 2001). A growing literature documents the added value of more information on civic engagement, showing citizens exposed to salient ballot measures (initiatives and referenda) and associated media campaigns have increased political knowledge (Smith 2002; Smith and Tolbert 2004).

While the research on the effects of the Internet is sparse, there is good reason to believe that online news consumption is particularly likely to increase knowledge. Like newspapers, the Internet is a reading-intensive medium that requires literacy for effective use (Mossberger, Tolbert, and Stansbury 2003; Warschauer 2003).[2] Reading involves higher information-processing skills, including those related to memory (Healy and McNamara 1996; Kyllonen and Christal 1990). Studies have demonstrated that more learning occurs from reading about politics in newspapers than from watching television (Smith 1989). Though based on descriptive statistics, recent Pew data support this assertion that individuals who consumed news online showed higher levels of knowledge and recall about the 2004 elections than those who relied on traditional media (Pew 2004a).

The Internet should also stimulate civic engagement by generating political discussion. Like other forms of media, the Internet provides individuals with information that facilitates discussion. Research shows that information obtained from the media encourages political dialogue (e.g., Chaffee and McLeod 1973; Beck 1991; Mondak 1995; Huckfeldt and Sprague 1991). Indeed, Steven Chaffee and Jack McLeod (1973, 243) found that individuals seek media to provide political information for partisan arguments to help support their positions during interpersonal discourse. Jeffery Mondak (1995) also concludes that individuals invoke information obtained from the media to support their positions. Yet unlike other forms of media, the Internet creates immediate opportunities for convenient, flexible, and inexpensive interpersonal communication through e-mail, listservs, and chat rooms. The convenience and speed of e-mail communication should encourage greater political discourse (on e-mail contacting, see Thomas and Streib 2003).

There are several reasons why the Internet may have a more visible influence on aspects of civic engagement than does traditional mass media. The Internet may have a greater impact than television on *political knowledge*, as do other reading-intensive media like newspapers. Media use in general facilitates political discussion, but as the Internet offers interactive opportunities for participation, so it should lead to higher levels of *political discussion*. Political interest is possibly the most important of the three dimensions of engagement analyzed here. The more diverse and ideological content available online may stimulate greater *political interest*. Research has found citizens exposed to ballot propositions (often over controversial topics) and associated media campaigns express a greater interest in politics overall (Smith and Tolbert 2004).

In summary, we hypothesize that citizens using online political information are more likely to be knowledgeable about politics, interested in politics, and occupied with discussion about politics more frequently. Paul Freedman, Michael Franz, and Kenneth Goldstein (2004) offer a similar informational hypothesis about the link between exposure to information and knowledge, and an engagement hypothesis about exposure to information and interest.[3] No previous research has proposed or established this relationship between the consumption of online political information and civic engagement, measured as knowledge, interest, and discussion. Young people are most likely to use online news (Pew 2004b), so this may predict future trends. We further test the effects of possible interactions between age and the use of online news.

Approach

To assess these hypotheses, we analyze data from the 2000 American National Election Studies (NES) survey, a 2002 Pew Internet and American Life Daily Tracking survey, and a 2004 Pew Research Center for the People and the Press survey.[4] Data from the 2000 NES allow us to assess the impact of consuming political information online on the respondents' political engagement, political knowledge, and political interest using the same survey and set of control variables. Data from the Pew studies allow us to assess the impact of consuming political information online on the respondents' political interest (2002 and 2004) and political knowledge (2004). These national opinion data allow us to measure relationships between the Internet and civic engagement over time. The data are not available to test all aspects of civic engagement across all years.

There are three dependent variables: political discussion, political knowledge, and political interest. We measured the first, political discussion, by the individual response to the 2000 NES question that asks the number of days (0 to 7) during the previous week that they discussed politics with friends or family. To measure respondent political knowledge, we created count variables indicating the number of factual questions they answered correctly in the 2000 NES and the 2004 Pew survey. These count variables range from 0 to 6 for the 2000 NES, and 0 to 2 for the 2004 Pew survey.[5] To measure respondent interest in politics, we created ordinal variables indicating their level of interest in the election. For the 2000 NES analysis, this variable is coded 1 for the respondents who were "not very interested," 3 for the respondents who were "interested," and 5 for the respondents who were "very interested" in the 2000 election. The dependent variables measuring interest in the

2002 and 2004 Pew surveys are coded similarly, with higher values indicating that respondents followed the 2002 midterm elections and the 2004 Democratic presidential nomination more closely.[6]

To measure the main independent variable, the consumption of political information online, we use a question in all the surveys that asked about reading election news from online sources. Respondents who read election news online were coded 1, and 0 otherwise. Unfortunately, this blunt measure does not allow us to observe how frequently the respondents read about politics online or how important they consider online sources relative to traditional ones.[7] Nevertheless, measuring the online readership of political information in this way provides for conservative tests of our hypotheses. By collapsing individuals who read about politics online habitually with those who do so infrequently, and those who consider online news sources as gospel with those who view them skeptically, we are less likely to observe a relationship between online readership and forms of political engagement even if there is one. If we do observe a relationship, then, it should demarcate the lower bounds of the impact of reading about politics online on civic engagement. Our models also include a host of attitudinal and demographic control variables, with question wording and coding discussed below.

One hurdle to assessing the hypotheses that consuming political information online increases these forms of engagement is that the consumption of online news is positively related to other variables in our analysis—for example, education. Therefore, we need to account for this endogeneity to avoid overstating the influence of reading about politics online on the dependent variables and to test against reverse causality. To do so, we use a two-staged estimation procedure for limited dependent variables employed in previous research (Alvarez and Glasgow 2000).[8] In the first stage, we use logistic regression to estimate the use of online news (see table 3.A.5), obtaining predicted values of whether the respondents read political news online. We then substituted these values for the endogenous variables when estimating the second-stage models. In the second-stage models, we estimate the frequency with which the respondents discussed politics during the prior week, the level of political knowledge the respondents possessed, and the respondents' political interest.

The following section provides a detailed explanation of our coding of the control variables. For those who are less interested in the methodological issues, you may skip to the "Results" section that follows.

Discussion of Variable Coding

In the analyses, we control for a variety of attitudinal and demographic characteristics of the respondents. For the 2000 NES data, these include the following demographics: educational attainment using a 7-point scale on which higher values indicate higher attainment levels; gender using a dummy variable assuming the value of 1 for the female respondents; race using dummy variables indicating that the respondents were African American, Asian American, or Latino (1 if yes; 0 otherwise) with non-Hispanic whites as the reference group; age using the respondents' age in years; and income using a 22-point scale on which higher values indicate higher incomes. To control for the likelihood that partisans discuss politics more frequently than nonpartisans, we created a dummy variable assuming the value of 1 if individuals were strong Democrats or Republicans, and 0 otherwise.[9] We control for the degree to which the respondents consume information about politics from traditional media sources by including a variable indicating the number of days during the previous week in which the respondents read the newspaper or watched the national nightly news. We control for external political efficacy by summing the scores from two 5-point scales that range from "strongly disagree" to "strongly agree" with the statements, "People don't have a say in government," and "Public officials don't care about people like me," creating a 2–10 scale. Finally, in the separate analyses of discourse, knowledge, and interest using the 2000 NES data, we control for each dependent variable as an independent variable—for example, in estimating discourse, we control for knowledge and interest as independent variables.

For the 2002 and 2004 Pew analyses, we controlled for the respondents' demographic characteristics as follows: education using a 7-point scale with larger values indicating higher levels of education completed on the part of the respondents; income using an 8-point scale on which higher values indicate higher family income levels; race using a series of dummy variables measuring whether the respondents were African

American, Asian American, or Latino (1 if yes; 0 otherwise) with non-Hispanic whites serving as the reference group; gender using a dummy variable assuming the value of 1 for the female respondents; and age using the respondent's age in years. For both 2002 and 2004, we controlled for respondent partisanship by creating two dummy variables, each assuming the value of 1 if the respondents were Democrats and Republicans, and 0 otherwise (with Independents as the reference category). For the 2002 data, we controlled for respondent consumption of other news by creating two dummy variables assuming the value of 1 if the respondents had read the newspaper or watched a national television news program the day prior to being surveyed, and 0 otherwise. For the 2004 data, we controlled for this propensity by creating two dummy variables indicating whether the respondents obtained most of their news about the presidential campaign from newspapers (1 if yes; 0 otherwise) and television (1 if yes; 0 otherwise). Finally, for the 2004 analysis of political knowledge, we controlled for respondent political interest; since there was no variable measuring respondent knowledge in the 2002 data, however, we could not control for it in the 2002 analysis of interest.

Results: How the Internet Matters for Civic Engagement

The findings summarized below and in the appendix tables are second-stage estimates of the impact of online election news on civic engagement.[10] In table 3.A.1 (column 1), the dependent variable is coded so that higher scores are associated with an increased frequency of political discussion, modeled with Poisson regression. Political knowledge is measured as a count of the number of six questions correctly answered, with results reported in tables 3.A.1 (column 2) and 3.A.4. Since we measure political interest on an ordinal scale, we employ ordered logistic regression to estimate the impact of consuming political information online on interest. We report coefficients of this relationship in tables 3.A.1 (column 3, 2000), 3.A.2 (2002), and 3.A.3 (2004).

The evidence that online news is related to civic engagement is persuasive (see tables 3.A.1–3.A.4). In the "what matters" table below, we find that the consumption of online news increases political discussion, knowledge, and interest over time as well as in high-information

Box 3.1
What Matters for Civic Engagement, 2000, 2002, 2004

Second-stage estimates from tables 3.A.1–3.A.4. Only statistically significant relationships are summarized below.

Year	Political Discussion	Political Knowledge	Political Interest
2000			
Online News	Yes	Yes	Yes
Newspapers	Yes	Yes	No
Television News	Yes	Yes	Yes
2002			
Online News			Yes
Newspapers			No
Television News			Yes
Young*Online News			No
2004			
Online News		Yes	Yes
Newspapers		No	Yes
Television News		No	Yes
Young*Online News		Yes	No

Note: Young*Online News notes the interaction between age and the use
of online news.

presidential elections (2000) and lower-information midterm (2002) or
primary elections (2004). Online news compares favorably with other
sources of news, and has positive spillover effects on civic engagement
in all three elections. There are a number of other factors that influence
civic engagement, as the regression tables in the appendix indicate. These
include strong partisanship, age, gender, race, ethnicity, education, income, and political efficacy. Below, however, we focus on the effects of
news consumption in different types of media, and the interaction between age and the use of online news for political discussion, knowledge,
or interest.

**The Internet provides individuals with information that fosters discus-
sion** Viewing Internet election news is positively associated with the

frequency of political discussion, after controlling for traditional media consumption along with individual demographic and partisan factors. This suggests the Internet may promote political discussion by providing supplementary information (measured by Internet news).

Political interest and knowledge are also positively linked to discussion, supporting previous research showing that the three variables are interrelated (Weaver 1996). Both newspaper usage and television news were found to be a significant predictor of political discussion, suggesting that news in general helps to stimulate political discussion through information.

Online news promotes political knowledge   Viewing online election news is positively related to increased political sophistication. The use of the Internet for political information is important for increasing citizen political knowledge, consistent with recent Pew (2004a) reports based on descriptive statistics. This finding is robust over time (2000–2004) and corroborates the result that Internet news is related to discussion. Also, the model shows that both television and newspaper news are positively related to enhanced political knowledge (Delli Carpini and Keeter 1996), contrary to previous research (Smith 1989). The finding that online news is positively associated with political knowledge, even after controlling for television news and newsprint, suggests that the Internet may be providing different sources of information above and beyond what can be gathered from traditional media forms (see Pew 2004a).

Consuming political information online increases interest in politics   Over time (2000, 2002, and 2004) individuals who use online news express more interest in politics in general, holding other factors constant. This is in contrast to the findings for newspapers. In all three years, viewing television news was positively associated with heightened political interest, while newspaper consumption was important in only one year (2004). The interactivity of this new medium and the visual images it offers may stimulate interest in politics and engagement, like television. We find the Internet may also engage the disengaged in politics (cf. Graf and Darr 2004). The strong statistical relationship repeated in three surveys over a four-year period lends confidence to the finding that the consumption of online news does indeed contribute to a general interest in politics.

Overall, the use of online news encourages civic engagement Our findings confirm some previous research and descriptive data reported by Pew (2004a) that did not control for overlapping factors, such as income, education, and media consumption. Together, the consistent results over multiple years provide strong evidence that the respondents using the Internet for news have an increased political sophistication,

Box 3.2
What Matters: Impact of Online News Consumption on Political Discussion and Knowledge

	Discussion (2000)	Knowledge (2000)	Knowledge (2004)
Estimated News Consumption	Prob. Number of Discussions	Prob. Number of Correct Answers	Prob. Number of Correct Answers
High	4.18 (.261)	2.03 (.181)	.77 (.181)
Mean	3.69 (.087)	1.63 (.055)	.48 (.066)
Low	3.49 (.106)	1.48 (.067)	.43 (.064)
High-Low (Absolute Change)	0.69	0.55	.34
High-Low (Relative % Change)	19.77%	37.16%	79.07%

Note: Predicted probabilities estimated with Clarify based on coefficients in tables 3.A.1–3.A.4. Numbers in parentheses are standard errors for the predicted probabilities. "High" and "low" Internet use represent changes from the maximum (1) of the predicted probability of reading online news to the mean (baseline) to the minimum (0) for this variable. For the 2000 NES data, we hold age, income, efficacy, political knowledge, television and newspaper consumption, and education to their means. Political interest was set at its median. Gender was set at female, and race/ethnicity was set at white non-Hispanic. Simulations are estimated for not-strong partisans. For the 2002 and 2004 Pew surveys we hold age, income, and education at their means. Political interest was set at its median, gender was set at female, and race/ethnicity was set at white non-Hispanic. Television and newspaper consumption as primary media for following the elections was set at yes (1). Simulations are estimated for nonpartisans.

a heightened interest in politics, and a greater propensity to discuss politics—three critical ingredients necessary for sustaining informed participation.

The preceding "what matters" table provides a measure of the predicted magnitude of the effect of online news on increased political discussion and knowledge. Predicted probabilities (simulated from the multivariate regression coefficients) show that the Internet can have a visible positive impact on a critical set of factors that mobilize citizens to be involved in politics.

The influence of online news consumption on civic engagement is sizable   Online news users are 20 percent more likely to engage in political discussion each week, and 37 percent more knowledgeable about politics in the 2000 elections, all else being equal. Similar substantive effects are found for political interest, but they are not reported here due to space constraints. Parallel findings are found using the Pew data, with online news users 80 percent more knowledgeable about the 2004 primary elections, all else being equal. Moveon.org's widely publicized online Democratic presidential primary before the official Iowa caucus and New Hampshire primary, in which Howard Dean and John Kerry emerged as the front-runners, may have contributed to this large effect. The findings connect digital citizenship to enhanced civic engagement across all three dimensions. Next, we examine the influence of online news on civic engagement among the young.

Engaging the Young Online

The Internet has become an important source of election news for all ages, but young people continue to go online for political news at higher rates than do older people. Nearly a third of those age eighteen to twenty-nine say they got most of their election news online in 2004, up from 22 percent in November 2000. That compares with 21 percent of those age thirty to forty-nine, and smaller percentages of older people, who get most of their election news from the Internet (Pew 2004b). Given that the young are more likely to use online election news, they may become politically engaged via online communication (Lupia and Baird 2003).

We test this hypothesis with an interaction term of age multiplied by the predicted probability of reading online news. These conditional effects models are reported in the second column of tables 3.A.2–3.A.4 for the Pew 2002 and 2004 data, and discussed in the text for the NES data.

The Internet is associated with greater increases in political knowledge among the young   We find support for the hypothesis that the relationship between online news consumption on knowledge is contingent on age and that younger people using this medium are more politically sophisticated (see second column of table 3.A.4). The inverse and statistically significant interaction term for the Pew 2004 data indicates that young people who use online news are more likely to be politically sophisticated than older people who read online news. This may be because the young use the Internet more intensively (Mossberger, Tolbert, and Stansbury 2003) and for a broader range of activities (Horrigan 2004), or because they have lower levels of political knowledge to begin with (Putnam 2000). In general, political knowledge increases over time, so online news may have a greater effect in increasing the political sophistication of the young. Since the young have more to learn, the effect of exposure to information may be greater.

An analysis of the 2000 NES data (not reported due to space constraints) indicates that young people who use online news are more knowledgeable than other age groups using the same medium.[11] An analysis of the two surveys conducted four years apart confirms the same pattern, but the results are more pronounced in 2004, reflecting the increased use of Internet news by the young over time.

Young people have the same levels of political interest as others who consume online news   Yet the association between reading news online and political interest does not appear to be contingent on age. Young people who read news online are not more interested in politics, as evidenced by the nonstatistically significant interaction terms in both the 2002 and 2004 Pew survey analysis (see second column of tables 3.A.2 and 3.A.3). The consumption of online news appears to have a similar predicted effect in engaging both young and old in politics.

Digital Citizenship and Civic Engagement

The potential impact of online news on civic engagement has not been previously explored over time or across the various dimensions of engagement. We offer a theoretical account for why the use of the Internet for political information should foster civic engagement, and we find support for this assertion. This chapter expands on the findings in previous research showing that the use of online news can increase voter turnout and political participation (Krueger 2002; Bimber 2003; Tolbert and McNeal 2003). Because civic engagement is necessary for sustained participation, this research strengthens and explains prior results on participation. The findings also run counter to some conclusions about the impact of the Internet on engagement (Putnam 2000; Margolis and Resnick 2000) and democracy (Norris 2001; Sunstein 2001). Our results point to the promise of the Internet, in contrast to arguments that new online forms of communication will do little to reverse, and may even exacerbate, long-term reductions in social capital and civic engagement.

Individuals who consume political information online are more likely to participate in political discussions, have higher levels of political knowledge, and have more acute political awareness, as measured by political interest. We find these results all the more compelling since we observe this relationship even without more precise measures of the frequency of use and the importance that individuals ascribe to what they read online. With more exacting measures of online news consumption, the effect we find should be even more pronounced.

We can explain these results in relation to the ways in which other media affect civic engagement. Online news reduces the individual costs of acquiring information, facilitates discussion, and increases the benefits of political participation by magnifying political interest. In addition to reducing information costs, the Internet may provide alternative or more diverse information than mainstream media. This research is consistent with a growing body of literature on the importance of information in participation and civic engagement (Alvarez 1998; Bowler and Donovan 1998; Grofman 1995; Lassen 2005; Lupia 1994; Luskin 1987, 1990; Lupia and McCubbins 1998; Popkin 1991). Paul Freedman, Michael Franz, and Kenneth Goldstein (2004) focus on information as the ingredient that makes "democracy possible." If online news creates richer political environments, stimulating interest in politics and political discussion, the Internet may in part serve to counteract a three-decade trend of declining engagement (Verba, Schlozman, and Brady 1995; Putnam 2000).

Despite the disparities in Internet use, there is cause for optimism. The rate at which individuals view political information online has been rising and continues to increase, especially for the young. The impact of digital citizenship is most profound for young people. The young—a demographic group with the lowest civic and political participation—have the highest probability of seeking online political news and becoming active in politics online. Because the young are more likely to have technology access and use online news (Lupia and Baird 2003; Mossberger, Tolbert, and Stansbury 2003; Lenhart 2003), the consequences for the sustained engagement of future generations are significant. This chapter revealed important evidence (measured with an interaction term) that online news may be especially beneficial for the young, related to increased political sophistication among this age group, and perhaps more permanent changes in civic engagement for the future.

Civic engagement provides a foundation for participation, based on an attachment to the political community, as envisioned by civic republicans. The next chapter addresses different forms of political communication on the Internet, to find out whether or how they can translate civic engagement into political participation.

4

The Benefits of Society Online: Political Participation

Citizen participation is at the heart of democracy.
—Sidney Verba, Kay Schlozman, and Henry Brady, *Voice and Equality: Civic Voluntarism in American Politics*, 1995

Voting is by a substantial margin the most common form of political activity, and it embodies the most fundamental democratic principle of equality.
—Robert Putnam, *Bowling Alone*, 2000

The previous chapter explored the benefits of online news for civic engagement—that is, for political knowledge, interest, and discussion. In this chapter, we ask whether the Internet's potential for enhancing civic engagement also leads to greater participation in democratic politics. As mentioned in chapter 3, there is some support already for the contention that the Internet does indeed encourage political participation. But existing studies have mainly confined themselves to the influence of either Internet access or online news consumption (Krueger 2002; Bimber 2001; Norris 2001; Tolbert and McNeal 2003). We expand on the current studies of participation by investigating and comparing the effects of chat rooms and e-mail as well as online news.

Probing the possible effects of chat rooms and e-mail allows us to better understand the influence of the interactive, two-way character of communication over the Internet. Online activities also represent different forms of communication in other ways. Reading online political news is mass communication; participating in a political chat room is small group communication; and e-mailing about politics and elections is interpersonal communication. Each form of online communication has a different primary goal (becoming informed, social discourse, and mobilization). Given these distinctions, it seems realistic to assume that dissimilar forms of online communication have varying effects on electoral participation. Do political chat rooms foster participation by creating opportunities for dialogue and debate, consistent with theories of deliberative democracy? Does e-mail mobilization (receiving and sending e-mail for and against political candidates) mimic other forms of mobilization (face-to-face, phone, etc.) that have been found to increase turnout and participation? Do the convenience and flexibility of online news increase turnout by reducing the costs of becoming politically informed? This chapter will ask which type of online activity has the greatest potential for influencing voter turnout. As the Putnam quote above shows, voting is considered by political scientists to be the core activity in the exercise of democratic participation. It is also the most widespread political activity.

Political participation requires motivation, capacity, and mobilization, according to Sidney Verba, Kay Schlozman, and Henry Brady (1995, 3). The last chapter demonstrated that online news can contribute to political interest (motivation) and political knowledge (one aspect of capacity). Prior research suggests a connection between the informational capacity of online news and political participation. Currently, we know much less about whether the Internet also provides interpersonal exchanges and networks that can mobilize participation as well as inform.

Because political participation and Internet use are affected by many of the same factors, such as age, education, and income, we again use two-stage models to analyze the data in this chapter. By examining Pew survey data collected immediately after the 2000, 2002, and 2004 elections, we are able to take into account the growth in Internet users and the political uses of the Internet over this period. We can also investigate the differences for Internet use between midterm congressional elections and presidential elections where participation is traditionally higher. Some conflicting findings about the impact of the Internet can be attributed to differences in the types of elections being held (Jackson 1997).

In the next section, we use theories of political communication, especially those concerned with the impact of the media on participation, to consider how the Internet could influence participation. Communication mechanisms may provide a means of connecting more general knowledge, discussion, and interest (civic engagement) to the specific decision to vote. We compare chat rooms, e-mail, and online news in terms of their potential linkages to participation. Finally, we discuss our findings in terms of existing inequalities in political participation, and the ways in which the Internet may shape future participatory opportunities.

Technology, Communication, and Participation

Historically, innovation in telecommunications technology has prompted speculation on how it will affect democratic participation. The values of civic republicanism have long colored debates over the public merit of technologies that promote new forms of mass communication, such as radio and television. We are at such a crossroad with the Internet. Typically, preliminary forecasts are optimistic, predicting that new technology will usher in a more democratic system. Unfortunately, no innovation in telecommunications has yet realized the potential contribution to democracy envisioned by proponents. This is in part because each form has evolved more readily into a commercial enterprise than a channel for political dialogue. Commercialization, while certainly present, may not have the same effects on the Internet. In contrast to other forms of media, business interests have not found a way to make advertising in conjunction with online news very profitable (Lupia and Baird 2003). This may allow for a greater focus on information content.

The Internet also differs from previous forms of mass media because it represents both a two-way network for communication and a medium for information. As such, it is capable of fostering discussion through chat rooms, mobilization through e-mail, and information gathering through online news. These different modes of use may have varied effects on political participation such as voting. Media theories relating to deliberative democracy, mobilization, and information subsidy predict ways in which these aspects of the Internet might stimulate political participation.

Chat Rooms, Deliberative Democracy, and Participation

Do political chat rooms foster political participation by creating opportunities for dialogue and debate, consistent with theories of deliberative democracy? Chat rooms are online meeting places where individuals with similar interests can hold a conversation. In this synchronous form of computer-mediated communication, participants interact on a real-time basis (Riva and Galimberti 1998). A typical chat room runs continuously, but occasionally an "event" will be scheduled where individuals will come together to discuss a specific topic. Specialists on the subject will often be invited to field questions, and moderators will also take part, overseeing the conversation in order to keep it on track. If properly carried out, such discussions can elicit solutions to problems or bring important topics to the forefront. If not carefully monitored, dozens of people may try to respond at once, resulting in the visual equivalent of noise (Gorski and Brimhall-Vargas 2000).

Because chat rooms operate in real time, their discussions suggest the discourse of the salons of the 1890s that the early proponents of deliberative democracy idealized. Advocates of deliberative democracy such as James Bryce (1888), Gabriel Tarde (1899), and John Dewey (1927) argued that the media play a critical role in promoting political discussion and participation. Underlying the theory of a deliberative democracy is the notion that citizens willingly and openly take part in the discussion of politics. The sharing and discussion of political information lead to the formation of opinions that ultimately translate into political participation. The media act to fuel the democratic process. The purpose of news is to provide the public with conversational topics, as the stories and events presented by the media are used as the basis of dialogue. During a discussion, ideas are shared and opinions take shape. Political attitudes and beliefs develop from conversations that then lead to political behavior. This perspective is unique in that it does not treat discussion as an intervening variable. The media nourish and support conversation, while discourse is the crucial factor that motivates participation (Barber 1984; Dryzek 1990, 2000; Elster 1998; Fishkin 1993, 1995; Gutmann and Thompson 1996; Habermas 1996; Katz 1992; Page 1996).

Chat rooms are a virtual means of bringing participants together for the discussion and opinion formation that sows the seeds of participation. Unlike earlier gathering places, chat rooms are open twenty-four hours a day, seven days a week, and every day of the year. The dress code is less formal than for the salon of earlier times (pajama-clad members are welcome), and you do not have to take part in the conversation in order to seem polite. Listening in often occurs without direct participation.

Stereotypes about chat room use and users have led some to believe that this form of discussion will have little effect on political participation. Among these preconceptions is the view that individuals who use chat rooms are lonely and bored as well as incapable of interacting under typical social situations. Research, however, indicates that participants in online discussions are not unlike the general public (for a review, see McKenna and Bargh 2000). Another stereotype is that chat room discussion is inferior to face-to-face conversation as a form of interaction (see chapter 3, "Debates over Civic Engagement, Social Capital, and the Internet").

Despite the perceived benefits of face-to-face interaction, there is evidence that chat room discussions have their own advantages. Chat room exchanges start more quickly and are often more straightforward than face-to-face meetings (Peris et al. 2002). This may be because of what is known as the familiarity effect. Individuals are more likely to perceive others as friendlier or more trustworthy if they seem more familiar (Cialdini 1990). In chat rooms, you can listen in on conversations and read people's thoughts as they tumble down the screen. This allows individuals to become acquainted with and form opinions about each other long before they interact through actual discussion online. The familiarity engendered through chat rooms helps to jump-start conversations that would be harder to initiate in person. For a further review on the advantages of online discussions, see chapter 3 ("Why Would Online News Enhance Engagement?").

The current research on chat rooms indicates that the conversations should resemble social discussions that might occur in a local pub or other physical settings. If so, then the impact of chat rooms should be analogous to the discourse described by deliberative democracy theory. The conversations in political chat rooms should help individuals sort out conflicting ideas and come to conclusions that will determine how they will vote, or will motivate them to take political action.

E-mail, Mobilization, and Participation

Does e-mail mobilization (receiving and sending e-mails for and against political candidates) resemble other forms of mobilization that have been found to increase turnout and participation? Like chat rooms, e-mail is a form of online communication, but the similarities end there. Asynchronous computer-mediated communication includes e-mails, listservs, bulletin boards, and other types of communication that take place via the Internet and do not require real-time interaction. For this reason, e-mail compares more closely to telegraph messages than conversations. Unlike chat room conversations, these messages can be stored, saved, deleted, retrieved, or forwarded. They may contain attachments with data or text that can be edited, or copied and pasted into other text (Gorski and Brimhall-Vargas 2000). Another difference between chat rooms and e-mail is that from the beginning, political actors recognized the possibilities of e-mail for political mobilization.

The interactive character of the Internet makes possible direct appeals for participation. Since the 1960s, there has been a persistent trend of declining political participation and civic engagement in U.S. politics (Putnam 2000; Burnham 1982; Piven and Cloward 1988; Rosenstone and Hansen 1993). There are numerous explanations for this decline (see, for example, Nye, Zelikow, and King 1997; Putnam 2000). One view is that the dominance of the media in electoral campaigns has diminished the mobilization efforts of parties and interest groups (Davis 1994; Croteau and Hoynes 2000). While the media may have played a minimal role in influencing political behavior and attitudes in the first half of the twentieth century (Lazarsfeld, Berelson, and Gaudet 1948), the events of the 1960s and 1970s changed the role of the media in politics. The 1960s ushered in a volatile era of mass mobilization in the United States with the civil rights, antiwar, and women's movements, among others—broadcast on televisions around the country (Delli Carpini and Keeter 1996). Changes in election laws and campaign finance reforms transferred much of the power over elections to candidates and the media. Advances in technology further aided this transfer of power with the widespread use of sophisticated opinion polls changing the way the media covered elections (Kerbel 1995, 67–71). Television allowed voters to see and hear the candidates from the comfort of their own homes, lessening the importance of political parties for promoting candidates.

Prior to the 1960s, political parties expended a major portion of their energy on get-out-the-vote drives and other recruitment activities. With candidate-centered and media-intensive elections, partisan mobilization efforts (especially get-out-the-vote drives and door-to-door canvasing) diminished substantially. Early research indicated a positive correlation between party recruitment efforts and voter turnout (see, for example, Kramer 1970). Later studies took the analysis a step further by trying to quantify the impact of political party activities on political behavior. A seminal work by Steven Rosenstone and John Mark Hansen (1993) found that the drop in mobilization efforts accounted for more than half of the loss in voter turnout. This argument indicates that the perceived relationship between the media and political participation may be spurious. Turnout has been harmed not by what the media are doing but by what political parties and interest groups have stopped (or limited their efforts in) doing.

Researchers have yet to investigate the influence of online mobilization efforts. But there is a history of empirical studies indicating the importance of recruitment activities. Beginning with Gerald Kramer (1970), scholars have shown that mobilization activities and voter turnout are positively related. In addition to Kramer, a multitude of researchers (e.g., Cain and McCue 1985; Caldeira, Clausen, and Patterson 1990; Huckfeldt and Sprague 1991; Rosenstone and Hansen 1993; Gerber and Green 2000) have found that individuals who are contacted by parties or candidates are more likely to vote. This research has been corroborated by studies on diverse topics such as blood donation (Jason et al. 1984) and recycling (Reams and Ray 1993), which have shown the significance of recruitment activities in obtaining participation.

The Internet opens new venues for mobilizing political participation. E-mail has been used either to campaign more efficiently and cost-effectively, or in an attempt to mobilize constituents. Examples of e-mail use for mobilization can be found as early as the 1992 presidential election when Jerry Brown maintained an e-mail address for communicating with the general public (McDermott 2000). While Brown's use of e-mail for campaigning was novel for the time, numerous other examples would follow.

When Jesse Ventura ran for governor of Minnesota in 1998 as an independent candidate, he campaigned on a shoestring budget. To contain costs, he drove his recreation vehicle from rally to rally, and at every stop, he signed up supporters to an e-mail list. As election day approached, he regularly sent out messages to mobilize followers

(Thompson 2002, 4). This strategy helped Ventura win on a budget that would not have sustained a victory in the past. As creative as Ventura was, Maria Cantwell went further in her effort to unseat Senator Slade Gorton (R-WA) in 2000. Her campaign included an e-mail listserv that permitted discussion between her campaign staff and supporters. E-mail allowed her to respond quickly to the television ads of her opponents. Cantwell's aggressive use of e-mail might have been the deciding factor in her narrow two thousand–vote victory over Gorton (Thompson 2002, 4). These examples illustrate that e-mail has allowed challengers, independents, and underfunded candidates the opportunity to launch effective campaigns.

It is not just challengers and candidates on a budget who have realized the potential of the Internet. Interest groups are using the Internet as another tool to make a political statement or lobby for change. In 1999, the National Education Association used e-mail to lobby Congress to kill a Republican-sponsored bill to end a federal requirement that Internet service providers give schools a discounted rate. The lobbying effort inundated Congress and the Federal Communications Commission with over twenty-two thousand messages from concerned school administrators and parents. Civil liberty groups used a similar tactic to shelve a Federal Deposit Insurance Corporation effort to relax customer privacy regulations (Engardio et al. 1999, 145–146).

The activities of left-leaning Moveon.org offer other examples of online grassroots work. Among the policy issues this online group has taken up is the war on Iraq. In October 2002, it gave over $1 million to candidates opposed to the war, and on February 26, 2003, it organized a "Virtual March on Washington" where its members jammed Senate and White House phone lines with calls and faxes in opposition to the war (Institute for Politics, Democracy, and the Internet 2003, 13). Key to mobilizing the membership is a Web site where members can sign petitions, receive encouragement to write or phone their representatives and newspapers, and make donations to specific candidates or causes. The group spent approximately $21,346,000 in issue advertising during the election using money raised through e-mail appeals for donations (Center for Responsive Politics 2005).

The adoption of e-mail as a tool to mobilize activists and voters has expanded with each election cycle. By the end of 2003, more than eleven million people had visited the sites of 2004 presidential candidates (Cornfield 2004, 33). Visiting a Web site has become a first link between candidates and supporters. If an individual signs up for a candidate's listserv, they will receive campaign messages and appeals for donations throughout the election campaign (Cornfield 2004). These examples all provide anecdotal evidence for the potential of e-mail as a campaign tool and suggest that the impact of e-mail on voting in future elections could be substantial. The research (e.g., Rosenstone and Hansen 1993) demonstrates that contact either from a party or a candidate can make a considerable difference in voter turnout.

Online News, Information Subsidy, and Participation

Do the convenience and flexibility of online news increase turnout by reducing the costs of becoming politically informed? Online news most closely resembles traditional media in its potential to reduce the information costs of participation, and we turn to media-system dependency theory to examine the possible impact of political news and information on the Internet. Individuals need more information than they can obtain due to costs in money and time, and so they rely on the media to reduce the costs of an information search (DeFleur and Ball-Rokeach 1989, 248–251). Because the Internet provides the public with information more quickly and efficiently, with a greater diversity of sources, it is more likely to be adopted and also change patterns of behavior. For media-dependency and other information-subsidy theories, online news primarily affects participation by lowering information costs and making the net benefits of participation higher. This differs from the role of online news in promoting civic engagement, where information, diversity, and content can lead to greater discussion, more in-depth knowledge, and more acute interest.

While the Internet has this potential, media-system dependency theory tells us that social forces can mediate these likely effects, and the systems of media, politics, and economics are interdependent in any society. In the United States, the mass media have played a critical role in providing electoral information since the 1960s. Prior to this time, political parties offered the primary means of linking citizens with politics, through both information and mobilization. Michael Robinson (1976) became the first of many to blame the media for decreasing voter turnout because it provides insufficient information for citizens to take part effectively in the electoral process. With revenue as the major objective of commercial television, informing the public has taken a backseat to entertainment, in Robinson's view. Other research has presented a countervailing body of evidence that suggests voters do learn from the media (for a review, see Weaver 1996).

There is some interesting evidence on how the Internet may lower information costs for many users. Arthur Lupia and Tasha Philpot (2002) conducted a Web-based experiment exposing twelve hundred respondents to nine different news and political information Web sites. Their experiments indicated that when individuals perceived a site to be effective (to provide information faster, easier, and more accurately), that site was more likely to generate greater interest and an increased probability of participation. While Lupia and Philpot (2002) did not directly show that online news was influencing political behavior, their findings did give some hint of the circumstances under which online political news can make a difference. Lupia and Philpot (2002) demonstrate that efficiency is a key.

An advantage that the Internet has over other forms of media for efficiency is its speed, convenience, currency of information, links to diverse types of information, and a greater variety of sources (see chapter 3, "How Online News Differs"). Survey research also supports this conclusion, as figure 4.1 shows using Pew survey data from 2000, 2002, and 2004. We calculate simple percentages to show the reasons why individuals are going online to get election news for 2000, 2002, and 2004.

As suggested by Lupia and Philpot, figure 4.1 indicates that efficiency is an important consideration for those who read news on the Internet. Convenience was the most-cited reason for going online for political news in all years. Of those using the Internet for political news, the proportion basing their choice on the ease of use was 56 percent in 2000, 57 percent in 2002, and 48 percent in 2004. Frustration with traditional media was the second-most-cited reason; 29 percent in 2000, 43 percent in 2002, and 33 percent in 2004 said that they turn to the Internet because other forms of media are inadequate. The percentage indicating that traditional media were insufficient was considerably higher in 2002. This may reflect low media attention during off-year elections. In addition, some respondents said that the Internet provides information that

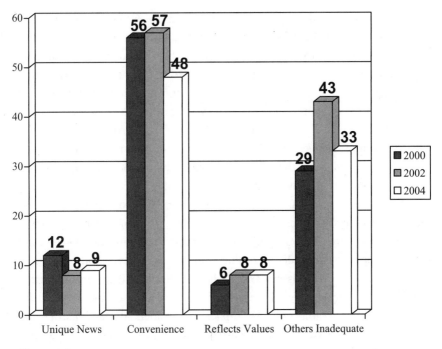

Figure 4.1
Why Do Individuals Go Online For Election News? Reason for Using Online News
Sources: *The Internet and American Life Daily Tracking Survey*, September–December 2000, *The Internet and American Life Daily Tracking Survey*, October–November 2002, and *The 2004 Postelection Survey*, Pew Internet and American Life Project.

they cannot get anywhere else—12 percent in 2000, 8 percent in 2002, and 9 percent in 2004. A minority of the respondents (6 percent in 2000, and 8 percent in both 2002 and 2004) indicated that they use online news because it allows them to choose the news that reflects their values instead of being subjected to a variety of viewpoints. This offers little support for the views of some scholars (e.g., Sunstein 2001) who have argued that the Internet has a detrimental effect on democracy. Overall, the Internet is not limiting the topics and viewpoints that citizens encounter.

What is the evidence on the use of online news and political participation? There is a small body of research showing a positive relationship between political action and online news (Krueger 2002; Bimber 1999,

2003; Thomas and Streib 2003). Research by Caroline Tolbert and Ramona McNeal (2003) suggests that the Internet may enhance citizen information about candidates and elections, and in turn stimulate increased participation. Using NES data from 1996 to 2000, they find that the respondents with access to the Internet and online political news were much more likely to report voting in the 1996 and 2000 presidential elections. There was no significant effect during the 1998 midterm elections, between presidential campaigns. This poses the question, however, of whether the Internet influenced political participation, or whether political activists happened to be more likely to be online. The authors used a two-stage model for the year 2000 to isolate cause and effect (to control for simultaneity problems), and logistic regression to hold factors other than Internet use constant. Voting increased even after controlling for other demographic and attitudinal variables (see also Bimber 2003). Previous research indicates that the likely impact of the Internet on voting varies by electoral context, with online political information having the greatest impact in presidential elections. This is consistent with a version of media-dependency theory: surge-and-decline theory. While media may lower information costs, for many voters the benefits of participation are sufficient only in higher-stakes elections, such as presidential races (Campbell 1966, 42–43).

Approach

This chapter explores the impact of Internet use on voting and political participation, as a core dimension of citizenship. Little previous research on the effects of the Internet on political participation has distinguished between various forms of online behavior, such as the use of e-mail, chat rooms, and news sites. These activities represent different forms of political communication, ranging from interpersonal interaction to mass media. The contribution of this research is to gauge the impact of these varying dimensions of online political communication on participation.

To examine these activities, we use three postelection national telephone surveys (2000, 2002, and 2004) conducted by the Pew Internet and American Life Project.[1] As in the previous chapter on civic engagement, the research design used here allows us to measure the effects of

Internet use on political participation over time, with an emphasis on comparing low-information midterm (2002) and high-information presidential elections (2000 and 2004).

Our primary outcome variable is voting in the three elections, which is constructed as a binary variable where 1 indicates that the individual both voted in the election and was registered to vote, and 0 otherwise. The variable was created in this manner instead of coding it 1 for voting and 0 otherwise to help control for response bias—an individual lying if they believe their answer is socially unacceptable. The overreporting of voting is a common problem in survey research.

A limitation of the previous analysis of civic engagement was the rough measure of Internet use: reading online news. This chapter refines the previous analysis by measuring the independent effects of three forms of online communication on voting in elections: reading online news, participating in political chat room discussions, and sending or receiving e-mail supporting or opposing a candidate for office. For each year, three separate multivariate regression models are estimated.

A second common problem in previous studies is self-selection, or the possibility that individuals who engage in online political activities may be more interested in politics, may be younger, or may be different in some other ways. To control for selection bias (or endogeneity), we use two-stage causal modeling and multivariate analysis (logistic regression). Each explanatory variable (reading online news, political chat room discussion, and e-mailing about political candidates) is constructed as the predicted probability of taking part in an online political activity from a first-stage binary logistic model. This is the same method used in chapter 3. Factors related to online political activities, such as education, are included in the first stage. Internet access in the first stage was controlled for using a dummy code 1 for Internet access and 0 otherwise.[2] The 2000 survey contains fewer questions about traditional political activities, such as political interest and party mobilization, which are included in the 2004 survey.

The following section provides a detailed explanation of our coding measurement of the control variables. For those who are less interested, you may skip to the "Results" section that follows to review the evidence and our conclusions.

Discussion of Variable Coding and Measurement

A number of variables are used to control for individual-level attitudinal and demographic factors. Previous research (e.g., Rosenstone and Hansen 1993; Lewis-Beck and Rice 1992) found that socioeconomic factors, particularly income, influence decisions on whether or not to vote. To control for the possible impact of income on voting, an ordinal scale for income included in the surveys was incorporated into the models. Income is measured on an 8-point scale, where 1 indicates that the family income ranges from $0 to $10,000, and 8 signifies a family income of $100,000 or more. Scholars (e.g., Texeira 1992) have identified party loyalty as an important determinant of participation. To control for partisanship, dummy variables were included for Democrats and Republicans, with Independents serving as the reference group. Survey data suggest that voting increases steadily from eighteen to sixty-five years of age and then levels off. A logarithmic relationship was the most efficient way of modeling this relationship between voting and age, and was calculated by taking the log of age in years.

Education is measured using a 7-point scale, ranging from an eighth-grade education or less to a PhD. Since women are more likely to vote than men, a dummy variable for gender is coded 1 for females and 0 for males. To control for race and ethnicity, dummy variables were included for African Americans, Asian Americans, and Latinos with non-Hispanic whites as the reference group. In 2002, Asian Americans were dropped from the model for chat rooms because of collinearity. General media consumption was controlled for using two variables (nightly television news and newsprint). In 2000, dummy variables were used to control for both measures of media consumption. For newspapers, the variable was coded 1 if the respondent had read the newspaper the previous day and 0 otherwise. Similarly, television news was coded 1 if the respondent had watched the national nightly news the previous day and 0 otherwise. In 2002, dummy variables were coded 1 if the medium was one of the top two forms of media used by the individual to follow the news and 0 otherwise. Although the 2000 survey did not include a political interest variable, there is one available in the 2002 survey. For the 2002 models, political interest is controlled for using a 4-point ordinal scale of responses ranging from none to quite a bit for the question, "How much thought did you give to the midterm election?"

By merging the survey data with state-level data, the models explore two aspects of the state environment in which individuals make choices about participating in elections. The first is exposure to direct democracy. Previous research (Tolbert, McNeal, and Smith 2003; Smith and Tolbert 2004) indicates that individuals residing in states with frequent exposure to ballot initiatives have a higher probability of voting. The number of initiatives appearing on the state ballot during the election year (National Conference of State Legislatures 2004) is used to measure exposure to direct democracy. The second state-level variable is state racial diversity. Kim Quaile Hill and Janet Leighley (1999) provide evidence that states with a higher racial diversity have significantly lower turnout rates. The state racial context is measured by an index of racial and ethnic percentages, created for the fifty states using demographic data from the 2000 census on the size of the African American, Latino, Asian American, and non-Hispanic white populations (cf. Hero and Tolbert 1996).

Results: How Does the Internet Influence Voting?

In each model reported in tables 4.A.1, 4.A.2, and 4.A.3, the dependent variable is coded so that higher scores are associated with the increased probability of voting. Since the dependent variable is binary, the models are estimated using logistic regression. The findings suggest that the Internet may be more helpful in stimulating increased voting during presidential elections than midterm ones.

All online activities are linked to increased voting, but during presidential election years only For 2000 and 2004, the respondents who took part in any of the three online activities were significantly more likely to report voting, controlling for other factors (age, income, education, gender, partisanship, and state contextual factors). None of the online political activities were associated with increased voting in the 2002 midterm election. These findings are consistent with previous research. Tolbert and McNeal (2003) found that individuals who viewed political news on the Internet were more likely to vote in the 1996 and 2000 presidential elections, but not in the 1998 midterm election. Similarly, Bimber (2001) found no relationship between voting and online news during the 1998 election. This suggests that the Internet may not be able to overcome a lack of interest associated with low salience political events such as midterm elections, consistent with surge-and-decline theory.

Together, these findings support the three hypotheses introduced at the beginning of the chapter. The first hypothesis is that the Internet has the potential for increasing the probability of voting by mobilization vis-à-vis political discussion in a social environment made possible by political chat rooms. The second hypothesis is that the Internet might increase the probability of voting through e-mail mobilization, which can be used to mimic the purposive face-to-face mobilization efforts of political parties in the past. The third hypothesis is that the Internet has the potential for increasing the probability of voting by providing information needed to make informed decisions about voting. Even though there is support for these hypotheses, the findings for 2002 qualify the results. These online activities are more likely to be related to participation during high-interest elections.

This is the first study to demonstrate the positive association between e-mail and chat rooms and voting   While this analysis confirms previous research on the influence of online political news in presidential elections, it is the first to show that individuals who engage in interpersonal e-mail communication for and against candidates, and who take part in political chat rooms, are also more likely to vote, holding other factors constant.

Political communication on the Internet parallels the effects of television on political participation   In addition to showing a positive relationship between voting and the Internet, in two of the three elections studied (2000 and 2002) we find a positive relationship between reading the newspaper and voting, but not in 2004. Television news was associated with increased participation in the presidential elections (2000 and 2004), but not in the 2002 midterm election. Online political activities appear to mirror the impact of television, with increased importance for voter turnout during high-information presidential elections.

Demographic variables also influence voting   The findings for individual demographic variables are in the expected direction and consistent with previous research on class biases in voting (Campbell et al. 1960; Wolfinger and Rosenstone 1980; Piven and Cloward 1988). Older individuals, the affluent, those more interested in the election, and those with a higher education are more likely to vote in U.S. elections over time. As in prior studies, partisans, whether Republican or Democrat, were more likely to vote than Independents (Donovan and Bowler 2003). State racial diversity played an important role in electoral behavior, with residents of states with a higher racial diversity less likely to vote in 2000 and 2002 (see also Hero and Tolbert 1996; Hill and Leighley 1999). Asian Americans were consistently less likely to vote than the reference group, non-Hispanic whites. Party mobilization by phone or mail was also related to increased political participation. Party contact was found to be positively related to voting in 2004, the only year in which these questions were asked.

In summary, the use of online political news, chat rooms, and e-mails is associated with increased voting in presidential elections. The results indicate that the Internet is related to the increased likelihood of voting through its ability to facilitate discussion, mobilize participation via e-mail, and provide for a greater variety of sources of information. The results support previous research that found an association between Internet use and voting (Krueger 2002; Tolbert and McNeal 2003; Bimber 2003), and extend our knowledge about this relationship by revealing potential causal mechanisms.

How Much Do Forms of Online Communication Matter for Voting?

While the findings indicate a positive relationship between all three of the Internet activities and voting, it is not likely that each activity is equally related to voter turnout. To illustrate the extent to which online communication and information is associated with increased voting, the coefficients reported in table 4.A.1 were converted to the predicted probabilities of voting in the 2000 presidential elections (King, Tomz, and Wittenberg 2000). The simulations compare the probability of voting for individuals who do and do not engage in the three forms of online political activities. The probability simulations were calculated holding

Box 4.1
What Matters: Use of Online News and the Expected Probability of Voting (2000)

Predicted Probability of Reading Online News	TV News/ Newspaper	No TV News/ Newspaper	TV News/ No Newspaper	No TV News/ No Newspaper
Low	75.8% (.030)	64.5% (.040)	68.7% (.027)	56.0% (.036)
Medium	85.6% (.027)	77.8% (.037)	80.9% (.029)	71.0% (.040)
High	91.7% (.030)	86.6% (.046)	88.7% (.039)	82.1% (.056)
Difference (High-Low)	15.9%	22.1%	20.0%	26.1%

Note: Standard deviations are in parentheses. To simulate different levels of Internet exposure, the predicted probability of seeing election information was set at 0, 0.5, and 1. Values for log age, education, income, initiative use, and minority diversity were set at their mean. Gender was set at female, race/ethnicity at non-Hispanic white, and political party at Independent. Estimations were produced using Clarify: Software for Interpreting and Presenting Statistical Results, by Michael Tomz, Jason Wittenberg, and Gary King.

the variables for log age, education, income, state racial diversity, and initiative use at their mean values. Gender was set at female, race at non-Hispanic white, and partisanship at Independent. The expected probabilities were calculated for different combinations of television news and newspaper usage, varying the use of online news from none (0) to average (.5) to very high (1).

The magnitude of the effect of Internet news depends on other forms of media consumption Comparing similar individuals who regularly read online news (high) with those who do not (low), the probability of voting increases by between 16 and 26 percent, depending on the respondent's other forms of media consumption. After holding other factors constant, the effects of online political news translated into an increased probability of voting of 16 percent for individuals who also rely on television and newspapers for news, and 21 percent for those who rely on newspapers but not television. Reading online news also translates into an approxi-

Box 4.2
What Matters: E-mail Mobilization and the Expected Probability of Voting (2000)

Predicted Probability of E-mail Mobiliza-tion	TV News/ Newspaper	No TV News/ Newspaper	TV News/ No Newspaper	No TV News/ No Newspaper
Low	77.8% (.026)	67.3% (.036)	70.8% (.024)	58.6% (.033)
Medium	96.5% (.029)	94.2% (.045)	95.0% (.038)	91.9% (.058)
High	99.1% (.019)	98.6% (.030)	98.8% (.025)	98.0% (.038)
Difference (High-Low)	21.3%	31.3%	28.0%	39.4%

Note: Standard deviations are in parentheses. To simulate different levels of Internet exposure, the predicted probability of e-mail mobilization was set at 0, 0.5, and 1. Values for log age, education, income, initiative use, and minority diversity were set at their mean. Gender was set at female, race/ethnicity at non-Hispanic white, and political party at Independent. Estimations were produced using Clarify: Software for Interpreting and Presenting Statistical Results, by Michael Tomz, Jason Wittenberg, and Gary King.

mately 20 percent increased probability of voting for those who use television but not newspapers, and 26 percent for those who do not get news from either television or papers. Thus, online news is the most important for increasing voting among those who rely on this medium exclusively for political information.

E-mail has an even greater influence on voter turnout than online news The probability of voting increases between 21 and 39 percent, comparing individuals who regularly send and receive political e-mails with those who rarely do. After holding other factors constant, the effect of political e-mail use translates into an increased probability of voting of 21 percent for individuals who also rely on television and newspapers for news, and 31 percent for those who rely on newspapers but not television. It also translates into an approximately 28 percent increased probability of voting for those who use television but not newspaper, and a 39 percent improvement for those who do not get

Box 4.3
What Matters: Chat Room Discussion and the Expected Probability of Voting
(2000)

Predicted Probability of Chat Room Participation	TV news/ Newspaper	No TV News/ Newspaper	TV News/ No Newspaper	No TV News/ No Newspaper
Low	79.0% (.025)	68.8% (.034)	72.4% (.022)	60.5% (.031)
Medium	99.3% (.014)	98.9% (.023)	99.1% (.020)	98.5% (.032)
High	99.8% (.008)	99.8% (.012)	99.8% (.012)	99.7% (.018)
Difference (High-Low)	20.8%	31.0%	27.4%	39.2%

Note: Standard deviations are in parentheses. To simulate different levels of Internet exposure, the predicted probability of political chat room participation was set at 0, 0.5, and 1. Values for log age, education, income, initiative use, and minority diversity were set at their mean. Gender was set at female, race/ethnicity at non-Hispanic white, and political party at Independent. Estimations were produced using Clarify: Software for Interpreting and Presenting Statistical Results, by Michael Tomz, Jason Wittenberg, and Gary King.

news from either television or papers. As for online news, the impact of e-mail use is intensified among those who do not regularly consume television and newspaper news.

The association between chat rooms and voting is even stronger than online news consumption and voting   When participation in political chat rooms increased from low to high, the probability of voting rose between 21 and 39 percent. After holding other factors constant, the effect of political chat room discussion translates into an increased probability of voting of 21 percent for individuals who also rely on television and newspapers for news, and 31 percent for those who read newspapers but do not watch television news. It also leads to an approximately 27 percent increased probability of voting for those who use television but not newspapers, and a 39 percent difference for those who do not get news from either television or papers. The effects of political chat room discussion on voting are comparable to those of e-mail use, and both are larger than the effects of reading online news.

The contribution of this research is to gauge the relationship between varying forms of online communication and voting. Our analysis reveals that individuals using all three forms of online activity for political information are more likely to vote, demonstrating the mobilizing potential of the Internet. Not only do varying forms of Internet use matter; the substantive impact is also large. Holding other factors constant, individuals who regularly read news, communicate through e-mail, or participate in chat rooms online are significantly (16 to 39 percent) more likely to vote than those who do not. The consequences for U.S. democracy are significant, particularly for the young, who are more likely to be online, but also less likely to engage in voting and other forms of political participation (Mossberger, Tolbert, and Stansbury 2003). Given the close presidential elections of 2000 and 2004, the findings are crucial, showing that politics online matters for politics off-line. The Internet can have a positive effect on political participation, most clearly in presidential elections.

Understanding the Internet's Benefits for Participation

Politics online clearly encourages both civic engagement and participation. In this chapter, we find that the Internet promotes voting as well as political knowledge, interest, and discussion. Previous research (Krueger 2002; Bimber 2003; Tolbert and McNeal 2003) indicates that there is a positive association between political participation and the Internet. This chapter goes further by exploring whether Internet activities may influence participation in varied ways, and finds that chat rooms and e-mail are even more important for voter turnout than online news. The literature on the connection between online media and political participation suggests three possible explanations for the effects of the different forms of Internet communication we have studied.

The first is derived from the theory of deliberative democracy, which argues that the media do not have a direct relationship with political participation. Instead, the media only provide topics that stimulate social discourse, which is the mechanism that influences political activities. This theory predicts that the Internet should facilitate political participation through opportunities for individuals to meet and take part in discourse through chat rooms. We indeed find that participation in political chat room discussions leads to an increased probability of voting in both the 2000 and 2004 presidential elections.

The second way in which the Internet may increase participation is through the mobilization efforts of parties and interest groups. Before the changes in campaign finance laws and election rules during the 1960s and 1970s, political parties engaged in substantial mobilization through get-out-the-vote drives and door-to-door canvasing. Once these laws weakened the power of parties, mobilization efforts were reduced. At the same time, voter turnout dropped off. Authors such as Rosenstone and Hansen (1993) contend that there is a direct correlation between these two events. Parties, candidates, and interest groups have now found new methods of mobilizing voters through e-mail appeals to vote, register, give money, or donate time. Our analysis reveals that sending and receiving e-mails in support of or opposition to political candidates is statistically associated with an increased probability of voting in the two recent presidential elections. This indicates the power of mobilization online.

The third explanation focuses on information costs. According to information-subsidy theories, such as media dependency, citizens need more information than they can themselves obtain due to the costs (money and time). The public relies on the media to provide them with the information they need in a manner that will reduce costs (Gandy 1982). Because the Internet is capable of providing information almost instantly, easily, and from an almost endless variety of sources, one would expect it to encourage political action by lowering the cost of becoming informed about elections. Figure 4.1 shows that individuals seeking online news for political coverage cited the inadequacy of traditional media coverage as an important reason for turning to the Internet. Individuals using online news were statistically more likely to vote in the two recent presidential elections, lending support to the argument that online news reduces the cost of participation. But consistent with surge-and-decline theory, the value of online news (as well as chat rooms and e-mail) declines during less salient, nonpresidential elections.

This chapter supports all three explanations for the effects of the Internet (social discourse, mobilization, and information), but it is difficult to predict which will have the greatest impact on the political landscape in the future. Probability simulations based on the regression coefficients show that each online activity can increase the probability of voting between 16 and 39 percent during presidential elections. Chat rooms and e-mail had a somewhat greater influence on voting than online news. Yet those who participate in chat rooms or appear on listservs may also have more activist orientations than those who read only online news.

The Internet fosters participation in three ways: by offering information to help make informed decisions and promote discussion, by supplying outlets such as chat rooms that permit individuals to meet and discuss politics, and by providing interest groups, candidates, and parties a means for revitalizing the mobilization efforts of earlier eras through e-mail. This sets the Internet apart from traditional media forms and demonstrates that the benefits of Internet inclusion extend beyond what any other single form of mass communication can facilitate. Like the New England town meetings that have helped to inspire U.S. ideals of civic republicanism, the Internet provides a new forum for political information and interaction.

Across the previous chapters, we can see that digital citizenship supports the achievement of equal opportunity in the liberal tradition, and civic engagement and political participation in the republican tradition. The effects of Internet use are substantial for wages, especially for minorities and less-educated workers. They are considerable for civic engagement and voting as well, even surpassing the influence of more traditional media. Moreover, the increases in civic engagement are clearest for the young, who tend to be among those who are least likely to participate or be knowledgeable. The Internet not only exercises an independent effect on economic opportunity and political engagement but it also affects those for whom changes will make the most difference— disadvantaged workers and the youngest citizens. The remainder of the book considers patterns of exclusion from society online and the consequences of that exclusion.

Methods Appendix

As a comparison to the 2000 probability simulations of voting reported in the chapter, below we show similar simulations based on the 2004

Box 4.A.1
What Matters: Online News and the Expected Probability of Voting (2004)

Predicted Probability of Reading Online News	Mobilized by Both Phone and Mail	Mobilized by Phone	Mobilized by Mail	No Phone or Mail Mobilization
Low	85.0% (.037)	74.0% (.057)	74.7% (.056)	59.7% (.066)
Medium	92.4% (.018)	85.9% (.031)	86.3% (.031)	75.9% (.042)
High	96.2% (.013)	92.7% (.024)	92.9% (.024)	86.8% (.038)
Difference (High-Low)	**11.2%**	**18.7%**	**17.7%**	**27.1%**

Note: Standard errors are in parentheses. To simulate different levels of Internet exposure, the predicted probability of seeing election information was set at 0, 0.5, and 1. Values for log age, education, income, initiative use, and minority diversity were set at their mean. Political interest and the measures of media consumption were set at their median. Gender was set at female, race/ethnicity at non-Hispanic white, and political party at Independent. Estimations were produced using Clarify: Software for Interpreting and Presenting Statistical Results, by Michael Tomz, Jason Wittenberg, and Gary King.

survey data. Differences in the availability of control variables mean that 2004 models do not exactly replicate those from 2000. To illustrate the extent to which online activities can increase voting in 2004, the coefficients reported in table 4.A.3 for the online political activities were converted to predicted probabilities of voting (King, Tomz, and Wittenberg 2000). Probability simulations were calculated holding the variables for log age, education, income, state racial diversity, and initiative use at their mean values. Political interest and the five measures of media consumption were held at their median values. Gender was set to female, race at non-Hispanic white, and partisanship at Independent. Expected probabilities were calculated for different combinations of party mobilization varying the use of online news from none (0) to average (.5) to very high (1).

Box 4.A.1 estimates the probability of voting during the 2004 presidential election varying reading online political news. Individuals who

Box 4.A.2
What Matters: E-mail Mobilization and the Expected Probability of Voting
(2004)

Predicted Probability of E-mail Mobilization	Mobilized by Both Phone and Mail	Mobilized by Phone	Mobilized by Mail	No Phone or Mail Mobilization
Low	85.5% (.035)	74.9% (.054)	75.3% (.053)	60.7% (.063)
Medium	93.8% (.016)	88.4% (.029)	88.6% (.027)	79.7% (.040)
High	97.4% (.012)	94.8% (.023)	95.0% (.022)	90.5% (.039)
Difference (High-Low)	**11.9%**	**19.9%**	**19.7%**	**29.8%**

Note: Standard errors are in parentheses. To simulate different levels of Internet exposure, the predicted probability of seeing election information was set at 0, 0.5, and 1. Values for log age, education, income, initiative use, and minority diversity were set at their mean. Political interest and the measures of media consumption were set at their median. Gender was set at female, race/ethnicity at non-Hispanic white, and political party at Independent. Estimations were produced using Clarify: Software for Interpreting and Presenting Statistical Results, by Michael Tomz, Jason Wittenberg, and Gary King.

regularly read online news (high) have an increased probability of voting by between 11 and 27 percent, compared to a similar individual who does not read online news (low). It also illustrates the influence that party mobilization has on activities. The difference in the probability of turnout increases between 9 and 25 percent between those who are not mobilized and those who are mobilized by both phone and mail, depending on the level of online media consumption.

Next we estimate the substantive effect of sending or receiving e-mails for or against candidates on the probability of voting in the 2004 elections. Probability simulations suggest that when e-mail use increases from low to high, the probability of voting increases by between 12 and 30 percent. After holding other factors constant, the effect of political e-mail use translates into an increased probability of voting of 30 percent for individuals who are not mobilized by parties and 20 percent for those only contacted through mail. It also produces an approximate 20 percent

Box 4.A.3
What Matters: Chat Room Discussion and the Expected Probability of Voting
(2004)

Predicted Probability of Chat Room Participation	Mobilized by Both Phone and Mail	Mobilized by Phone	Mobilized by Mail	No Phone or Mail Mobilization
Low	91.6% (.018)	84.2% (.033)	84.6% (.030)	73.2% (.040)
Medium	98.8% (.011)	97.7% (.023)	97.8% (.023)	95.6% (.042)
High	99.7% (.008)	99.3% (.016)	99.4% (.015)	98.7% (.029)
Difference (High-Low)	8.1%	15.1%	14.8%	25.5%

Note: Standard errors are in parentheses. To simulate different levels of Internet exposure, the predicted probability of seeing election information was set at 0, 0.5, and 1. Values for log age, education, income, initiative use, and minority diversity were set at their mean. Political interest and the measures of media consumption were set at their median. Gender was set at female, race/ethnicity at non-Hispanic white, and political party at Independent. Estimations were produced using Clarify: Software for Interpreting and Presenting Statistical Results, by Michael Tomz, Jason Wittenberg, and Gary King.

increase in the probability of voting for those who are mobilized through phone only, and 12 percent for those who are contacted by political parties by both phone and mail.

Finally, box 4.A.3 shows the impact of political chat rooms on the probability of voting in 2004. When comparing an individual who regularly uses political chat rooms to one who does not, the probability of voting increases by between 8 and 26 percent. After holding other factors constant, the effects of political chat room discussion translated into an increased probability of voting of 26 percent for individuals who were not contacted by political parties and 15 percent for those who were mobilized by mail alone. Chat rooms account for a 15 percent increase in the probability of voting for those who were mobilized through phone contact, and an 8 percent increase for those who were contacted by political parties using both phone and mail.

Based on the available data, online election news was found to increase the probability of voting between 16 and 26 percent in the 2000 election, all else being equal. The data also suggested that e-mail contact increases the probability of voting between 21 and 39 percent in the 2000 presidential elections, while online political chat room discussion was associated with an increased probability of voting between 21 and 39 percent, holding other factors constant. A glaring difference between the 2000 and 2004 results is that the 2000 model indicated that the online political activities could have a greater impact on the probability of participation by as much as 39 percent, while the 2004 results suggest an upper bound of 30 percent. One possible explanation for this difference is that in 2000, traditional party mobilization could not be controlled for, and researchers (e.g., Rosenstone and Hansen 1993) identify this factor as one that is crucial in predicting participation. Because there were no available mobilization variables in the 2000 data set, expected probabilities were calculated for different combinations of media consumption instead of party mobilization varying the use of online news from none (0) to average (.5) to very high (1).

5

From the Digital Divide to Digital Citizenship

with Bridgett King

Now that a large number of Americans regularly use the Internet to conduct daily activities, people who lack access to those tools are at a growing disadvantage. Therefore, raising the level of *digital inclusion*—by increasing the number of Americans using the technology tools of the digital age—is a vitally important national goal.

—U.S. Department of Commerce, *Falling through the Net: Toward Digital Inclusion*, 2000

Changes have clearly occurred since the first report issued by the U.S. Department of Commerce (1995) describing information technology have-nots in urban and rural areas, yet we have not achieved the goal of digital inclusion that the federal government set at the beginning of the millennium. Current surveys from the Pew Internet and American Life Project show that 73 percent of Americans say that they go online at least occasionally in some setting, but this falls considerably short of widespread digital citizenship, as we have defined it (Madden 2006). In this chapter, we examine some trends over time and review prior research on digital inequality before analyzing patterns of access and use in the 2003 CPS. Smith's (1993) concept of ascriptive hierarchy emphasizes the role of disparities based on gender, race, and ethnicity, and we pay particular attention to discussing the role these factors play in exclusion from society online.

To better understand the overlapping effects of many influences, we conduct separate multivariate analyses for various segments of the U.S. population: African Americans, Latinos, less-educated individuals, younger people, and older ones. These subsample analyses allow us to explore differences in factors that influence technology use *within groups*.

Are there gender differences among African Americans or Latinos? Are there racial and ethnic cleavages in Internet use even when only poor or less-educated people are considered? When we examine digital citizenship among younger individuals, do we see the fault lines historically based on race, ethnicity, and class receding? To answer these questions, we use the CPS of October 2003, which has over 103,000 respondents and is unrivaled in its ability to provide representative samples of all of these subgroups in the population. While there may have been some recent growth in the Internet population since late 2003, these changes have not fundamentally transformed the deep-rooted disparities we reveal here. Before discussing the CPS, we turn to Pew data to compare patterns of use among different groups in the population since 2000.

Descriptive Data: Trends over Time

Despite our concerns about the validity of occasional usage as a primary measure of Internet involvement, the Pew Internet and American Life Project is the best source for tracking Internet use over time, and the project produces high-quality survey data on a rich variety of topics regarding the Internet. Box 5.1 below shows Internet use by different groups of the population from 2000 through 2006. According to Pew, the change in question wording in 2005 did not substantially alter the patterns of who is online and who is not (Fox 2005).

Several demographic trends emerge.[1] Women and men are about on a par for having used the Internet. Older individuals have also increased their presence online. Those in the age fifty to sixty-four category have now nearly caught up to the average for the population, and almost one-third of those who are sixty-five or older now use the Internet. Those respondents who are seventy or older account for a large part of the drop-off in this category (Fox 2005).

On the other hand, most people under thirty in the United States report some experience with the Internet—88 percent for this age group. This raises the possibility that there are fewer differences among young people; that race and ethnicity, for example, are no longer important determinants for occasional Internet use. We examine this possibility later in the chapter, using the 2003 CPS. Pew surveys show little change

Box 5.1
Who Goes Online?

Group	% Online in the Year...						
	2000	2001	2002	2003	2004	2005	2006
Overall	46	59	61	63	63	68*	73
Men	49	60	62	65	66	69	74
Women	44	58	59	61	61	67	71
Whites	48	61	62	64	67	70	73
Blacks	35	50	48	51	43	57	61
Hispanics**	40	53	61	62	59	70	76
18–29	64	75	78	83	78	84	88
30–49	56	68	70	73	74	80	84
50–64	36	58	55	59	60	67	71
65+	12	17	22	22	25	26	32

For 2005 and 2006: "Do you use the Internet, at least occasionally? Do you send or receive e-mail, at least occasionally?"

Prior to 2005: "Do you ever go online to access the Internet or the World Wide Web, or to send or receive e-mail?"

* 2005 Internet use in this box is based on the May–June 2005 survey, which showed that 68 percent of Americans had used the Internet at least occasionally. Box 1.1, earlier in the book, used the tracking surveys, which contain somewhat different questions, and which showed that 67 percent had used the Internet in February–March 2005.
** English-speaking Hispanics only.
Note: The data for the year 2000 is from March 2000, which was the first survey reported by the Pew Internet and American Life Project. The 2001 data are from August–September. Data from the following years are approximately one year apart: September 2002, August 2003, May–June 2004, May–June 2005, and February–April 2006. For most of the surveys included here, it can be said with 95 percent confidence that the error attributable to sampling and other random effects is plus or minus 2 or 3 percentage points. Samples are weighted to correct for known biases.

between 2003 and 2005 among young people (only 5 percent), so the 2003 analysis should represent current trends.

For some groups, the gap in Internet use seems to be narrowing, but this is not true for all. African Americans are increasing their Internet use, with 61 percent online (or occasionally online) in 2006 in comparison to 35 percent in 2000. The group that most clearly gained in Internet users with the 2005 wording change emphasizing occasional use is African Americans. This suggests less frequent use, perhaps in venues other than home. Yet even as occasional users, African Americans still lag considerably (by more than 10 percent) behind the 73 percent of whites who are Internet users. Technology disparities based on race and ethnicity persist despite overall growth, demonstrating a pattern consistent with Smith's (1993) tradition of ascriptive hierarchy.

The Pew data show that English-speaking Latinos may have recently surpassed whites in Internet use, but these findings are subject to some debate. A recent bilingual study conducted by Pew found that only 56 percent of Latinos reported using the Internet occasionally in comparison with 71 percent of non-Hispanic whites (Fox and Livingston 2007). The Pew English-only data do not give us an accurate picture of the Latino population as a whole. The size of the sample for each survey—about one to four thousand respondents—can also create problems in generalizing to subsamples, such as Latinos.

In contrast, the large-sample October 2003 CPS, conducted in both English and Spanish, revealed that 38 percent of Latinos reported Internet access at home in comparison with 65 percent of non-Hispanic whites (see box 5.2 below). Demonstrating the limitations of their measures for Latinos, Pew data from the same time period show no appreciable difference between English-speaking Latinos and non-Hispanic whites.

For 2006, there are still noticeable gaps based on income and education, even as more individuals of all backgrounds go online. According to the Pew 2006 survey, only 64 percent of those with a high school education report using the Internet, in comparison to 91 percent of college graduates. Similarly, only 53 percent of those with annual household incomes of $30,000 or less use the Internet—considerably below the 73 percent of all Americans who are online in some fashion (Madden 2006).

Box 5.2
Descriptive Statistics (Percentages) for General Population versus Disadvantaged Population Subsamples

	General Population	African Americans	Latinos	Less Educated	Poor	Older	Younger
Internet Access at Home							
Yes (%)	60	40	38	43	36	42	61
No (%)	40	60	62	57	63	58	39
Frequency of Internet Use over Last Year							
At Least Once a Day	35	21	18	20	20	18	42
At Least Once a Week but Not Every Day	19	16	13	13	13	11	21
At Least Once a Month but Not Every Week	4	5	2	4	3	3	5
Less Than Once a Month	2	3	2	3	2	2	3
No Internet Access	40	55	64	60	60	66	29
Reason for No Internet Use							
Costs Are Too High	9	20	22	14		7	13
Lack of Confidence	2	2	3	3		4	.99
Don't Need It; Not Interested	16	18	15	23		32	10
Privacy and Security Concerns	.35	.39	.34	.35		.34	.35

Box 5.2
(continued)

	General Population	African Americans	Latinos	Less Educated	Poor	Older	Younger
Concern That Children Will Access Inappropriate Sites	.41	.47	.69	.49		.22	.40
Have Access Elsewhere	.83	.60	.66	.54		.59	1
Lack of Time to Use Internet	.90	1	.95	1		1	1
Language Barriers	.20	.09	1	.35		.23	.30
No Computer/Inadequate Computer	9	15	17	13		11	11
Not in Universe/Did Not Answer Question	60	40	39	42		43	61

Note: Based on the October 2003 CPS Computer and Internet Supplement of 103,000 total respondents.

The 2003 CPS: Home Access and Digital Citizenship

Box 5.2 shows in greater detail the descriptive data for the 2003 CPS summarized here. Using a somewhat higher bar, Internet use at home, the CPS showed that African Americans and Latinos were only about two-thirds as likely as other Americans to go online at home, and a little less than two-thirds as likely to use the Internet daily. Similar disparities based on age, income, and education are present in both the 2003 CPS and the 2006 Pew. In comparison with 60 percent of the population as a whole, only 43 percent of the less educated (those with a high school education or less) and only 36 percent of the poor (those with annual incomes of $20,000 to $25,000) had home Internet access. Although 35 percent of the population can be classified as digital citizens, the figure is between 18 and 21 percent for African Americans, Latinos, the poor, the less-educated, and the oldest quartile of the sample. The analyses discussed later in this chapter confirm that most of these differences persist for home use and digital citizenship, even when we use appropriate statistical controls.

Importantly, the CPS includes questions about why individuals do not use the Internet. We report these simple percentages below, for they reveal some interesting information on the barriers to access, motivation, and interest.

Minorities remain off-line because of costs, while older and less-educated Americans cite a lack of interest   African Americans and Latinos were much more likely than others to say that the costs are too high (20 and 22 percent, respectively, in comparison with 9 percent of the population overall). The highest proportions of those who say they don't need the Internet are age fifty-eight or older (32 percent),[2] or have a high school education or less (23 percent). Not all disparities, then, are the same, as low incomes seem to be greater hurdles for disadvantaged minorities, and a lack of interest is associated with older and less-educated respondents. Recognizing different causes for technology disparities is crucial for public policy solutions. Smith's argument about the U.S. tradition of ascriptive hierarchy also assigns special significance to inequalities based on race, ethnicity, and gender, which we review before further examining the 2003 CPS.

The Role of Race and Ethnicity

What explains differences in technology access, use, and skill based on race and ethnicity? Some accounts stress racial and ethnic differences in attitudes or awareness, or the perceived relevance of the medium among minorities, while others show systematic dissimilarities in the opportunities available in impoverished communities.

Robert Fairlie (2004) analyzed the 2000 CPS in an effort to explain the lower rates of home access among minorities. He did not examine technology use, as we do here. But his use of the CPS is of particular interest for the purposes of comparison. Variations in income, education, and occupation contribute substantially to lower rates of home computer and Internet access among minorities, according to Fairlie (2004), but they do not entirely explain the contrasts between African Americans, Latinos, and the rest of the population. Mexican Americans have the lowest rates of access, and Fairlie believes language barriers may partly explain these results. A recent Pew study on Latinos also identifies language as a significant influence on Internet use, controlling for other variables (Fox and Livingston 2007). Fairlie (2004) concluded that we do not know much about why race and ethnicity influence home access.

Some social scientists have hypothesized that the lower rates of access and use among African Americans and Latinos are due to differences in motivation or cultural perceptions (including their views of the relevance of content on the Internet) (Kretchmer and Carveth 2001). For example, Jan Van Dijk (2005, 40) says that the differences between African Americans, Latinos, and other Americans are sufficiently large that we must assume that they are cultural. He cites a study (Stanley 2001), in which some African American male respondents expressed the sentiment that computers were for girls. In part, this reflected expectations about the jobs that were available, and the attitude that men performed manual labor. Many of the other studies citing negative attitudes about the relevance or lack of interest are based on narratives from some qualitative interviews. While these can provide insights about some individuals who are nonusers (and how race may influence reasoning), we must ask the extent to which these findings are representative, even for nonusers. How far do they get us in explaining the persistence of racial and ethnic disparities? The CPS, for example, shows that of course some African Americans and Latinos (as well as whites) have no interest in the Internet. But there is no real difference between minorities and whites in terms of interest, whereas there are major distinctions in interest based on education. There are, however, sizable racial and ethnic gaps in terms of the sensitivity to costs for Internet access and the lack of a computer. Are these factors—cost sensitivity and the lack of a working computer—simply another form of lack of interest, though?

Survey research paints a different picture: that African Americans and Latinos have more positive attitudes toward technology, despite lower rates of access, use, and self-reported skill. National survey data indicate that African Americans, and to a lesser extent Latinos, are even more likely to believe in the benefits of computers and the Internet than similarly situated whites. This is particularly true for African Americans when the respondents are asked about technology and economic opportunity—getting a job, getting a raise, starting a business, and so on. African Americans express more willingness to use public access sites (Mossberger, Tolbert, and Stansbury 2003). Among those who do not currently use computers or the Internet, African Americans more frequently say that they will go online someday (Lenhart 2003). Latinos are more likely than other groups to believe that you need the Internet to keep up with the times, controlling for other factors. In other respects, however, their attitudes do not differ from other Americans, who are on the whole optimistic about information technology.

Comparing behavior, African Americans are more likely than white Americans to use the Internet for a job search or to take online classes (Spooner and Rainie 2000; U.S. Department of Commerce 2002). These relationships are statistically significant, controlling for other factors, again indicating that African Americans connect technology use with economic advancement (Mossberger, Tolbert, and Stansbury 2003). More recent data confirm that this pattern has continued over time. In 2005, 67 percent of African American Internet users had looked for a job online, compared to 39 percent of white Internet users and 54 percent of English-speaking Latino Internet users. (While African Americans are most likely to search online for jobs, Latinos also engage in online job search at higher rates than non-Hispanic whites.) As online education has grown, African Americans still remain ahead. As of 2005, 18 percent of African American Internet users reported having taken an online course for credit, in comparison with 11 percent of white Internet users.[3] The motivation to overcome barriers of discrimination in the job market likely accounts for these positive attitudes toward technology and economic opportunity, and higher rates of Internet use for job search and distance learning. After World War II, African Americans also exploited the educational benefits of the GI Bill at higher rates than white veterans, in an analogous effort to secure greater economic opportunity (Hacker, Mettler, and Pinderhughes 2005).

How can we explain this contradiction between more positive attitudes and lower rates of access, use, and skill? Karen Mossberger, Caroline Tolbert, and Michele Gilbert (2006) hypothesized that the place of residence matters because it can influence opportunities to learn about technology in schools, public access sites, social networks, and jobs. Using hierarchical linear modeling to analyze national opinion data merged with zip code–level data, the authors demonstrated that race at the individual level is no longer significant in predicting access or use once we control for contextual variables such as the median income or the percentage of high school graduates in the respondent's zip code. In other words, persistent and significant racial differences in technology use for African Americans are caused by the limitations of living in segregated, high-poverty neighborhoods, rather than by race per se (Mossberger, Tolbert, and Gilbert 2006). For Latinos, ethnicity as well as place is still important—perhaps because of language, as Fairlie (2004) suggested. African Americans living in middle-class neighborhoods are actually somewhat more likely than similarly situated whites to have a home computer (Mossberger, Tolbert, and Gilbert 2006).

Surveys comparing communities in northeastern Ohio recently found that residents in poor African American communities were more likely than individuals in other poor neighborhoods to use the Internet even if they did not have access at home *or* work, and that living in an area with a high proportion of African Americans was a statistically significant predictor of use outside home or work, controlling for other factors (Mossberger, Kaplan, and Gilbert 2006). Demonstrating clear effort to participate as digital citizens, residents relied on networks of friends and relatives as well as public access sites to go online when they could. The high dependence on social networks recalls other patterns of resource sharing and "kinship" in poor communities (Stack 1974). One advantage of such arrangements is informal learning about technology, or the creation of communities of practice (Van Dijk 2005, 91; Warschauer 2003, 121). The problem, however, is that these individuals used the Internet sporadically. This underscores the need to measure the frequency of use rather than just occasional use. Those without home or work access were more likely to go online just a few times a month. It was also clear from both survey data and interviews with library officials that there were longer waiting times along with strains on public resources in these heavily African American neighborhoods with high demand. The story of these northeastern Ohio communities encapsulates the contradictions of race, where positive attitudes and motivation are hampered by a lack of resources for poor minorities.

The Role of Gender

The most recent data show that U.S. women are just as likely to be online as men. But gender matters for Internet use in other ways. Men are traditionally more intensive users who go online more frequently and engage in a greater number of uses (DiMaggio et al. 2001; Boneva, Kraut, and Frohlich 2001; Katz and Rice 2002, 41; Fallows 2005; Bimber 1999). These findings raise questions about possible skill disparities between men and women.

What is the evidence on gender and skills? Survey data reveal almost no substantive difference between men and women in self-reported technical competence, information literacy, or the ability to use the Internet to find information (Mossberger, Tolbert, and Stansbury 2003). According to a recent study that compared self-assessments and actual performance in searching for information online, there were no real differences in the actual performance of men and women, once age, education, and other influences were taken into account. Yet women underestimate their skill, and this may even limit use due to a feeling of inadequacy online (Hargittai and Shafer 2006).

Limited time and family responsibilities may account for these differences in use, rather than skill. A higher percentage of parents than nonparents have computers and the Internet in their homes, and married individuals also have higher rates of access (Lenhart 2003; Fairlie 2004). But parenthood may have a constraining effect on use, especially for women, as experience and time are important predictors of use (Howard, Rainie, and Jones 2001, 403). Surveys have shown that 83 percent of women who reported limited access and guilt about the time away from family responsibilities were parents of young children, or had five or more children (Burke 2001). Single women, especially single mothers, are less likely to use the Internet (Bucy 2000; U.S. Department of Commerce 1998).

Research shows differences in online activities, but also increasing use by women. Females are most interested in the communication capabilities of the Internet for meeting new people and staying in touch with them, and are more frequent users of e-mail than men (Jackson et al. 2001; Fallows 2005; Boneva, Kraut, and Frohlich 2001, 538). Women go online more often for health information, religious information, jobs searches, and playing games online; men seek financial/stock-trading information, read general and sports news, shop on the Internet (including online auctions), and visit government Web sites (Howard, Rainie, and Jones 2001; Fallows 2005). Differences in activities do not necessarily reflect disparities in skill or access, or a lack of interest in the medium. Women in general, like African Americans and Latinos, are also more likely to believe that information technology is important for economic opportunity (Mossberger, Tolbert, and Stansbury 2003).

In fact, recent surveys reveal that both African American and younger women surpass males in their peer groups in terms of the percentage who are Internet users (Fallows 2005). The research cited in Deborah Fallows (2005) does not control for factors other than gender and race, however. In the following section, we consider many influences on technology use in order to isolate their effects using appropriate controls.

Approach

In order to explore home Internet access—and more important, daily Internet use—we turn to the most recent comprehensive survey data available: the October 2003 CPS supplement on information technology conducted by the U.S. Census Bureau. The national random sample survey includes over 103,000 respondents. As mentioned in chapter 2, the large sample allows a rigorous empirical test of what demographic, economic, and geographic factors predict digital citizenship. In this chapter, we are especially concerned with taking an in-depth view of access and daily use among less-educated, minority, and poor Americans. We use statistical models to predict the probability of home Internet access and the frequency of Internet use, including daily use.

We analyze these data in two ways. First, we estimate multivariate regression models to predict technology access and use for the general population. Second, because of the unique large-sample CPS data, we are able to estimate multivariate regression models on subsamples of the population—that is, predicting what factors increase technology access and use among only African Americans, Latinos, or the less educated. We also compare factors related to Internet use among younger and older people. This allows us to isolate the factors predicting technology use more accurately than previous research.

Two primary dependent (or outcome) variables are examined. The CPS asked the respondents about whether the "Internet at home was used." A little more than 62,000 individuals (or 59 percent) said yes and approximately 42,000 (or 40 percent) indicated no. As of 2003, we can be fairly confident that roughly 60 percent of the U.S. population used the Internet at home. This variable was recoded so that "yes" responses were coded 1 and "no" responses were coded 0.

But home access may obscure more critical questions of use. Daily Internet use, our proxy for digital citizenship, requires skill and literacy, and serves as our second dependent variable. The CPS asked the respondents about their "Internet use and access over the last year." This variable was coded so that higher values measured more frequent Internet use with the respondents coded 4 ("at least once a day"), 3 ("at least once a week but not every day"), 2 ("at least once a month but not every week"), 1 ("less than once a month"), and 0 ("no Internet access"). As of 2003, 34.5 percent of the population (or 36,000 respondents) used the Internet at least once every day. These daily users can be classified as digital citizens, regularly using the Internet for work and/or home activities with high levels of technology skills. This 34.5 percent of the population who are digital citizens is much lower than the 60 percent of the population with home Internet access. The next section describes in greater detail other variables included in the study and how they are measured. Readers who are less interested in the methodological issues, as before, may want to turn to the following section on "Results."

Discussion of Methods and Variable Coding

Our primary independent (or predictor) variables measure demographic factors traditionally associated with the digital divide, such as income, education, age, and race/ethnicity. Compared to standard surveys, our national opinion data include large and representative samples of African Americans and Latinos. Of the 103,000 total sample, 10 percent (or 10,113) reported being of Hispanic origin, and almost 10 percent (or 9,920) reported being black, allowing for separate statistical analyses of these groups.[4] These sample sizes are larger than the 2002 Black National Election Study, for example.

The statistical models include many socioeconomic control variables—such as age, education, income, and geographic location—that have been identified as significant in previous digital inequality research. Variable coding generally mirrors that discussed in chapter 2. Age is measured in years. The educational attainment of the respondent is measured on a 5-point ordinal scale ranging from 1 (less than a high school degree) to 5 (a bachelor's degree or higher). Income is measured as the total family annual income on an ordinal scale ranging from $2,500 (coded 1) to over $150,000 (coded 16). Geography/location is measured with binary variables for urban and suburban residents, with rural residents and those who did not identify their location as the reference group (coded as 0). It is not possible to identify more specific zip code or census tract information for CPS respondents (as used in Mossberger, Tolbert, and Gilbert 2006), so this chapter uses more general measures of place (as in Fairlie 2004). Because having children has been shown to be important in technology access for adults (Lenhart 2003; Fairlie 2004), we include a binary variable measuring whether the respondent has a child under the age of eighteen living at home. Parents with children are coded 1, and all others are coded 0. Marital status may also be crucial in technology use, especially because married couples often have higher incomes (Fairlie 2004). We use a binary variable for married, with non-married respondents (widowed, divorced, separated, or never married) as the reference category coded 0. Married is also the modal category, with 59 percent of the respondents reporting being married.

An advantage of the CPS data beyond standard surveys is the detailed employment information. We again use the eleven industry and occupation job categories measuring a respondent's primary occupation.[5] We expect that the management, professional, sales, and office/administrative categories would have the highest technology use. Using listwise deletion, our overall models have nearly eighty-five thousand cases.

Results: Home Internet Access for the General Population

We first examine the general trends predicting home Internet access for the general population, shown in table 5.A.1. Since the dependent variable—home Internet access—is binary, logistic regression coefficients are estimated. Column 1 provides the baseline model for the general population. Overall, the disparities are similar to those reported in previous research, including Fairlie's (2004) analysis of the 2000 CPS.

Gender is not a factor in access, but age, income, education, race, ethnicity, and location matter While women are statistically less likely to have home Internet access than men, the substantive magnitude of this effect is small (only a 2 percent difference). Racial gaps remain, however, as Latinos and African Americans are considerably less likely to have home access. These models based on large-sample sizes provide additional evidence that home access continues to be in part defined by race and ethnicity, even after controlling for the respondent's socioeconomic status and place of residence.[6] Using a large-sample survey conducted in both English and Spanish reveals that Latinos are in fact disadvantaged in terms of access. We also see that younger individuals are considerably more likely to have home Internet access, and suburban residents are more likely than those living in urban or rural areas to have access. Annual family income is a strong and independent predictor of the probability of having home access, as is a higher education.

Children, marriage, and some occupations increase the likelihood of home Internet access Consistent with the literature (Lenhart 2003;

Fairlie 2004), individuals with a child under the age of eighteen living at home are more likely to have Internet access at home, as are married respondents. Fairlie (2004) also found that occupation partly explained the disparities in home access. Here, we show in greater detail that the respondents with professional, management, service, sales, and secretarial/administrative occupations are all more likely to have Internet access at home, holding other factors constant.

Results: Home Internet Access for Disadvantaged Populations

Another way to understand technology access rates is to conduct statistical tests where only subgroups of the population are included—such as African Americans, Latinos, the less educated, or the poor. The models discussed below provide a superior test of what factors increase home Internet access for disadvantaged subpopulations.

African Americans
The most revealing analyses are reported in the remaining columns of table 5.A.1. Column 2 includes only African Americans, a critical subpopulation in the United States. There are distinct similarities and differences with the general population in what predicts home Internet access among this group, suggesting additional barriers faced by African Americans.

Many of the factors that affect the population as a whole influence access among African Americans   We see that education, income, and age are important for predicting technology access in this subsample, as they are among the general population. Young African Americans are more likely to have home access as well as those residing in suburbs compared to urban or rural areas. Marriage and having a child under the age of eighteen residing at home increases the probability of access for this group, as for the population as a whole.

Occupations matter less for home access for African Americans   Beyond those employed in professional occupations, employment does not appear to translate into an increased probability of home access, as it does when we consider the entire population. For the overall sample, the respondents employed in management, service, sales, and secretarial occupations were more likely to have home access. Among African Americans, though, only those in professional positions are more likely to have Internet access. Perhaps African Americans in service, sales, and secretarial positions are relegated to jobs within these categories that have limited technology use or lower pay. The descriptive statistics presented in box 5.2, for example, suggest that cost is a primary factor limiting home access for this minority group, and labor market discrimination may blunt the expected impact of technology-intensive occupational categories.

Latinos

Few scholars have studied Internet use among Latinos in much detail, and thus we know relatively less about this minority group than African Americans.[7] Yet Latinos are now the largest minority in the United States (Hero 1992), and because of larger families and higher birthrates, their share of the population is increasing dramatically. Partially because of language barriers, they have the lowest educational attainment rates of any minority group. It is important and revealing to study the Latinos in our sample to see what factors predict home Internet access.

Home access for Latinos differs from the general population in terms of the effects of age, marriage, and residence Mirroring the traditional digital divide, education and income are important; educated, more affluent Latinos are more likely to have home Internet access. These findings illustrate that technology disparities based on poverty or a lack of skill are unlikely to disappear. But surprisingly, age is not a divide. Young Latinos are not more likely to have home access than older Latinos. Marriage per se does not increase the probability of access, but having a child does. Geographic location does not affect this subpopulation, as Latinos residing in rural, urban, and suburban areas have statistically indistinguishable access rates.

Latinos contrast with African Americans on occupational factors Unlike for African Americans, occupation does matter in predicting home Internet access. Latinos working in professional, management, sales, and secretarial occupations all have an increased probability of home access, and so occupational influences for Latinos resemble patterns for the general population. This suggests that African Americans may face more discrimination in the labor market than Latinos, particularly within white-collar occupations.

Less-Educated and Low-Income Americans

Column 3 in table 5.A.1 examines the almost 35,000 respondents in our sample who have only a high school degree or less. These less-educated and presumably lower-skilled workers face increased barriers to home Internet access. Here we see almost an exact mirroring of the factors predicting home Internet access among the overall population: age, income, place of residence, marriage, child, and occupation.

Racial inequalities are related to decreased access rates, even when studying only less-educated individuals or the poor   Race and ethnicity magnify the disadvantage among the less educated. Latinos with only a high school degree have a lower probability of home access than similarly situated whites with only a high school degree. Similarly, among the less educated, Africans Americans have a lower probability of home Internet access than whites. We see the same results among the poor (column 4), or those families earning $35,000 per year or less (which corresponds to the federal poverty line for a family of four). The coefficients for African Americans and Latinos are negative and statistically significant, indicating that among the poor, African Americans and Latinos have a lower probability of home Internet access than poor whites. What these data reveal is that patterns of inequalities in the overall population are replicated in disadvantaged subpopulations.

Results: Digital Citizens as Daily Internet Users

A central premise of this book is that measuring access alone may neglect important variations in technology use and skill. Table 5.A.2 explores the factors that predict digital citizenship or daily Internet use. Since the dependent variable is a 5-point ordinal scale, ordered logistic regression coefficients are reported. The highest values on this scale measure daily Internet use (which can occur anywhere). The lowest values on this scale indicate no Internet use.

General Population

Column 1 in table 5.A.2 provides our baseline model for the total population of almost 85,000 respondents.

Factors critical for home Internet access matter also for the frequency of use, but their effects are magnified   Latinos and African Americans have considerably lower probabilities of being daily Internet users than whites. Asian Americans are no different than whites in the probability of being digital citizens. A higher education, greater income, youth, and a suburban or urban location increase the frequency of Internet use; notice that urban and suburban residence increases the frequency of use, whereas only suburban residence increased the probability of home Internet access. Occupation again matters, with those in professional, management, service, sales, and secretarial positions significantly more likely to be daily users than those in production occupations (the reference category).

Gender has a modest effect on digital citizenship, and the presence of children is associated with the decreased frequency of use   Females are less likely to be digital citizens than males, but the substantive size of this effect is small. The results showing that women have a lower frequency of use than men is consistent with the literature, which shows some differences in the frequency of use between men and women. While marriage increases the probability of being a digital citizen, having children under the age of eighteen at home reduces the likelihood of daily Internet use. This latter finding may reflect time constraints, as daily access to the Internet is twice as common at home as at work.

Substantive Size of Disparities in Who Has Digital Citizenship

Probability simulations are useful for understanding the substantive magnitude of the statistically significant differences reported above. They differ from the simple percentages reported earlier in the chapter because they show the effects of a given variable, holding other factors constant. Setting the explanatory variables at their mean or modal values reveals that the baseline probability of being a digital citizen (defined as daily Internet use) is 34 percent ($p = .004$) of the U.S. population. The estimates in this simulation are based on a white married female of an

Box 5.3
What Matters? Size of the Disparities in Digital Citizenship

Probability of Daily Internet Use			
Low Education (High School Graduate)	.22 (.004)	Black	.21 (.005)
High Education (Associate's Degree)	.44 (.005)	White	.34 (.004)
Diff Education (Low to High)	**+.22**	**Diff Ethnicity (Black to White)**	**+.13**
Old (63 Years of Age)	.21 (.003)	Latino	.18 (.004)
Young (29 Years of Age)	.49 (.006)	White	.33 (.004)
Diff Age (Young to Old)	**+.28**	**Diff Race (White to Latino)**	**+.15**
Poor ($20,000–25,000 Annual Income)	.23 (.004)	Asian	.28 (.007)
Rich ($75,000–100,000 Annual Income)	.45 (.005)	White	.33 (.004)
Diff Income (Poor to Rich)	**+.22**	**Diff Race (White to Asian)**	**+.05**

Note: Predicted probabilities estimated with Clarify. Numbers in parentheses are standard errors. Simulations assume a female respondent, with modal or mean values on all explanatory variables, varying education, age, income, and race/ethnicity. Simulations based on model presented in table 5.A.2, column 1.

average age, education, and income residing in the suburbs, and without children residing in the home.

The largest differences are based on age Varying the age of the respondents, but setting all other variables at the same mean/modal values, reveals similarly large substantive effects. An older respondent (sixty-three years of age, plus one standard deviation above the mean) has a 21 percent (p = .003) probability of digital citizenship, compared to a young respondent (twenty-nine years of age, minus one standard deviation from the mean) who has a 49 percent (p = .006) probability of being online every day—a 28 percent increased probability based on age alone. The young are considerably more likely to be digital citizens than older individuals.

Socioeconomic factors are nearly as important   If the respondent has only a high school degree (low educational attainment, minus one standard deviation from the mean), the probability of daily Internet use drops to 24 percent (p = .004). The same respondent with a higher education (an associate's degree, plus one standard deviation from the mean) has a 44 percent (p = .005) probability of being a digital citizen—a 22 percent increased probability based on education alone. Therefore, education accounts for a 22 percent difference in the probability of digital citizenship. This indicates skill is a critical dimension for participation online. Similarly, income is strongly associated with digital citizenship. The poor (an annual income of $20,000 to $25,000 minus one standard deviation below the mean) have a 23 percent (p = .004) probability of logging on every day, compared to the affluent ($75,000 to $100,000 in annual income, plus one standard deviation from the mean), who have a 45 percent (p = .005) probability of being daily Internet users—a 22 percent difference based on income alone.

Race and ethnicity are still substantial, even controlling for education and income   Race and ethnicity also exert independent effects, determining disparities in daily Internet use. Setting the explanatory variables at their mean or modal values reveals that African Americans on average have a 21 percent (p = .005) probability of being digital citizens, while Latinos have an 18 percent (p = .004) probability. Asian Americans have a 28 percent (p = .007) probability of daily Internet use, while whites (non-Hispanics) have a 34 percent (p = .004) probability. The gaps in daily use based on race/ethnicity range from 5 percent comparing Asian Americans to whites, to 15 percent comparing Latinos to non-Hispanic whites.

The gender gap has virtually closed in the frequency of use, just as it did earlier in access   In contrast to the large substantive gaps reported above, women have a 34 percent (p = .004) likelihood of being online every day compared to 35 percent (p = .004) for men—a 1 percent difference. While differences between men and women are statistically significant, their magnitude is now negligible in 2003.

Results: Digital Citizenship for Disadvantaged Groups

Again, the subpopulation analyses reported in the remaining columns of table 5.A.2 are illustrative.

Digital citizenship results emphasize the importance of access outside the home for African Americans   When the frequency of use includes use at work, home, or a public place, we see that African Americans (column 2) generally mirror the overall population. Younger, more educated, and more affluent African Americans have an increased probability of being digital citizens, as do those in management, professional, sales, and secretarial occupations, compared to production workers (the reference category). This pattern for use is different than the one we saw for *home Internet access* among African Americans, indicating that access for African Americans may be more likely to take place at work or a public place. African Americans residing in urban and suburban areas are more likely to be digital citizens than those residing in rural areas. If African Americans have considerably lower home Internet access rates, these combined findings suggest public access makes a difference for African American populations residing in urban areas. This lends greater generalizability to the northeastern Ohio neighborhood study mentioned earlier in this chapter. Place matters for Latinos, but in a reversal of the pattern for African Americans. Latinos residing in urban areas are less likely to frequently use the Internet compared to those residing in rural and suburban areas. If public access is more available in cities, Latinos may be less likely to use public access than African Americans.

African American women are more likely to be digital citizens   While women overall are basically similar to men, one striking difference among African Americans is the greater frequency of use for women. Digital citizens or daily Internet users are more likely to be African American females than males. More recent studies using descriptive statistics have reported more frequent use among African American women, but our analysis shows that these gender differences among African

Americans are significant, holding other factors constant. Stanley's (2001) interviews with African American men revealed some attitudes about technology use that may contribute to gender differences among African Americans, though they clearly do not account for racial disparities.

Factors predicting the frequency of use among Latinos largely resemble those for the general population   Digital citizenship for Latinos (column 3) also has some overlap with the general population, as the younger, more educated, and more affluent are more likely to be online every day. Employment and occupation continue to matter among Latinos, with those in professional, management, sales, and secretarial positions more likely to be frequent users.

Gender is not significant for digital citizenship for Latinos, but marriage is related to the decreased frequency of use   Gender is not a statistically significant predictor of daily Internet use among Latinos; women are not more likely to be frequent users than men, or vice versa, unlike African Americans. Marriage actually reduces the probability of daily Internet access among Latinos—the reverse of the general population.

Columns 3 and 4 of table 5.A.2 report models predicting the frequency of Internet use for the less educated (a high school degree or less) and the poor (annual household incomes of $35,000 or less).

Less-educated women spend more time online than less-educated men   Tracking the analysis of African Americans, we see that less-educated women are more likely to be digital citizens than less-educated men—the reverse of the results for the general population (column 3). This finding suggests that Internet use among less-educated women may be an important way to improve socioeconomic status. In contrast, among the poor (column 4), females are less likely than men to be daily Internet users. A traditional pattern of gender inequality is apparent among the poor.

Variation among the less educated and the poor follows more general patterns   Traditional influences on digital inequality shape digital citizenship among low-income and less-educated Americans, with age, occupation, race/ethnicity, and place of residence being key for the frequency of use. Among these subgroups, residing in suburban or urban areas increases the probability of digital citizenship compared to rural residence, and this mirrors the results for the general population. The young are more likely to be online in both of these subpopulations.

Service sector employment is associated with digital citizenship among the less educated and the poor, but not for minorities   Among the low-skilled and poor subsamples, even service occupations increase the probability of daily Internet use—a finding not replicated among African Americans or Latinos.

African Americans and Latinos use the Internet less frequently than other disadvantaged Americans   Again, the most striking finding is that poor and less-educated Latinos and African Americans are even less likely to be digital citizens than other disadvantaged Americans. Stated another way, even after controlling for education and income (socioeconomic status), race and ethnicity matter in predicting digital citizenship or daily Internet access. Beyond the digital divide in access, inequalities based on race and ethnicity drive participation online, consistent with Smith's notion of ascriptive hierarchy.

Results: Digital Citizenship for the Young and the Old

A crucial way to predict future technology inequalities is to study patterns of access and the frequency of use among the young (defined here as the bottom quartile of the population, or those thirty-two years of age or younger), and compare them to the oldest population quartile (age fifty-eight or older). Table 5.A.3 provides multivariate regression models predicting home Internet access among younger (column 1) versus older people (column 2) as well as digital citizenship for younger (column 3) and older respondents (column 4).

Evidence exists that disparities in access are not simply disappearing in the younger generation   Surprisingly, the factors predicting home Internet access among older and younger respondents are similar (columns

1 and 2). Increased education, affluence, suburban residence, and white race raise the probability of home Internet access whether one is young or old.

Education determines digital citizenship for the young and the old   But the models predicting the frequency of Internet use (columns 3 and 4, table 5.A.3) are even more revealing. Among the young (column 3), we find classic evidence of the digital divide in predicting digital citizenship by gender, race, income, and education. Although still significant, substantively wealth is less important for the frequency of use among the young (see smaller size of the regression coefficient for income for the young than the old—columns 3 versus 4). The size of the coefficients for education are almost identical across the two subgroups, however. Skill, measured by education, is critical for digital citizenship whether the respondent is young or old. Patterns of racial and ethnic inequalities are repeated here as well, with Latinos and African Americans less likely to have home access whether they are young or old, and less likely to be daily Internet users. This suggests that patterns of inequality will not disappear in the near future, even among the young. Despite the expansion of the online population among the young, classic patterns of inequality based on socioeconomic conditions, race, and ethnicity are readily apparent.

Older women, though, outpace older men in digital citizenship   In some ways, it is the older population sample that represents a break from traditional digital disparities. Among those fifty-eight years of age or older, women are more likely to be daily Internet users than men, paralleling the gender use patterns we found among African Americans and the less educated. Yet among those thirty-two years of age or younger, males are significantly more likely to be online than women. The effects of gender are varied, with women enjoying an edge among several of the less-connected subgroups.

These analyses illustrate that different predictors of digital citizenship shape patterns of access and use within subgroups of the population. Still, some core factors emerge repeatedly; in every case, education, income, race, and ethnicity define the chances for individuals to develop digital citizenship.

From the Digital Divide to Digital Citizenship: Persistent Inequalities

Even with the expansion of the online population in the United States, those who are low income, less educated, older, African American, and Latino continue to be less likely to have home computers or use the Internet frequently. These factors are all statistically significant using multivariate controls, measured across a number of models representing different segments of the U.S. population, for both use at home and the frequency of use.

Given the growth of information and opportunities online in the United States, we have defined digital citizens as those who use the Internet daily. The frequency of use is a better measure of capacity for digital citizenship than occasional use or access alone, although we know that the most frequent use occurs in the home, followed at some distance by work (U.S. Department of Commerce 2002). Frequent use implies basic skills for using technology, and as individuals gain experience, they deepen their activities online, undertaking more complex tasks while also using the Internet for work, study, or information search rather than just entertainment (DiMaggio and Celeste 2004).

When measured this way, only 21 percent of African Americans and 18 percent of Latinos were digital citizens in 2003, compared to 35 percent of the U.S. population overall (see table 5.A.1). Although recent Pew surveys estimate that close to half the population now uses the Internet daily, the evidence shows that gaps based on race, ethnicity, and socioeconomic status are not disappearing. Our analysis of younger and older people demonstrates that while income is somewhat less crucial for Internet use among the young, race, ethnicity, and education will continue to affect digital citizenship in the future. Whether the effects of income are truly fading remains to be seen, as college students are likely to have low incomes during their current stage in life, yet are intensely engaged online. The temporary economic status of highly educated college students may blur the significance of income for Internet use among the young.

Women, however, are nearly as likely to be digital citizens as men. After the access gap closed around the turn of the millennium, women continued to be less frequent users. By 2003, women were only about 1 percent less likely than men to be daily Internet users, controlling for other factors. Among some groups—African Americans, less-educated individuals, and older Americans—women are actually more likely to be digital citizens than men. For others, such as Latinos, there are no differences in the frequency of use based on gender. Women continue to earn considerably less than men despite their digital skills, as chapter 2 showed, and they are underrepresented in many technology occupations (Eccles 2005; Fountain 2001). But they have become equal participants on the Internet. The gender dimension of Smith's ascriptive hierarchy no longer represents a barrier for digital citizenship.

More enduring are those inequalities based on race and ethnicity. Even among the poor and less educated, African Americans and Latinos are doubly disadvantaged. Sizable gaps continue despite more positive attitudes toward technology among African Americans. Even though some progress is evident for minorities, we can see that for many their connections online are more tenuous. Among African Americans, digital citizens rely more heavily on access outside the home, and both African Americans and Latinos are more likely to cite the cost of technology as prohibitive. This differs from less-educated or older Americans, who are simply less interested in the Internet. Prior research has demonstrated that Latinos are clearly no less optimistic about information technology than other Americans (Mossberger, Tolbert, and Stansbury 2003), and yet they also lag considerably behind in digital citizenship. This contradiction between aspirations and results lends credence to claims that inequalities online replicate traditions of ascriptive hierarchy in U.S. citizenship.

Yet digital inequality reflects class or socioeconomic divisions not included in the notion of ascriptive hierarchy, as well following racial and ethnic divides. Race and ethnicity exercise an independent effect over and above income and education, but as prior research has shown, segregation and concentrated poverty explain these differences for African Americans, and a portion of the disparities for Latinos. It is poor minorities who confront the greatest barriers to digital citizenship, for they are most likely to live in communities with inadequate educational resources, to achieve lower rates of educational attainment, and to be excluded from technology-intensive jobs. Poverty limits home access and frequent use, and educational disparities constrain the development of the skills needed for digital citizenship. For low-income and less-educated Americans of all backgrounds, in both metropolitan and rural communities, poverty and unequal education diminish the potential for digital citizenship. Ascriptive hierarchy is alive and well, but it goes hand in hand with class inequality and an unfulfilled liberal tradition more generally. Unequal access to education and growing income inequality reveal the cracks in the liberal tradition promising an equal chance for all to succeed and prosper.

6

Broadband and Digital Citizenship

High-speed connections promise to enhance our Nation's productivity and economic competitiveness, improve education, and expand health care for all Americans. High-speed networks provide the power to erase geographic, economic, and cultural gaps.
—U.S. Department of Commerce, *A Nation Online*, 2004

Recent reports show that high-speed, or broadband, Internet access is proliferating in the United States, and that it is associated with a more frequent and sophisticated use of the Internet (Horrigan 2005; Fox 2005; U.S. Department of Commerce 2004). Broadband Internet service, which is most commonly available for home use through cable modems or digital subscriber lines (DSL), is technically defined by the Federal Communications Commission in terms of its speed of at least two hundred kilobits per second in one direction. But broadband's significance goes beyond its transmission speed, as it is also "higher-capacity, always-on, and interactive" (Alliance for Public Technology and Benton Foundation 2003). Broadband "fundamentally changes the way people use the Internet" (European Commission 2004, 1). Rather than merely providing a faster and better technological tool, broadband access may facilitate the migration of tasks and information online, improving digital skills that are important for economic opportunity and political participation. In other words, broadband access may promote frequent use and digital citizenship.

Despite the overall expansion of broadband access, systematic inequalities are apparent and also merit attention as a public policy issue. In multivariate analyses of Pew survey data from 2003 and 2005, we find that broadband access reflects many of the same gaps that are apparent in computer or Internet disparities, but that family structure and geographic areas also influence broadband adoption. In a separate analysis using a 2001 survey (Mossberger, Tolbert, and Stansbury 2003), we find a significant relationship between broadband access and the frequency of use, and broadband access and the likelihood that the respondents have engaged in political and economic uses of the Internet. We describe this as "digital experience." Previous reports using descriptive data have suggested a connection between broadband use and the range of activities that users undertake online (Horrigan 2004; U.S. Department of Commerce 2004, 7–8). Our analysis controls for other possible explanations, and provides stronger evidence of a link between broadband, digital citizenship, and experience and skill online.

The Benefits of Broadband Access and the Costs of Exclusion

The United States recently ranked twelfth in per capita broadband subscriptions (OECD 2005a), but some evidence indicates that broadband adoption may be growing. According to the Pew Internet and American Life Project, 42 percent of Americans had high-speed broadband connections by March 2006 (Horrigan 2006). Why has broadband not been more widespread in the United States? The reliance on private markets and the large geography of the United States emerge as topics of debates over the economics of broadband policy. Two dimensions that influence the individual adoption of broadband are its *availability* (including the presence of the necessary infrastructure) and *affordability*.

One limitation for the diffusion of broadband is the availability of the technology through cable, DSL, wireless, satellite, or other means of delivery. Cable modem access is available in 80 percent of the United States, and DSL is available in approximately 75 percent of the country (OECD 2004, 12, 13). The areas most likely to lack broadband access are rural and served by smaller regional carriers (Prieger 2003). Broadband availability currently depends on an approximate 3.5-mile distance from local exchange carriers for cable and DSL, creating a "last-mile bottleneck" for sparsely populated rural areas, where infrastructure investment has not been profitable (Prieger 2003; Ayres and Williams 2003). The availability of broadband affects the ability of businesses, government, and other institutions—as well as individuals—to take advantage of high-speed connections. Although programs such as E-Rate have aided schools and libraries in obtaining Internet access, only 34 percent of rural public libraries have bandwidth levels of 760 bkps (high speed), in comparison with 42 percent of libraries in the country that have this level of bandwidth (Bertot, McClure, and Jaeger 2005). Places lacking in broadband access may suffer in terms of local economic development, and the ability to deliver high-quality services such as health care and education for residents.

Price is also a consideration in broadband, which is more expensive than dial-up access. There has been some reduction in average prices, as less-expensive DSL overtook cable modems as the primary means of broadband access during 2005. Monthly service rates remain much higher, however, for high-speed access compared to a dial-up modem connection, so income is clearly one factor in broadband access. In 2004, broadband users reported an average monthly bill of $39, compared to an average monthly bill of less than $20 for a dial-up modem connection (Horrigan 2004). By 2006, the average monthly cost for broadband had declined to $36 per month. The growth of home broadband access among African Americans was particularly dramatic in this period of falling prices (Horrigan 2006). As the previous chapter showed, technology use among African Americans is especially sensitive to price.

The high-resolution, high-speed, and "always-on" capacity of broadband connections make it more likely that individuals will be digital citizens. Broadband encourages a more intensive use of the Internet and makes information more readily available. Beyond this, though, broadband may encourage the development of digital skills exhibited through the performance of a variety of activities online.

The Economic and Institutional Benefits of Broadband Use
There are collective benefits to broadband access as well as the enhancement of skills needed for digital citizenship. Broadband can be economically justified as a public policy issue if there are market failures that produce underinvestment and inhibit society's potential to capture the full benefits of the technology. International organizations such as the Organization for Economic Cooperation and Development as well as the European Commission of the European Union have promoted

increased broadband access among member states because of its potential for supporting cost savings and increased productivity. Research conducted by the Brookings Institution, the University of California at Berkeley, and the Momentum research group estimated that 61 percent of U.S. businesses have used the Internet, and have accumulated a cost savings of $155.2 billion (NetImpact 2002). One study has estimated the potential impact of broadband on the U.S. economy at $500 billion per year in gross domestic product within 15 to 25 years (Crandall and Jackson 2001). Others predict substantial economic benefits from broadband as well (Yankee Group 2001; Ferguson 2004, 6–7).

In addition to these early economic forecasts, some initial evidence is emerging to support the contention that broadband availability has positive economic effects. Studies of individual communities that had municipal broadband networks found greater business investment or higher retail sales in those communities in comparison with their neighbors (Strategic Networks Group 2003; Kelley 2003; Ford and Koutsky 2005). Recent national research using Federal Communications Commission data on broadband availability by zip code between 1998 and 2000 found positive economic effects, controlling for other factors. The authors concluded that communities with broadband enjoyed higher growth rates in the number of businesses in information technology–intensive sectors, the number of businesses in general, and employment overall (Lehr et al. 2005). In addition to the potential that broadband offers for economic development, the public benefits from broadband include innovative uses in schools and government agencies (Alliance for Public Technology and the Benton Foundation 2003; Telecommunications Industry Association 2003).

The Individual Benefits of Broadband Use: Reducing the Impact of Distance and Disability

There are other advantages that broadband offers for individual users as well as businesses, schools, and governments. Some of the most promising applications for broadband are in telemedicine, distance learning, and Internet accessibility for people with disabilities. For example, the improved resolution of broadband permits more accurate diagnosis over the Internet, and the high quality of broadband transmission also facilitates video sign language interpretation. Broadband opens up new possibilities for remote monitoring of patients in their homes. This could increase the feasibility of independent living for the elderly and others (National Academy of Sciences 2002, 117). Broadband is useful for protocol conversion for adaptive technologies for the visually impaired (for computer speech recognition or speech synthesis) (Telecommunications Industry Association 2003). Distance learning can be made more interactive through real-time video conferencing and video streaming. As more adult students have broadband in their homes, it becomes easier for distance educators to make fuller use of interactive technology (Alliance for Public Technology and the Benton Foundation 2003). Telecommuting is another application for broadband, and this could have special significance for residents of remote areas, or workers who are constrained by child or elder care needs (National Academy of Sciences 2002, 117). A recent study of the 2004 election conducted by the University of Michigan demonstrates that broadband users are more likely to be exposed to diverse viewpoints on policy issues and politics, controlling for other factors (Horrigan, Garrett, and Resnick 2004).

Convenience, Frequent Use, and Skill

More generally, accessing the Internet through broadband rather than narrow-band technology enhances information searches, the use of e-government sites, job searches, and virtually any activity on the Web (U.S. Department of Commerce 2004, 7–8). The convenience and quality of broadband may facilitate the more frequent use of computers and the Internet, and increased levels of technical or information skills.

Home broadband users are more likely to go online every day (77 percent) compared to dial-up users (56 percent)—a 21 percent difference as of the end of 2005 (Horrigan 2006). Across a range of activities, high-speed connections foster a migration of tasks to the Internet, such as work-related research and reading the news. These tasks can have implications for economic opportunity, political information, and participation. For instance, in 2004, 40 percent of broadband users got their news online, compared to 22 percent of dial-up users. Twenty-six percent of broadband users went online for work-related research on an average day, compared to only 14 percent of dial-up users. Similarly, 24 percent of broadband users researched a product online compared to 11 percent of dial-up users. Another study has found that on average, broadband users visit 90 percent more Web sites than dial-up users, al-though they spend 23 percent less time at each site (Rappoport, Kridel, and Taylor 2002). Higher-speed connections promote more extensive use of the Internet.

Using broadband is not conceptually different than using other modes of access to the Internet in terms of the skills or knowledge required. While high-speed Internet access alone does not address inequalities in basic and information literacies, some data (Horrigan 2005; Fox 2005; U.S. Department of Commerce 2004) suggest that broadband access is systematically associated with a more frequent and sophisticated online use. Given the benefits of broadband, what do we know about home access to broadband service?

Approach

To better understand patterns of exclusion online, we focus on whether the respondent has Internet access at home, comparing three groups of individuals: those with high-speed access, dial-up access, and no Internet access. We use an August 2003 national random digit-dialed telephone survey of 2,924 Americans age eighteen or older conducted by the Princeton Survey Research Associates for the Pew Internet and American Life Project. The data have a sampling error of plus or minus 2 percent. Additionally, we use a December 2005 national random digit-dialed tele-phone survey of 3,011 Americans age eighteen or older, also conducted by the Princeton Survey Research Associates for the Pew Internet and American Life Project. Following our examination of the patterns of broadband use in 2003 and 2005 is an exploration of the relation-ship between broadband and digital skills. The data used to study this relationship come from a 2001 national random digit-dialed telephone survey of 1,837 respondents, with an oversample drawn from all high-poverty census tracts in the forty-eight states, excluding Alaska and Hawaii.[1]

The dependent variable constructed from the 2003 and 2005 surveys is derived from the question, "Does the modem you use at home connect through a standard telephone line, or do you have some other type of connection?" Responses for a "DSL-enabled phone line," "cable modem," "wireless connection," and "T-1 or fiber optic connection" were coded 3, a "standard telephone line" was coded 2, and no access was coded 1. The dependent variable is nominal, coded 1 for no home Internet access, 2 for dial-up home Internet access, and 3 for broadband home Internet access. Since the dependent variable is nominal, measured in three mutually exclusive categories, multinomial logistic regression coefficients are reported.[2] The discussion in the "Results" section is based on the models reported in table 6.A.1 that include income, age, education, gender, race, ethnicity, geographic characteristics (urban, suburban, or rural), marital status, employment status, and the presence of children in the household (ages eleven and under, and twelve to seventeen).

The following section provides a detailed explanation of our methods and variable coding. As in other chapters, you may skip to the "Results" section that follows.

Discussion of Methods and Variable Coding

The coefficients from a multinomial logistic regression model can be used to calculate the predicted probabilities for each outcome. Some methodologists argue it is preferable to use the chi-square to determine the overall fit of the variable rather than relying on the significance of each coefficient, as this provides a stronger test of significance and allows for a comparison of the effects of a given variable across all possible outcomes (Long and Freese 2001). We thus calculate the predicted probabilities for all outcomes if a variable is statistically significant for one outcome for 2005. These probabilities are reported in box 6.1 below.

Explanatory or independent variables measure individual-level demographic and attitudinal factors. In both 2003 and 2005, binary variables measure gender, race, ethnicity, marital status, children, income, and employment. This means that they are coded as categories, with female, African American, Latino, Asian American, married, employed (either full-or part-time), government employee (2003 only), children eleven and under, and children ages twelve to seventeen, and 0 otherwise. The government employee category was not available for the 2005 and 2001

Box 6.1

What Matters: Who Is Least Likely to Have Broadband Internet Access at Home? (2005)

Poor Americans (28.3% for incomes of 20–30K vs. 50.3% for incomes 50–75k) **−22 point difference**

Older Americans (24.9% for 69 year olds vs. 55.8% for 33 year olds) **−30.9 point difference**

Less-Educated Americans (31.1% for high school diploma vs. 52.5% for bachelor's degree) **−21.4 point difference**

Children Ages 11 and Under (34.3% vs. 50.7% for those with children 12 to 17) **−16.4 point difference**

Asian Americans (29.7% vs. 41.9% for whites) **−12.2 point difference**

African Americans (28.7% vs. 41.9% for whites) **−13.2 point difference**

Not Married (38.6% vs. 41.9% for married) **−3.3 point difference**

Rural Residents (25.7% vs. 41.9% for those who live in suburban area) **−16.2 point difference**

Rural Residents (25.7% vs. 40.6% for those who live in urban area) **−14.9 point difference**

Note: See table 6.A.1, columns 3 and 4. We have calculated the probability of broadband home Internet access, holding other factors constant. Probabilities are based on a hypothetical respondent who is female, non-Hispanic white, with an average education, age, and income. The respondent was employed, married with no children, and a suburban resident.

---

surveys. For race, whites were the reference group, while for ethnicity, non-Hispanics were the reference group. For the ages of children, individuals with no children were the reference group. In the 2003 and 2005 surveys, income was measured on an 8-point scale by the total family income from all sources, before taxes, ranging from 1 = annual income less than $10,000 to 8 = $100,000 or more. Education was measured on 7-point scale from 1 = none, or grade one to eight, to 7 = postgraduate training/professional school after college. In the 2001 survey, education was measured on a 5-point scale with responses ranging from 1 = less than a high school degree to 5 = postgraduate work. In all the surveys, age was recorded in years. In the 2003 and 2005 Pew surveys, an additional variable was added to measure rural areas. Dummy variables for urban and suburban areas were coded 1, with rural residents as the reference group.

Results: Who Has Broadband Access at Home?

The results of the multinomial logistic regressions are reported in two columns in table 6.A.1, with the first column comparing dial-up Internet access versus no Internet access, and the second column comparing broadband Internet access versus no Internet access. Data for 2003 (columns 1 and 2) and 2005 (columns 3 and 4) are reported.

Broadband replicates patterns of Internet access more generally; gender is not a significant factor   Despite the growth of broadband, the findings from the 2003 and 2005 surveys parallel those based on previous research showing systematic inequalities in access to technology. Many of the statistically significant factors associated with high-speed Internet access at home follow the contours of the inequalities for computer and Internet access more generally. We find that in 2003 the poor, older respondents, the less educated, Latinos, and African Americans are statistically less likely to have home Internet access of any type—high-speed *or* dial-up—in comparison to the affluent, young, educated, and non-Hispanic whites. Those who were not married as well as those with children eleven and under were less likely to have broadband access, while those with children over eleven were more likely to have access. By 2005, marital status and Latino ethnicity were becoming less important determinants of access, while children were becoming more important ones. Despite the rapid growth in broadband adoption by African Americans in 2005, race was still a significant predictor of high-speed access at home.

Rural residents are less likely to have broadband access in 2003 and 2005   Rural respondents are significantly less likely than those residing in urban or suburban areas to have broadband access, but rural residents are not disadvantaged in terms of dial-up Internet access. These findings agree with the descriptive statistics drawn from the large-sample CPS in 2003 (U.S. Department of Commerce 2004, 4).

Measuring the Gaps: Estimates of the Magnitude for the Disparities
The boxes below are used to understand the relative size or substantive magnitude of the disparities discussed above. While the figures reported

in the boxes look like percentages, they are the predicted probabilities derived from simulations of the multinomial logistic regression coefficients for 2005 reported in table 6.A.1 (columns 3 and 4) using Clarify software. The simulations generating these estimates are based on mean/modal values for the explanatory variables resulting in a hypothetical respondent who is female, non-Hispanic white, employed, married, and childless, with an average education, age, and income. The respondent resides in a suburban area.

The probability simulations indicate that in 2005, the largest gap in home broadband access is based on age, with only a 25 percent probability of home access for older respondents (sixty-nine year olds, one standard deviation above the mean age in the sample) compared to a 56 percent probability of access for the young (thirty-three year olds, one standard deviation below the mean for age), all other factors held constant. This is a 31 percent difference based on age alone. The second-largest gap, however, is based on income. Lower-income respondents (with an annual income of $20,000 to $30,000) have a 22 percent lower probability of home broadband access than the more affluent respondents (with annual incomes of $50,000 to $75,000), all else being equal. The poor are less able to afford broadband access than those with higher incomes. A significant education gap emerges as well, with college graduates 21 percent more likely to have home broadband access than those with only a high school diploma.

The presence of children also plays an important role in home broadband access. Holding constant socioeconomic status, households with children under eleven had a 34.3 percent probability of broadband access at home, compared to 41.9 percent for those without children. Households with children twelve to seventeen were the most likely to have access, with 51 percent of this group having broadband at home. Thus, having older children in the home encourages the migration to broadband. Marriage is statistically significant, but it increases broadband access by only 3 percent.

African Americans are significantly less likely to have broadband access in 2005—13.2 percent less likely than whites. Asian Americans, who generally have equal or higher rates of Internet access than whites, lag behind in broadband adoption according to our analysis, as they are

12 percent less likely than non-Hispanic whites to have high-speed access at home.

Rural residence is slightly more important than race, as rural residence decreases broadband access by 17 percent in comparison with the suburban respondents, and by 14 percent in comparison with the urban respondents. In sum, the disparities in home broadband access largely mirror those reported in chapter 5 for digital citizenship or the frequency of Internet use.

Broadband Access, Digital Citizenship, and Technology Skills

Convenient access to the Internet, however, is only part of the equation. Access is undeniably important, but it is an incomplete description of the policy problem. Technology skills are critical for digital citizenship. Drawing on descriptive statistics that suggest broadband access may facilitate a more frequent and sophisticated use of the Internet (Horrigan 2004), we hypothesize that home broadband access promotes the acquisition of technology skills. Using unique 2001 national opinion data (reported in Mossberger, Tolbert, and Stansbury 2003), we analyze two dependent variables, measuring skills in two ways.

First, we measure the frequency of Internet use ranging from none (coded 0) to multiple times per day (coded 4.5). Since this variable approximates an interval level measure, it is estimated with an ordinary least squares regression. We have argued in this book that the frequency of use represents a basic ability to use the Internet, and we measure frequency here.

Another way to measure technology skills is by the range of uses of the Internet for tasks that are related to digital citizenship for economic opportunity or political participation. Given the assertions by John Horrigan (2004) about the greater range of activities among broadband users, we explore the relationship between broadband and the range of uses most closely related to the benefits of digital citizenship. For this second dependent skills variable, we create an index of digital experience by summing the responses to the following six questions: whether an individual can locate information on the Web, has searched for political information online, has searched for government information online, has

Box 6.2
What Matters: For Digital Experience and Frequency of Use (2001)

Who Is Most Likely to Use the Internet Daily?	Who Is Most Likely to Have Digital Experience?
Home Broadband Users	Home Broadband Users
Young	Young
Non-Hispanic Whites	Non-Hispanic Whites
Educated	Educated
Nonpoor	Nonpoor
Employed	Employed
	Males

Note: The only statistically significant differences are the ones reported above. See table 6.A.2.

seen an online political campaign ad, has searched or applied for a job online, and has taken a class online. Positive responses to each question were coded 1 (0 for negative responses), and then the six questions were summed to create an index ranging from 0 to 6. Since the index is a count of online activities, the statistical model is estimated using Poisson regression. The logic is similar to that used by Paul DiMaggio and Cora Celeste (2004) in their index of social capital and human capital-enhancing activities involved in the deepening of Internet use.

In table 6.A.2, column 1 presents a model estimating the relationship between home broadband access and the frequency of Internet use. Column 2 estimates a similar model, but the index of digital experience serves as our primary dependent or outcome variable to be explained. Do individuals with home broadband access have a wider range of experience using technology in their daily lives, controlling for basic demographic factors? What factors are associated with varying levels of digital experience (and technology skills) among the survey respondents?

Broadband is related to greater skill and digital citizenship, controlling for other factors   Table 6.A.2 (column 1) indicates that home broadband access is a positive and statistically significant predictor of the frequency of Internet use, consistent with the descriptive analysis reported by Pew (Horrigan 2004). Individuals with high-speed access at home are more likely to be frequent users of the Internet. Column 2 shows that broadband access is also a positive and statistically significant predictor of digital experience, as suggested by previous research (Horrigan 2004; Rappoport, Kridel, and Taylor 2002).[3] Individuals with home broadband access are more likely to report using the Internet for a range of political and economic activities, after controlling for demographic factors, partisan attitudes, and employment status. Both findings suggest that broadband access facilitates digital citizenship through frequent use and skill.

Income, education, age, and employment influence digital experience
Using multivariate regression techniques, we find that the young, the educated, and the affluent have more digital experience, more frequent use of the Internet, and likely greater levels of skill in using the Internet. These findings mirror the disparities for technology access in general. An interesting addition in the data here is that the unemployed are less likely to have digital experience, even controlling for income. This lends credence to the case that employment (and possibly Internet use at work) is related to technology skill—not just having broadband access at home.

Gender matters for digital experience, but not the frequency of use
Although women and men use the Internet with similar frequency (table 6.A.2), women have lower rates of digital experience than men. They are less likely than men to engage in a range of activities on the Internet, controlling for broadband use and other factors. These results are consistent with other studies that women use the Internet for a more restricted range of activities (Bimber 1999). As chapter 5 showed, however, these differences were narrowing by 2003.

Race, ethnicity, and digital skill are related   Racial and ethnic divisions emerge, as African Americans and Latinos are less likely than non-Hispanic whites to have digital experience and frequent Internet use. The findings on digital experience are similar to those for home computer access and the frequency of Internet use in the previous chapter, and consistent with previous research on the digitally disadvantaged.

Our questions measuring the frequency of Internet use and digital experience are similar to those asked in the Pew 2004 survey (Horrigan 2004) on the migration of tasks to the Internet, and our results based on multivariate analysis are consistent with the findings premised on the descriptive statistics from Pew and also the U.S. Department of Commerce (2004). In contrast to Pew, our sample for minorities and the poor is representative due to oversampling. The multivariate analysis confirms that broadband access is related to a more sophisticated (Horrigan 2004) and extensive use of the Internet (Rappoport, Kridel, and Taylor 2002).

Broadband Facilitates Digital Citizenship

We have provided empirical evidence that broadband use facilitates digital citizenship. Those who have high-speed connections are more frequent Internet users (Fox 2005), and our data show that broadband is significant for digital citizenship (or frequent use) as well as participation in economic and political activities online. While those who are most interested already in the Internet are likely to be broadband adopters, its speed and convenience may encourage greater use and skills acquisition for others.

Based on our analysis of survey data from 2003, we find that the disparities in broadband access largely follow the contours of the inequalities in general Internet access and skill. Additionally, the presence of children also plays an important part, and marriage has a modest influence on broadband adoption. The analysis based on the 2005 survey found similar results, but with Latino ethnicity and marital status acting as less of a barrier to broadband. By 2005, the presence of children ages twelve to seventeen in the household was more likely to increase broadband access in the home, while children eleven and under were more likely to decrease high-speed Internet access in the home. Asian Americans are less likely to have broadband in 2005, and African Americans are significantly less likely to have high-speed access in both years, even though they have been enthusiastic adopters as broadband prices have declined.

The place of residence matters for broadband, with individuals who live in rural communities less likely to have access. The rural disparities are primarily due to infrastructure needs. Ironically, it is rural regions that may have the most to gain from broadband, for it facilitates uses such as telemedicine at health clinics, teleconferencing at schools, telecommuting for those who are isolated from labor markets, and other practices that overcome distance. Broadband also promotes local economic development and employment, which are sorely needed in many rural communities (Lehr et al. 2005).

The wider diffusion of broadband holds the promise of increasing the social benefits of this technology and the spread of digital citizenship. The expansion of the market can stimulate research and development for new and innovative uses for broadband as well as improvements that simplify use (Ferguson 2004, 9; National Academy of Sciences 2002, 13–14). The next chapter considers policy options such as municipal broadband as a way to promote digital citizenship.

Public Education and Universal Access: Beyond the Digital Divide

Societies in which citizenship is a developing institution create an image of an ideal citizenship against which achievement can be measured and towards which aspiration can be directed.

—T. H. Marshall, "The Problem Stated with the Assistance of Alfred Marshall," 1949

New wireless and wired technologies allow local governments, schools, public-private partnerships and community groups to offer affordable, universal broadband access.

—Freepress, "Community Internet," 2006

I have indeed two great measures at heart, without which no republic can maintain itself in strength: 1. That of general education, to enable every man to judge for himself what will secure or endanger his freedom. 2. To divide every county into hundreds, of such size that all the children of each will be within reach of a central school in it.

—Thomas Jefferson to John Tyler, 1810

The necessary building blocks for citizenship in the information age are quality public education combined with universal access to the prevailing communication and information medium, the Internet. Over two centuries ago, Thomas Jefferson advocated for public education from the primary school to the university so that all citizens could enjoy full membership and participation in society. Today, quality public education fostering literacy and critical thinking skills must be matched with universal access with the goal of promoting digital citizenship.

In chapter 1, we made the argument that the occasional use of the Internet was insufficient for digital citizenship. The Internet has become such an indispensable source of information that some people rely on others to look up information online, or use the Internet at the homes of friends or relatives when they can. Others who lack access may inter-mittently visit the local library. But these individuals are not fully able to participate online, for they lack the skills and/or the means to use the Internet effectively. A better standard for measuring full participation, we believe, is the daily use of the Internet, which is most likely to occur at home and work. Recent surveys estimate that the percentage of Americans who go online daily is between 45 and 50 percent. At the same time that there is growth in occasional use, there may be wide differences in the ability of individuals to function effectively online. Jan Van Dijk (2005) has characterized this as a "deepening divide" in skills and usage at the same time that more people have some sporadic access or experi-ence on the Internet.

Digital citizenship requires both skills and access for regular and effec-tive use. Digital citizens are those who have the ability to read, write, comprehend, and navigate textual information online, and who have access to affordable broadband. Because of the Internet's significance for economic advancement as well as engagement and participation in U.S. democracy, we contend that digital citizenship is, in Marshall's terms, the ideal of citizenship in the twenty-first century. This concluding chapter recommends public policy at the federal, state, and local levels to achieve these aspirations through universal access and equal education. We again draw on the three traditions of citizenship in the United States (republicanism, liberalism, and ascriptive hierarchy) to justify the policy necessary to meet the ideal of digital citizenship. In doing so, we seek to move the policy debate from technical issues to normative concerns about more general social inequalities and the contribution that digital citizenship can make toward a more just society, worthy of our best traditions.

The Liberal Tradition of Citizenship: Equality of Opportunity for Economic Advancement

What role do information technology skills play in promoting economic opportunity, and how critical is equal access to those skills for disadvan-taged workers? Since the late 1990s, information technology (especially the Internet) has contributed to higher productivity and growth through investment and use in numerous sectors of the economy. The emergence of broadband has accelerated the possible benefits of technology use in the workplace.

Still, the benefits for individuals have been disputed by some economists, and most studies showing increased wages for computer use predate the Internet. Existing studies using national data on wages have not attempted to distinguish the gains for less-educated workers from the benefits for all employees. This is important for understanding the potential costs of exclusion from digital citizenship as well as its general benefits. Those who are less likely to have regular access and the ability to use the Internet effectively are also the most likely to have a high school education or less. The question, then, is whether Internet skills can contribute anything toward economic improvement and mobility for such workers? Internet use is spreading throughout many industries and occupations, but it continues to be most common in those professional and managerial job categories that also require higher education and other qualifications. The economic significance of the Internet might be expected to be weakest among those who have jobs requiring less education.

Yet we find that Internet use has substantial benefits for all workers (chapter 2), as it is associated with an average $118 per week increase in wages, controlling for other factors. This compares to a gain of approximately $340 per week for a four-year college degree in comparison with a high school diploma. Thus, technology use at work may account for more than a third of the earning power of a college degree. For less-educated workers, Internet use is also a crucial determinant of wages, and the premium is nearly the same—$111 per week.

Proportionately, the benefits of information technology skills are most consequential precisely for those who are least advantaged in the labor market. Among less-educated workers, the wage premium for Internet use is higher for minorities. Those who are already disadvantaged in the job market by discrimination suffer a compounded disadvantage from digital inequality.

Greater frequency of use is linked to further increases in the economic rewards for Internet use at work, as the Pew data show. This supports the assertion that regular, daily use is critical for economic opportunity. The significance of Internet use at the workplace persists across years, for both wages and income, and using multiple sources of data, including the full CPS sample. We control for a number of factors that are known to affect wages or income, including employer characteristics, occupation, education, race, ethnicity, and gender. Internet use consistently produces independent effects, over and above these other considerations. Moreover, our less-educated sample addresses the problem of endogeneity between Internet use and education, in contrast to earlier studies.

The liberal tradition of citizenship emphasizes the equality of opportunity as one dimension of personal liberty. In this view, citizens will naturally differ in their talents and preferences, but all deserve the chance to succeed through their own hard work. If the resources needed to compete economically are denied to some citizens, then liberal societies have cause for concern. Unequal resources for education or the development of digital citizenship undermine the ideal of equal opportunity. The results of our analysis indicate that Internet skills and their employment on the job not only enable individuals to compete but also matter most for those who suffer from other disadvantages in the job market. Information technology has contributed to economic change and greater inequality in the workforce in recent decades, but it can be a tool for leveling the playing field as well. Justice in the liberal tradition requires society to provide an equal chance for the least advantaged to succeed, according to John Rawls (1971). Our results show that digital citizenship is needed to prosper in the information economy, and that it matters most for those on the bottom of the economic ladder. •

The Republican Tradition of Citizenship: Civic Engagement and Participation

The Internet has provided new political information venues, sites for discussion, and networks for mobilization. Despite dire predictions by some that politics online would increasingly fragment the sense of political community (Sunstein 2001) or accelerate the decline in social capital (Putnam 2000), we find that Internet use actually increases civic engagement (chapter 3). At the individual level, citizens appear to gain political knowledge, increase the frequency of political discussions, and raise their political interest when reading news about politics online. The Internet's effect on political knowledge is greatest for the young, who are most likely to turn to the Internet as a source for political information. Young people are also the least likely to be knowledgeable about politics, so the Internet has the potential to fill an important gap. Members of generations "X" and "Y" (Putnam 2000) have the lowest engagement in politics and voting, yet they are the most frequent users of the Internet (Lupia and Baird 2003).

While information and knowledge are empowering, the evidence shows that all individuals (young and old) who read news online are more likely to discuss politics with friends and family, and express an interest in politics. Together, these three elements—knowledge, discussion, and interest—create the conditions for civic engagement. Such engagement is the foundation for a broad and lasting commitment to participate in the political life of the community.

The evidence that the Internet is linked to civic engagement is clear. The use of online news is consistently associated with all three elements of civic engagement across all three elections included in this study (2000, 2002, and 2004). Internet use has a substantial effect, producing on average up to 20 and 37 percent increases for discussion and knowledge, respectively, during the presidential election of 2000. The consumption of online news also increased interest in elections in 2000, 2002, and 2004, while traditional mass media, such as newspapers and television, had a less consistent effect. The heightened impact of online news may be due to its richer and more diverse information content, including foreign and domestic news sources.

Logically, the benefits of civic engagement should also be realized in the form of increased political participation, and we found abundant evidence that Internet use facilitates voting, the most common form of political participation in the United States (chapter 4). Just as online news is associated with civic engagement, it also leads to a greater likelihood of voting, at least during the two most recent presidential elections. These findings are consistent with some prior studies. Online news may reduce information costs for busy citizens through greater convenience, continuous availability, and a broader diversity of sources, promoting political participation.

In the chapter on participation, we investigated the impact of other sources of information and communication on the Internet—chat rooms and e-mail. These are unique and interactive forms of communication that separate the Internet from traditional mass media such as television, radio, and newspapers. Yet their influence on participation has been neglected so far, and we explore their potential to boost voter turnout. Political parties and interest groups may find new ways to reach citizens with their message, and mobilize them through the Internet and e-mail. Political debate in online chat rooms may supplement off-line discussions with friends and family, with new opportunities for deliberation. Such small group discussions may foster voter turnout as well.

We find that e-mail and chat rooms have an even greater effect on voting than online news, increasing the probability that an individual will vote in presidential elections by 20 to 40 percent (rather than 16 to 26 percent from reading online news), all other factors held constant. As with online news, the influence of chat rooms and e-mail was not significant during low-information midterm elections, only presidential ones. This suggests that low interest remains a barrier for participation in U.S. elections, and that the Internet is unlikely to compensate sufficiently for some institutional factors, such as uncontested or uncompetitive congressional races. Still, technology offers new and convenient ways for partisans to make information accessible, provide for deliberation, and mobilize participation—all of which have been shown in the past to enhance individual participation.

The results clearly demonstrate that the Internet contributes to the development of civic engagement among individuals and fosters political participation. Our findings are consistent for both civic engagement across three elections and voting in two recent presidential elections. The independent effects of Internet use stand out even after we have controlled for other explanations that are traditionally related to civic engagement and voting, such as age, education, income, race/ethnicity, partisanship, and the use of other media, such as television and newspapers. These findings persist even when we use two-stage multivariate regression models to control for selection bias (or endogeneity) in who uses online news. The statistical models separate the dual effects of factors such as education and income on both Internet use and outcomes, such as political knowledge, discussion, interest, or voting.

While our evidence on participation was limited to voting, the findings on civic engagement and previous research suggest that the Internet may facilitate other types of participation, such as campaigning, donating money, attending meetings or rallies, working for a party or candidate, or contacting political candidates (Tolbert and McNeal 2003; Bimber 1999, 2003). Different facets of the Internet may contribute toward the capacity of individuals to undertake these political activities.

The Internet can easily accommodate a plurality of political voices, but its greatest impact may be in making worldwide news and other sources of information easier to access, including foreign news. The effects of the Internet may not be so much in creating a "brave new world" of politics online as in promoting the availability of information and restoring some of the capacity of linkage institutions such as political parties. The presidential election of 2004 demonstrated this in a variety of creative ways.

Together, the results on voting and civic engagement indicate that political information and communication online have visible collective benefits for society as well. Jefferson's republican ideal of civic virtue requires a knowledgeable citizenry, deliberative democracy through the frequent discussion of politics, and civic duty. Voting, though it is merely one form of participation, has a special place in a democratic society as the ultimate exercise of the rights and responsibilities of citizens. Civic engagement implies long-term changes in democratic participation, beyond involvement in any particular election. With just over half of U.S. citizens turning out to vote in recent presidential elections, we are far from the republican ideal of the founders. In an age where political participation and civic engagement have been steadily declining, the Internet may hold promise for renewing republican traditions of citizenship. Current and future benefits for more widespread information and mobilization are encouraging, especially given the greater use and political knowledge for young people online. In this capacity, the regular and effective use of the Internet is a potentially democratizing resource.

Exclusionary Traditions and Digital Citizenship

The costs of digital exclusion add to the inequalities that disadvantaged groups already experience in access to education, jobs, and the political process. Smith (1993) contends that the exclusionary tradition of ascriptive hierarchy has long relegated people of color and women, among others, to the status of second-class citizenship. Rodney Hero (1998,

2007) builds on this work, arguing that racial inequality and economic stratification, manifest to this day, are traceable to the ascriptive hierarchy strand of U.S. political philosophy.

The patterns of inequality in society are clearly being replicated online—creating a virtual inequality. With a few exceptions, these patterns persist despite the growth of Internet use, and the fault lines are magnified when we consider digital citizenship, or daily Internet use, rather than home access alone, or sporadic use in any place. Nor are these disparities likely to disappear soon, given our analysis of technology access and use among young Americans.

Examining the large-sample 2003 CPS, we explored the factors that influence access and the frequency of use among technologically disadvantaged segments of the population: African Americans, Latinos, the less educated, and the poor. These multivariate subgroup analyses offer a more nuanced view of the relationships within groups and the intersection of overlapping inequalities. By comparing access and use among the youngest and oldest respondents, we can make some predictions about the future.

While age, income, and education explain the greatest disparities in both access and use, race and ethnicity are significant influences as well. The subsample analyses show that African Americans face greater hurdles for technology use than other groups. Fewer occupations increase technology access for African Americans, in comparison with Latinos or the general population. Home computer access is also lower for African Americans who live in urban areas, but not for Latinos. Technology use is more likely to occur outside the home for African Americans. This fits with the descriptive data from the 2003 CPS that indicate cost is a greater barrier for African Americans (and Latinos), and it confirms the patterns of high use outside the home observed in earlier studies of high-poverty, majority–African American neighborhoods. Dependence on use outside the home was distinctive in these African American communities, in comparison with other high-poverty neighborhoods. There are, however, some signs of hope. When we examine the frequency of use (with the highest category being daily use), white-collar occupations increase digital citizenship for African Americans. African American women are more likely to be digital citizens, suggesting that the use of technology may promote economic advancement for black women.

Few studies have examined the experience of Latinos in much detail. First, we show that Latinos continue to have substantially lower rates of access in comparison with the general population. The 2003 CPS was conducted in both English and Spanish, and unlike most Pew surveys, contains representative samples of Latino respondents. We discover that income and education shape both access and frequent use among Latinos, as for the population as a whole. Surprisingly, though, age is not a significant determinant of technology use once we take other variables into account. This suggests that young Latinos are not more likely to be digital citizens, and that caution is needed in predictions that gaps in access and use based on Latino ethnicity will disappear in the future. Latino men and women do not differ in access or frequent use in this population, compared to African Americans. By some standards, Latinos may lag behind African Americans in the transition to digital citizenship.

Lending support for Smith's concept of ascriptive hierarchy, our analyses of access and frequent use among less-educated and low-income Americans show that African Americans and Latinos compare unfavorably even within these groups. Poor and less-educated minorities continue to have lower access rates and use than those whites with similar education and income. These findings, based on our analysis of disadvantaged subgroups of the population, suggest how deep the disparities in technology access and use are for racial and ethnic minorities.

Time alone will not resolve the problem of digital inequality. Among young people as well as older respondents, income, education, race, and ethnicity form the basis for inequalities in access and digital citizenship. Although differences based on income are small for those under thirty, it is less than clear whether this is due to the low incomes of highly educated college students, or whether income is becoming less of a barrier for technology inclusion. The replication of other traditional technology disparities among the young based on education, race, and ethnicity, suggests that these gaps are unlikely to disappear soon.

In chapter 6, we explored an additional dimension of digital citizenship. Broadband access at home facilitates frequent use and promotes involvement in a greater variety of activities online, even when we control for skill-related variables such as education. Individuals with high-speed Internet connections are more likely to engage in online activities related to political participation and economic opportunity in our index of digital experience. Those who lack high-speed access at home are the same groups most likely to be excluded online more generally—individuals who are older, less educated, poor, African American, and Latino, with the addition of residents of rural areas. For rural Americans, the problem is inadequate infrastructure in sparsely populated places. For others, the barrier is the higher cost of broadband access, which discourages both those who cannot afford the monthly payment and those who have more sporadic interest in the Internet. Extending the reach of broadband is essential for regular and effective use, for skills and digital citizenship.

Ascriptive Hierarchy, Class, and the Costs of Exclusion

The concept of ascriptive hierarchy provides an explanation for some disparities online, insofar as they are rooted in more general patterns of disadvantage in education, employment, housing, and life chances. It focuses our attention on the continued significance of race and ethnicity in U.S. society, and the institutional barriers to addressing inequality. In the case of gender, the differences online are less pronounced. Women were slower to adopt computers and the Internet as a part of their daily lives, but have generally caught up in terms of Internet use, if not technology careers. Among some disadvantaged groups, women are in fact more likely to be digital citizens—if they are older, less educated, or African American.

Why have racial and ethnic differences endured on the Internet? One reason is that in U.S. society, race and ethnicity are tied to place and educational disparities in a way that gender is not. The quality of education varies considerably in the United States across communities because schools are to a large extent dependent on local tax revenues. Impoverished school districts, whether urban or rural, have fewer resources to devote to education. This effect is magnified in areas of concentrated poverty, which is an urban phenomenon that affects minorities disproportionately (Massey and Denton 1993, 12; Orfield and Lee 2005). Measures of educational attainment may mask real differences in the quality of education and the competencies achieved by students across districts. As we have emphasized, information literacy and education matter online.

Discrimination continues to influence access to jobs for minorities (Holzer 1996, 111, 113–114). Our findings here suggest that occupation may matter less for home access for African Americans because they remain on the bottom rung for pay within these occupations. Both African Americans and Latinos continue to earn much less than similarly situated whites, according to the 2003 CPS, even when we control for Internet use. Minorities are more sensitive to costs when it comes to technology, and are also the lowest paid.

As mentioned in chapter 5, some research finds race is less important in predicting technology access and use once we control for geographic factors (the wealth and educational attainment of the zip code) using multilevel models (Mossberger, Tolbert, and Gilbert 2006). Structural inequalities—such as discrimination on the job market and residential segregation—find new expression in society online and act as barriers to digital citizenship. Racial and ethnic discrimination (or ascriptive hierarchy) is clearly evident.

Yet it is also impossible to discuss digital inequalities without pointing to economic class, as Hero suggests. African Americans in white collar occupations are more likely to be digital citizens. Education and income have the most powerful effect on technology access and use, following age. Rural communities (which are often impoverished, too) suffer from inadequate infrastructure for broadband and higher costs for Internet access more generally (Strover 1999). Living in a poor community diminishes technology access and use for individuals of any race, although it is true that the interaction between race and community poverty intensifies this effect (Mossberger, Tolbert, and Gilbert 2006). Technology disparities partly reflect ascriptive hierarchies, but also the inequities endured by the poor and the unskilled more generally.

If Internet use enhances civic engagement and political participation, then exclusion from digital citizenship exacerbates existing inequalities that are based on race, ethnicity, income, and education. Our research shows that using the Internet for political information may encourage citizens to be more knowledgeable, interested, involved in political discussions, and likely to vote. Individuals and groups who are not making use of information technologies are likely to become increasingly marginalized in U.S. politics and policy debates.

Differences in the frequency and quality of participation count. As Sidney Verba, Kay Schlozman, and Henry Brady (1995, 11) have argued, it is the relative absence of the poor among other voices that diminishes their representation in public policy. To the extent that digital citizenship increases participation overall, the needs of the poor may be even more likely to be lost among other utterances. Political scientist E. E. Schattschneider (1960) long ago observed that the interest group system of pluralism on which U.S. politics is built speaks with an upper-class accent despite its outward commitment to the equal rights of citizenship. Digital inequality further isolates citizens from discussion and deliberation, the political knowledge that informs participation, and the networks that mobilize interest and activity. As a result, it further distances those who are not online from equal representation in the policy process and full participation in the political community.

The cost of digital exclusion in the new economy is likewise a redoubling of current disadvantages in the labor market. Unskilled positions requiring no Internet use still exist, but offer few possibilities for good wages, benefits, and upward mobility. Economic change over the past few decades has penalized less-educated workers, leading to reductions in real wages. Education matters more than ever for economic opportunity, but our research shows that Internet use plays a role, too, even for lower-skilled workers. The cost of exclusion from digital citizenship is the reduced capacity to compete for good jobs and earn a decent standard of living for those individuals lacking technology skills. Given these costs to individuals and society, more effective public policy is needed.

Programs to Address Digital Citizenship: Surveying the Policy Landscape

Policies to promote digital citizenship are piecemeal and underfunded. Existing programs demonstrate some accomplishments, especially in providing public access in libraries and increasing the presence of computers in public schools. Less easily solved are the issues tied to effective use and home access, although there are further needs for public access and technology use in schools as well. One recent policy development is the growth of municipal broadband. We believe that this has important implications for digital citizenship.

The Federal Role Has Diminished over Time

Federal policy is fragmented and has shifted significantly over time. Policy under the Clinton administration in the 1990s stressed public access strategies, emphasizing connectivity in libraries and schools over technical assistance and training. The E-Rate program, which was created by the passage of the Telecommunications Act of 1996, was established as a $2.25 billion annual fund to provide discounts to schools and libraries for connections to the Internet. Eligible costs include wiring, phone lines, and Internet access, but do not include computers, staff training, or support staff (McClure and Bertot 2002; Carvin, Conte, and Gilbert 2001). Two smaller federal programs, the Technology Opportunities Program and the Community Technology Centers Program, provided more flexible funding, but they have been completely or largely eliminated under the Bush administration (Dickard 2003; Edutopia News 2004).

Not all governments have turned their backs on issues of digital citizenship. During 2005, the British government launched an initiative to become the first country to close the digital divide, enlisting businesses, nonprofit organizations, and local authorities in the effort. The Blair government has announced that local authorities will provide universal local access to the Internet by 2008, public sector service delivery will be transformed through e-government, and the Internet will be used to address social exclusion more generally. The United Kingdom already has a relatively high rate of broadband access (the third highest among the G7 countries), but the government has identified persistent disparities, including the lack of necessary skills, as a barrier to economic development and realizing the full benefits of moving government services online. Plans include the expansion of UK Online Centres throughout the country, low-cost laptop leasing for students, and a Digital Challenge prize for local authorities (eGovernment News 2005; Prime Minister's Strategy Unit and Department of Trade and Industry 2005).

At the present time, there is little inclination at the federal level in the United States to launch such an initiative. Still, policies such as E-Rate, private efforts, and library programs have expanded public access over the past decade, and are important to consider as part of an overall policy to develop digital citizenship.

Public Libraries and Nonprofit Programs

Libraries have been an essential point of public access for computers and the Internet as well as potential sources for training and assistance in locating information online (Mossberger, Tolbert, and Stansbury 2003). In addition to the E-Rate program, the Library Service and Technology Act of 1996 distributes federal funds to states for local libraries. A recent Florida State University study showed that nearly 99 percent of public libraries now feature free Internet access, and library visits have doubled over the past dozen years, primarily due to information technology services (Gates Foundation 2005; Bertot, McClure, and Jaeger 2005). Studies conducted by the University of Washington revealed that 30 percent of library patrons have no other Internet access. This research found that job search is especially critical for low-income library users, and medical information searches are prevalent in rural areas. About a third of library patrons use public access computers to learn or practice computer skills (Gates Foundation 2004).

The expansion of public access is not always sufficient to meet demand, however, for 85 percent of libraries report that resources are insufficient for traffic at certain times of the day. Rural libraries are more likely to lack high-speed connections, and urban libraries often have too few workstations (Gates Foundation 2005; Bertot, McClure, and Jaeger 2005). Public libraries have clearly evolved as the main gateway for public access, but there are unmet needs, and challenges for maintaining staff and equipment in the future (Bertot, McClure, and Jaeger 2005; Gates Foundation 2004). These studies also underscore the continued lack of home access in poor communities.

Private giving and nonprofit efforts include programs run by large foundations and grassroots volunteers. Visible initiatives include the U.S. Libraries Program that the Bill and Melinda Gates Foundation (2004) has operated since 1997 to provide training, software, and technical assistance. Nonprofit organizations such as the Boys and Girls Clubs of America offer skill development programs located in low-income urban and rural areas, where exposure to technology is sorely needed. Despite cuts in federal funding for community programs, many nonprofit community technology centers offer training, help with job search and résumé writing, and literacy education. CTCNet, an umbrella organization with over a thousand participating centers, surveyed its members in summer and fall 2005. It found that about half of the responding organizations had uncertain or perilous funding situations, and that two-thirds were in need of additional staff and space to meet the demand for their services (CTCNet 2006).

The Bush administration, with the No Child Left Behind Act, has focused its technology priorities on K–12 education. While education is critical, the current policy provides insufficient resources for promoting digital citizenship among youth.

Education and Technology

There has been notable progress in providing more technology in the schools. Yet access to hardware and wiring has not necessarily translated into effective technology skills for students. In 1998, there were 12 students for each computer in U.S. schools—a figure that dropped to 4.8 students per computer by 2002. As a result of the E-Rate program, 92 percent of schools had Internet access available for classroom instruction by 2002 (Kleiner and Lewis 2003).

Just as critical, however, is the need to integrate information technology into the curriculum, as a way of developing student skills. A 2002 survey of 811 school districts by the National School Boards Foundation found that only 18 percent of teachers used the Internet for class demonstrations and presentations. Barely 8 percent incorporated the Internet into class projects and only 7 percent employed it for student research activities. Inadequate training may be preventing teachers from using information technology to develop the capacities of their students (National School Boards Foundation 2002).

Some provisions of the No Child Left Behind Act, such as the Technology Literacy Fund, provide support for the use of technology in education. The act allocates money to schools for a broader variety of Internet resources such as teacher training, support staff, and software. This has not provided a windfall for technology or other improvements in K–12 schools, though, for state and local governments have loudly complained that the federal government has failed to supply adequate funding in general for meeting the requirements of the No Child Left

Behind Act (MacPherson 2004). Low-income rural and urban districts are likely to be faced with the greatest challenges in meeting standards for reading and math as well as providing information technology skills. Hardware and software are ineffective without technology skills, including basic literacy.

The obvious gaps in public policy are for programs that foster technical competence and information literacy among adults and children. In poor communities, this cannot be addressed without taking into account fundamental inequalities in education. Technical solutions are not enough, if schools lack the resources to give all children a firm foundation in literacy and academic skills. Equal access to educational opportunities should include more support for schools in poor communities, and more assistance to low-income students seeking adult education, further training, and postsecondary education. As the chapter on the economy showed, the continued availability of education is important for less-educated workers, and for meeting the challenges of economic and technological change. Education also enhances the likelihood of civic engagement and political participation. Increased technology access will do little without widespread literacy and access to quality education.

The overall picture, then, is that the progress made over the past few years is real but incomplete. Voluntary efforts and libraries have extended public access, and there are now more hardware and Internet connections in the schools. Yet federal efforts have withered, and fundamental educational disparities remain. We do not claim to be education policy experts and so hesitate to offer precise solutions in this area, but we recognize that education provides the foundation for digital citizenship in an information society.

Another need is for universal access that extends broadband to all areas of the country and makes high-speed connections affordable for all. The frequent use of technology is necessary for digital citizenship and is most likely to occur at home. Public access has a key role to play, but should be seen as a bridge to digital citizenship.

Universal Access Policy: Community Internet
Local governments are filling the access gap by providing broadband through municipal networks. Some municipal networks offer wired broadband services; in 2004, there were a little under two hundred

wired municipal providers. These tend to be in municipalities where there is already a public electric utility, and in smaller, rural communities that would otherwise lack broadband access (Gillett 2006). More recently, however, wireless technologies have shifted the terrain for providing high-speed Internet access in rural areas and large cities as well. Wireless technologies have several advantages over the wired broadband networks. First, they do not require a license from the Federal Communications Commission, as they can be used in the unlicensed spectrum. This makes them cheaper and easier to implement. Second, they can often use existing infrastructure to mount equipment to broadcast signals, including streetlights and buildings. This can be an advantage in cities, where critical infrastructure is already controlled by municipalities. Third, the wireless technologies solve the last-mile problem and are cheaper than wired networks (Tapia, Stone, and Maitland 2005).

Investment in municipal wireless is expected to top $4 billion between 2006 and 2010. There are now three hundred cities in the United States with municipal wireless networks or proposals for such networks. Philadelphia, San Francisco, Portland (Oregon), Dayton, Minneapolis, Chicago, Atlanta, Los Angeles, and Houston are among the large cities that have initiatives at some stage (Hamblen 2006).

The objections raised to municipal broadband include competition with private sector providers and fiscal considerations for local governments. Urged on by private telecommunications providers, many states have passed or are currently considering legislation to restrict the municipal provision of broadband by imposing conditions such as feasibility studies, referenda, and so on. Some federal legislation to regulate or ban municipal broadband has been debated as well (Tapia, Stone, and Maitland 2005). But municipal broadband has tended to provide high-speed access in places that are not served by the market, and the presence of a municipal provider does not preclude market provision (Hauge, Jamison, and Gentry 2005). In many areas, cities collaborate with private service providers, offering access to existing infrastructure in return for low rates for the city or residents. In San Francisco, Google plans to offer free wireless access to all residents in return for advertising rights. According to Sharon Gillett (2006), the policy issue is not competition with the private sector but avoiding a long-term monopoly provision by private sector partners.

Community Internet—whether wireless or not—is often attractive to municipalities because of its potential to lure businesses or lower costs for municipal services such as policing. But it also holds the promise of providing ordinary citizens with free or affordable universal access to high-speed connections. We support free municipal broadband as a way to extend high-speed access and develop widespread digital citizenship. Bills for monthly Internet services are often a greater obstacle for connectivity for low-income households than the one-time purchase of a computer (Mueller and Schement 2001). The provision of municipal broadband by itself, however, may be insufficient to promote digital citizenship. Cities like Philadelphia and Chicago are also considering initiatives in low-income communities that will provide training and support services for computer novices.

Policy innovation has historically occurred subnationally in the decentralized U.S. system of federalism, and local governments have a critical interest in ensuring universal access and effective Internet use. Governments can better implement e-government solutions with widespread Internet use by citizens, and they can also encourage greater civic engagement and participation more generally, as our research shows. Local schools can be effortlessly connected to universities, museums, and resources anywhere on the globe. In the pursuit of economic growth, broadband provides high-tech infrastructure for local businesses and encourages the development of workforce skills among citizens. In short, municipal broadband promotes digital citizenship, and generates benefits for economic opportunity and political participation. We recognize that it is a partial solution, which may not be implemented evenly across the country. Yet state and federal policies should encourage this development rather than inhibit its growth. It does not address fundamental problems in public education, but it can make a significant contribution toward fostering digital citizenship nonetheless.

From Economic Efficiency to the Just Society: Foundations for Public Policy

Most economists would agree that public policy has a role in fostering Internet access and skills if there are positive externalities or spillover effects of Internet use, such as economic growth and a better-informed citizenry. Utilitarian philosophy would justify universal access, skill, and education in the interest of the greater social good. But there are also arguments for public policy to expand technology access based on the equality of opportunity (liberalism), civil rights (as an antidote to ascriptive hierarchy), and democratic governance (civic republicanism). The benefits of Internet use and the costs of exclusion from society online raise fundamental questions of empowerment and participation. Digital citizenship is facilitated by both technology access and skill. Social inequalities such as poverty, illiteracy, and unequal educational opportunities, prevent all Americans from enjoying full participation online and in society more generally. Marshall referred to citizenship as a "developing institution" against which "achievement can be measured and towards which aspiration can be directed" (1992, 18). Citizenship in the information age underscores the need for educational opportunity, and the capabilities to enjoy the rights and fulfill the duties of membership in a changing society.

Appendix: Multivariate Regression Models

Table 2.A.1
The Effect of Technology Use at Work on Weekly Earnings (General Population), Current Population Survey 2003

Covariates	Computer Use at Work		Internet/E-mail Use at Work		Online Courses	
	b (s.e.)	p > z	b (s.e.)	p > z	b (s.e.)	p > z
Computer Use at Work	101.60 (7.67)	.000				
Internet/E-mail Use at Work			118.27 (8.12)	.000		
Online Courses					38.69 (17.35)	.026
Female	−208.36 (7.86)	.000	−205.22 (7.82)	.000	−205.40 (7.88)	.000
Age	4.86 (.24)	.000	4.83 (.24)	.000	4.90 (.24)	.000
Latino	−52.30 (9.23)	.000	−55.38 (9.20)	.000	−61.63 (9.30)	.000
Asian American	−51.92 (15.05)	.001	−52.99 (14.97)	.000	−56.09 (15.18)	.000
African American	−65.17 (10.05)	.000	−64.12 (10.02)	.000	−74.23 (10.06)	.000
White (Reference Category)						
Education	88.68 (3.12)	.000	85.93 (3.14)	.000	96.65 (3.11)	.000
Urban	49.90 (8.90)	.000	48.55 (8.88)	.000	51.18 (8.94)	.000
Suburban	99.37 (7.44)	.000	98.33 (7.43)	.000	100.67 (7.48)	.000
Management	319.29 (16.65)	.000	311.82 (16.62)	.000	357.85 (16.36)	.000
Professional	163.05 (14.35)	.000	163.36 (14.14)	.000	193.12 (14.18)	.000
Service	−16.12 (14.35)	.129	−18.36 (10.58)	.084	−17.81 (10.77)	.098
Sales	75.11 (14.29)	.000	76.98 (14.14)	.000	98.85 (14.45)	.000
Secretary	−40.81 (11.42)	.000	−37.58 (11.19)	.001	−1.90 (11.08)	.863

	Model 1		Model 2		Model 3	
Farming	−74.22 (22.47)	.001	−79.79 (22.74)	.000	−81.67 (22.93)	.000
Construction	67.36 (14.55)	.000	61.22 (14.74)	.000	54.09 (14.66)	.000
Repair	−.97 (15.27)	.949	3.98 (15.27)	.794	9.43 (15.44)	.541
Transportation	17.64 (14.78)	.233	16.22 (14.74)	.271	9.39 (14.87)	.000
Production (Reference Category)						
Federal Government	189.68 (27.57)	.000	195.96 (24.68)	.000	181.02 (24.68)	.000
Local Government	15.95 (16.82)	.343	21.19 (16.89)	.210	13.17 (16.91)	.463
Private Sector	88.76 (14.47)	.000	97.14 (14.56)	.000	81.69 (14.50)	.000
State Government and Nonprofits (Reference Category)						
Information Industry	−15.50 (24.90)	.534	−14.92 (24.68)	.545	−13.00 (24.90)	.602
Full-time	379.59 (7.15)	.000	373.93 (7.14)	.000	395.17 (7.14)	.000
Part-time (Reference Category)						
Constant	−253.68 (23.42)	.000	−250.66 (23.36)	.000	−250.60 (23.60)	.000
N	**14851**		**14851**		**14851**	
F	389.96	.000	389.61	.000	379.35	.000
R^2	.41		.41		.40	

Note: Unstandardized regression coefficients with robust standard errors in parentheses to control for heteroskedasticity. Probabilities based on two-tailed tests. 2003 CPS data, October Supplement on Information Technology. Variables appearing in boldface are statistically significant (throughout appendix).

Table 2.A.2
The Effect of Technology Use at Work on Weekly Earnings for the Less-Educated Population (High School Degree or Less), Current Population Survey 2003

Covariates	Computer Use at Work		Internet/E-mail Use at Work		Online Courses	
	b (s.e.)	p > z	b (s.e.)	p > z	b (s.e.)	p > z
Computer Use at Work	89.76 (8.81)	.000				
Internet/E-mail Use at Work			111.33 (10.61)	.000		
Online Courses					63.11 (24.85)	.011
Female	−133.73 (8.51)	.000	−133.78 (8.48)	.000	−126.95 (8.57)	.000
Age	2.92 (.24)	.000	2.92 (.24)	.000	2.93 (.25)	.000
Latino	−72.15 (9.58)	.000	−74.13 (9.55)	.000	−84.40 (9.65)	.000
Asian	−46.45 (18.02)	.010	−50.98 (17.66)	.004	−52.02 (18.25)	.004
Black	−27.07 (11.49)	.019	−26.89 (11.50)	.019	−35.48 (11.54)	.002
White (Reference Category)						
Urban	12.15 (9.70)	.210	11.20 (9.70)	.248	13.05 (9.81)	.183
Suburban	44.68 (8.41)	.000	44.86 (8.38)	.000	45.98 (8.48)	.000
Rural (Reference Category)						
Management	223.69 (27.28)	.000	219.24 (27.08)	.000	258.94 (27.01)	.000
Professional	72.71 (23.60)	.002	78.39 (23.11)	.000	98.82 (23.35)	.000
Service	−70.22 (10.95)	.000	−73.51 (10.92)	.999	−73.41 (11.12)	.000
Sales	−2.98 (15.12)	.844	−23.96 (12.35)	.053	15.26 (15.54)	.326
Secretary	−26.02 (12.45)	.037	−23.96 (12.35)	.053	9.94 (12.01)	.408

Farming	−131.90 (22.50)	.000	−135.47 (22.85)	.000	−138.13 (22.80)	.000
Construction	61.15 (15.83)	.000	53.23 (15.85)	.001	51.34 (15.98)	.001
Repair	28.65 (18.49)	.121	30.57 (18.55)	.099	39.99 (18.58)	.031
Transportation	2.63 (15.43)	.864	−.12 (15.34)	.994	−2.04 (15.50)	.895
Production (Reference Category)						
Federal Government	76.71 (31.89)	.016	86.86 (31.86)	.006	66.81 (31.61)	.035
Local Government	−2.20 (23.34)	.925	2.60 (23.50)	.912	.07 (23.74)	.998
Private Sector	1.48 (19.76)	.940	8.73 (19.93)	.661	−3.38 (20.11)	.866
State Government and Nonprofits (Reference Category)						
Information Industry	1.20 (23.49)	.959	5.01 (23.23)	.829	3.31 (23.71)	.889
Full-time	290.63 (7.31)	.000	289.01 (7.28)	.000	301.61 (7.34)	.000
Part-time (Reference Category)						
Constant	180.45 (25.30)	.000	184.94 (26.38)	.000	195.50 (26.69)	.000
N	5960		5960		5960	
F	161.22		158.44		154.25	
R^2	.32		.32		.30	

Note: Unstandardized regression coefficients with robust standard errors in parentheses to control for heteroskedasticity. Probabilities based on two-tailed tests. 2003 CPS data, October Supplement on Information Technology.

Table 2.A.3
Impact of Internet Use at Work on Personal Income, Pew Internet and American Life 2002 and 2005

| | Income in 2002 | | | | Income in 2005 | | | |
| | Model 1 (Internet Use at Work) | | Model 2 (Frequency of Use at Work) | | Model 3 (Internet Use at Work) | | Model 4 (Frequency of Use at Work) | |
Covariates	b (s.e.)	p > z	b (s.e.)	p > z	b (s.e.)	p > z	b (s.e.)	p > z
Internet Use at Work	.31 (.058)	.000			.76 (.121)	.000		
Frequency of Internet Use at Work			.06 (.016)	.000			.14 (.022)	.000
State Economic Factors								
Information Technology Jobs in Respondent's State	.14 (.082)	.078	.13 (.083)	.095	.35 (.093)	.000	.34 (.093)	.000
Unemployment Rate in Respondent's State	.09 (.059)	.119	.08 (.060)	.139	−.02 (.045)	.648	−.02 (.045)	.580
Individual Demographics								
Male	.34 (.094)	.000	.34 (.095)	.000	.46 (.094)	.000	.46 (.094)	.000
Age	.03 (.004)	.000	.03 (.004)	.000	−.01 (.002)	.000	−.01 (.002)	.000
Education	.28 (.035)	.000	.32 (.035)	.000	.49 (.029)	.000	.48 (.029)	.000
Latino	−.31 (.178)	.073	−.33 (.175)	.060	−.79 (.218)	.000	−.78 (.218)	.000
African American	−.34 (.161)	.032	−.32 (.152)	.043	−.96 (.167)	.000	−.96 (.166)	.000
Asian American	−.40 (.340)	.233	−.50 (.354)	.159	−.25 (.340)	.460	−.24 (.343)	.481

	b (SE)	p	b (SE)	p	b (SE)	p	b (SE)	p
Respondent's Occupation								
Professional	.44 (.121)	.000	.50 (.120)	.000				
Manager	.48 (.145)	.001	.59 (.144)	.000				
Owner	.78 (.283)	.006	.80 (.301)	.008				
Clerical	−.30 (.173)	.084	−.25 (.172)	.143				
Sales	.08 (.176)	.641	.12 (.178)	.468				
Type of Organization (Government Reference Categories)								
Large	.51 (.131)	.000	.48 (.131)	.000				
Medium	.27 (.156)	.078	.28 (.156)	.069				
Small	.15 (.142)	.076	.22 (.141)	.118				
School/Nonprofit	−.46 (.159)	.004	−.44 (.158)	.005				
Geographic Area								
Urban	−.01 (.134)	.902	−.03 (.136)	.793	.10 (.131)	.446	.10 (.131)	.446
Suburb	.33 (.118)	.004	.33 (.118)	.005	.37 (.121)	.002	.38 (.121)	.002
Constant	1.00	.013	.95	.018	2.32	.000	2.36	.000
N	1493		1492		1689		1689	
F	26.88	.000	26.20	.000	61.23	.000	62.74	.000
Adjusted R^2	.26		.25		.26		.26	

Note: Unstandardized regression coefficients with robust standard errors in parentheses to correct for heteroskedasticity. Reported probabilities based on two-tailed tests. Pew Internet and American Life, *May 2002 Workplace E-mail Survey*, and Pew Internet and American Life, *Major Moments Survey, February–March 2005*. The dependent variable is the respondent's income in 2002 and 2005.

Table 2.A.4
The Effect of Technology Use at Work on Annual Household Income (General Population), Current Population Survey 2003

Covariates	Computer Use at Work b (s.e.)	p > z	Internet/E-mail Use at Work b (s.e.)	p > z	Online Courses b (s.e.)	p > z
Computer Use at Work	.84 (.03)	.000				
Internet/E-mail Use at Work			.81 (.03)	.000		
Online Courses					21 (.05)	.000
Female	−.40 (.02)	.000	−.38 (.02)	.000	−.37 (.02)	.000
Age	.02 ($.11^{-2}$)	.000	.02 ($.11^{-2}$)	.000	.02 ($.11^{-2}$)	.000
Latino	−1.17 (.04)	.000	−1.21 (.04)	.000	−1.26 (.04)	.000
Asian American	−.29 (.06)	.000	−.29 (.06)	.000	−.33 (.06)	.000
African American	−1.21 (.05)	.000	−1.21 (.05)	.000	−1.28 (.05)	.000
White (Reference Category)						
Education	.52 (.01)	.000	.52 (.01)	.000	.59 (.01)	.00
Urban	.31 (.03)	.000	.30 (.03)	.000	.32 (.03)	.000
Suburban	1.20 (.02)	.000	1.20 (.02)	.000	1.22 (.02)	.000
Management	1.11 (.06)	.000	1.09 (.06)	.000	1.39 (.06)	.000
Professional	.75 (.06)	.000	.76 (.06)	.000	.98 (.06)	.000
Service	−.33 (.06)	.000	−.35 (.06)	.000	−.36 (.06)	.000
Sales	.36 (.06)	.000	.39 (.06)	.000	.56 (.06)	.000
Secretary	.25 (.06)	.000	.32 (.06)	.000	.57 (.06)	.000

	Model 1		Model 2		Model 3	
Farming	−.84 (.16)	.000	−.91 (.16)	.000	−.94 (.16)	.000
Construction	.16 (.07)	.022	.11 (.07)	.118	.06 (.07)	.392
Repair	.30 (.07)	.000	.34 (.07)	.000	.39 (.07)	.000
Transportation	$-.68^{-2}$ (.07)	.928	−.02 (.07)	.713	−.07 (.07)	.332
Production (Reference Category)						
Federal Government	1.05 (.07)	.000	1.04 (.07)	.000	1.04 (.07)	.000
Local Government	.44 (.05)	.000	.46 (.05)	.000	.47 (.05)	.000
Private Sector	.35 (.04)	.000	.38 (.04)	.000	.35 (.04)	.000
State Government and Nonprofits (Reference Category)						
Information Industry	.04 (.09)	.614	.04 (.09)	.673	.05 (.09)	.558
Full-time	.55 (.04)	.000	.56 (.04)	.000	.69 (.04)	.000
Part-time (Reference Category)						
Constant	6.79 (.10)	.000	6.90 (.10)	.000	6.77 (.10)	.000
N	55471		55471		55471	
F	796.33	.000	806.09	.000	760.20	.000
R^2	.24		.24		.23	

Note: Unstandardized regression coefficients with robust standard errors in parentheses to control for heteroskedasticity. Probabilities based on two-tailed tests. 2003 CPS data, October Supplement on Information Technology.

Table 2.A.5
The Effect of Technology Use at Work on Annual Household Income for the Less-Educated Population (High School Degree or Less), Current Population Survey 2003

Covariates	Computer Use at Work		Internet/E-mail Use at Work		Online Courses	
	b (s.e.)	p > z	b (s.e.)	p > z	b (s.e.)	p > z
Computer Use at Work	1.11 (.05)	.000				
Internet/E-mail Use at Work			1.18 (.05)	.000		
Online Courses					1.18 (.05)	.000
Female	−.26 (.04)	.000	−.25 (.04)	.000	−.25 (.04)	.000
Age	−.01 $(.11^{-2})$	.000	−.01 $(.11^{-2})$	.000	−.01 $(.11^{-2})$	.000
Latino	−1.31 (.05)	.000	−1.35 (.05)	.000	−1.35 (.05)	.000
Asian American	.12 (.09)	.185	.11 (.09)	.248	.11 (.09)	.248
African American	−1.61 (.06)	.000	−1.63 (.06)	.000	−1.63 (.06)	.000
White (Reference Category)						
Urban	.26 (.05)	.000	.25 (.05)	.000	.25 (.05)	.000
Suburban	1.28 (.04)	.000	1.28 (.04)	.000	1.28 (.04)	.000
Rural (Reference Category)						
Management	1.57 (.09)	.000	1.59 (.08)	.000	1.59 (.08)	.000
Professional	1.21 (.10)	.000	1.30 (.10)	.000	1.30 (.10)	.000
Service	−.23 (.06)	.001	−.23 (.06)	.001	−.23 (.06)	.001
Sales	.41 (.08)	.000	.50 (.08)	.000	.50 (.08)	.000
Secretary	.80 (.07)	.000	.92 (.07)	.000	.92 (.07)	.000

Farming	−.58 (.17)	.001	−.62 (.17)	.000	−.62 (.17)	.000
Construction	.39 (.08)	.000	.34 (.08)	.000	.34 (.08)	.000
Repair	.52 (.10)	.000	.59 (.10)	.000	.59 (.10)	.000
Transportation	.46 (.08)	.000	.47 (.08)	.000	.47 (.08)	.000
Production (Reference Category)						
Federal Government	1.40 (.15)	.000	1.43 (.15)	.000	1.43 (.15)	.000
Local Government	.64 (.10)	.000	.70 (.0)	.000	.70 (.10)	.000
Private Section	.32 (.06)	.000	.37 (.06)	.000	.37 (.06)	.000
State Government and Nonprofits (Reference Category)						
Information Industry	−.17 (.13)	.214	−.17 (.13)	.205	−.17 (.13)	.205
Full-time	1.16 (.05)	.000	1.23 (.05)	.000	1.23 (.05)	.000
Part-time (Reference Category)						
Constant	8.13 (.08)	.000	8.14 (.08)	.000	8.14 (.08)	.000
N	38481		38481		38481	
F	476.45		477.84		477.84	
R^2	.19		.19		.19	

Note: Unstandardized regression coefficients with robust standard errors in parentheses to control for heteroskedasticity. Probabilities based on two-tailed tests. 2003 CPS data, October Supplement on Information Technology.

Table 3.A.1
Impact of Online News on Political Engagement: Political Discussion, Knowledge, and Interest, National Election Study 2000 (Second-Stage Estimates)

Covariates	Political Discussion		Political Knowledge		Political Interest	
	β (s.e.)	p > z	β (s.e.)	p > z	β (s.e.)	p > z
Reading Online News (Predicted Probability)*	.18 (.075)	.017	.31 (.109)	.005	3.03 (.322)	.000
Traditional Media						
Newspaper Consumption	.02 (.005)	.000	.02 (.007)	.002	−.01 (.022)	.532
Television (National) Consumption	.02 (.005)	.000	.02 (.007)	.003	.15 (.023)	.000
Demographic Controls						
Strong Partisan	.07 (.029)	.019	.12 (.040)	.003	.61 (.135)	.000
Age	−.003 (.001)	.001	.006 (.001)	.000	.03 (.005)	.000
Female	.06 (.029)	.030	−.32 (.040)	.000	.13 (.124)	.307
Latino	.02 (.055)	.769	−.29 (.091)	.002	.48 (.236)	.044
African American	−.13 (.050)	.009	−.29 (.078)	.000	.81 (.204)	.000
Asian American	−.07 (.104)	.515	.01 (.131)	.969	−1.38 (.441)	.002
Education	.01 (.011)	.211	.13 (.015)	.000	−.12 (.048)	.013
Income	.02 (.004)	.000	.01 (.005)	.307	−.02 (.018)	.234
Political Efficacy	.02 (.006)	.004	−.02 (.009)	.013	−.06 (.028)	.030
Political Knowledge	.04 (.010)	.000			.23 (.044)	.000
Political Discussion			.03 (.008)	.000	.24 (.024)	.000

	Model 1		Model 2		Model 3	
Political Interest	.16 (.012)	.000	.10 (.018)	.000		
Constant 1	.37 (.092)	.000	−.70 (.132)	.000	1.23 (.375)	.000
Constant 2					4.23 (.397)	
N	1309		1309		1309	
Pseudo R^2	.10		.16		.22	
LR Chi^2	674.14	.000	794.08	.000	590.53	

Note: Unstandardized Poisson regression coefficients with standard errors in parentheses for models estimating political discussion and knowledge. Unstandardized ordered logistic regression coefficients with standard errors in parentheses for models for political interest. Reported probabilities are based on two-tailed tests. 2000 NES, postelection study.

* The predicted probability for reading online political news was constructed from a logistic regression model, where reading online political news was the dependent variable, and independent variables included female, national television news consumption, newspaper consumption, political interest, age, education, income, Internet access, strong partisan, efficacy, political interest, African American, Asian American, and Latino. In the model reported in column 3, political interest is not used in calculating the first-stage estimates.

Table 3.A.2
Impact of Online News on Political Interest, Pew Internet and American Life 2002 (Second-Stage Estimates)

Covariates	Political Interest β (s.e.)	p > z	Conditional Effects Model β (s.e.)	p > z
Reading Online News (Predicted Probability)*	**13.72 (.639)**	**.000**	**11.78 (1.62)**	**.000**
Traditional Media				
Newspaper Consumption	.11 (.129)	.402	.11 (.129)	.385
Television (National) Consumption	.40 (.124)	.001	.40 (.123)	.001
Demographic Controls				
Democrat	.12 (.150)	.442	.13 (.150)	.390
Republican	.17 (.146)	.252	.17 (.146)	.236
Age	.07 (.004)	.000	.06 (.004)	.000
Female	.46 (.119)	.000	.45 (.119)	.000
Latino	.26 (.222)	.235	.27 (.221)	.230
African American	.33 (.207)	.117	.31 (.207)	.134
Asian American	−.32 (.391)	.410	−.31 (.392)	.427
Education	−.16 (.042)	.000	−.16 (.042)	.000
Income	−.12 (.032)	.000	−.12 (.032)	.000
Age*Online News Consumption			.05 (.038)	.200
Constant 1	−.74 (.291)		−.87 (.313)	
Constant 2	3.73 (.305)		3.57 (.330)	
Constant 3	4.03 (.307)		3.86 (.332)	
N	**1867**		**1867**	
Pseudo R^2	.34		.34	
LR Chi^2	1210.65	.000	1212.30	.000

Note: Unstandardized ordered logistic regression coefficients with standard errors in parentheses. Reported probabilities are based on two-tailed test. *The Internet and American Life Daily Tracking Survey, October–November 2002,* Pew Research Center for the People and the Press.
* The predicted probability for reading online political news was constructed from a logistic regression model, where reading online political news was the dependent variable, and explanatory variables included female, national television news consumption, newspaper consumption, age, education, income, Internet access, Democrat, Republican, African American, Asian American, and Latino.

Table 3.A.3
Impact of Online News on Political Interest, Pew Research Center 2004 (Second-Stage Estimates)

Covariates	Political Interest		Conditional Effects Model	
	β (s.e.)	p > z	β (s.e.)	p > z
Reading Online News (Predicted Probability)*	**11.10 (.519)**	**.000**	**12.21 (1.029)**	**.000**
Traditional Media				
Newspaper Consumption	1.30 (.212)	.000	1.32 (1.029)	.000
Television (National) Consumption	2.34 (.193)	.000	2.36 (.193)	.000
Demographic Controls				
Democrat	.77 (.144)	.000	.78 (.144)	.000
Republican	.70 (.142)	.000	.66 (.142)	.000
Age	.05 (.004)	.000	.05 (.005)	.000
Female	.42 (.123)	.001	.43 (.123)	.001
Latino	1.06 (.243)	.000	1.08 (.244)	.000
African American	.41 (.203)	.045	.41 (.203)	.047
Asian American	−.71 (.478)	.112	−.78 (.479)	.102
Education	−.35 (.045)	.000	−.34 (.045)	.000
Income	.01 (.029)	.755	.01 (.029)	.616
Age*Online News Consumption			**−.03 (.021)**	**.204**
Constant 1	2.87 (.345)		3.09 (.386)	
Constant 2	5.06 (.367)		5.29 (.410)	
Constant 3	8.13 (.413)		8.35 (.450)	
N	**1241**		**1241**	
Pseudo R^2	.28		.28	
LR Chi^2	925.64	.000	927.24	.000

Note: Unstandardized ordered logistic regression coefficients with standard errors in parentheses. Reported probabilities are based on two-tailed tests. *Cable and Internet Loom Large in Fragmented Political News Universe Survey*, January 11, 2004, Pew Research Center for the People and the Press.

* The predicted probability for reading online political news was constructed from a logistic regression model, where reading online political news was the dependent variable, and explanatory variables included female, national television news consumption, newspaper consumption, age, education, income, Internet access, Democrat, Republican, African American, Asian American, and Latino.

Table 3.A.4
Impact of Online News on Political Knowledge, Pew Research Center 2004 (Second-Stage Estimates)

Covariates	Political Knowledge b (s.e.)	p > z	Conditional Effects Model b (s.e.)	p > z
Reading Online News (Predicted Probability)*	.54 (.244)	.028	1.89 (.514)	.000
Traditional Media				
Newspaper Consumption	−.11 (.112)	.309	−.07 (.114)	.552
Television (National) Consumption	−.11 (.107)	.303	−.05 (.110)	.635
Demographic Controls				
Democrat	−.05 (.086)	.558	−.04 (.086)	.648
Republican	−.02 (.086)	.800	−.01 (.086)	.877
Age	.02 (.002)	.000	.03 (.003)	.000
Female	−.37 (.075)	.000	−.44 (.076)	.000
Latino	−.05 (.224)	.025	−.44 (.225)	.054
African American	−.46 (.159)	.004	−.46 (.159)	.004
Asian American	−.23 (.338)	.506	−.28 (.339)	.409
Education	.14 (.028)	.000	.15 (.027)	.000
Income	.09 (.017)	.000	.10 (.017)	.000
Political Interest	.33 (.053)	.000	.30 (.053)	.000
Age*Online News Consumption			−.03 (.009)	.003
Constant	−3.56 (.219)	.000	−3.93 (.256)	.000
N	1241		1241	
Pseudo R^2	.17		.17	
LR Chi^2	463.90	.000	463.92	.000

Note: Unstandardized ordered logistic regression coefficients with standard errors in parentheses. Reported probabilities are based on two-tailed tests. *Cable and Internet Loom Large in Fragmented Political News Universe Survey*, January 11, 2004, Pew Research Center for the People and the Press.
* The predicted probability for reading online political news was constructed from a logistic regression model, reported in table 3.A.5, where reading online political news was the dependent variable, and explanatory variables included female, national television news consumption, newspaper consumption, age, education, income, political interest, Internet access, Democrat, Republican, political interest, African American, Asian American, and Latino.

Table 3.A.5
Who Reads Online News, 2000–2004? First-Stage Models, (First-Stage Estimates)

Covariates	2000 NES		2002 Pew		2004 Pew	
	b (s.e.)	p > z	b (s.e.)	p > z	b (s.e.)	p > z
Traditional Media						
Newspaper Consumption	.04 (.005)	.168	.34 (.158)	.034	−.43 (.036)	.036
Television (National) Consumption	−.01 (.031)	.776	.19 (.163)	.257	−1.28 (.164)	.000
Demographic Controls						
Strong Partisan	.38 (.169)	.025				
Democrat			.22 (.240)	.282	−.29 (.166)	.081
Republican			.35 (.183)	.057	−.47 (.168)	.005
Age	−.04 (.006)	.000	−.03 (.006)	.000	−.02 (.005)	.000
Female	−.40 (.029)	.009	−.42 (.150)	.005	−.54 (.138)	.000
Latino	.01 (.297)	.968	−.18 (.305)	.550	−.88 (.274)	.001
African American	−.10 (.297)	.734	−.19 (.309)	.542	−.13 (.217)	.562
Asian American	.32 (.551)	.561	−.21 (.542)	.705	.31 (.437)	.473
Education	.22 (.056)	.000	.18 (.054)	.001	.27 (.048)	.000
Income	−.02 (.611)	.434	.09 (.042)	.027	.27 (.048)	.000
Political Efficacy	−.03 (.036)	.390			.07 (.034)	.045
Political Interest	.31 (.061)	.000	.92 (.091)	.000	1.11 (.086)	.000
Internet Access	20.59 (172)	.990	19.37 (151)	.990	19.513 (120)	987

Table 3.A.5
(continued)

Covariates	2000 NES b (s.e.)	p > z	2002 Pew b (s.e.)	p > z	2004 Pew b (s.e.)	p > z
Constant	−20.82 (172)	.990	−24.31 (151)	.987	−22.985 (120)	.985
N	1333		1863		1241	
Pseudo R²	.51		.40		.46	
LR Chi²	599.220	.000	501.633	.000	808.017	.000

Note: Unstandardized logistic regression coefficients with standard errors in parentheses. Reported probabilities are based on two-tailed tests. 2000 NES, postelection study; *The Internet and American Life Daily Tracking Survey, October–November 2002*, Pew Research Center for the People and the Press; *Cable and Internet Loom Large in Fragmented Political News Universe Survey*, January 11, 2004, Pew Research Center for the People and the Press.

Table 4.A.1
The Impact of Internet Activities on the Probability of Voting, Pew Internet and American Life 2000 (Second-Stage Estimates)

Covariates	Voting b (s.e.)	p > z	b (s.e.)	p > z	b (s.e.)	p > z
Reading Online News (Predicted Probability)*	1.31 (.438)	.003				
E-mail Mobilization (Predicted Probability)*			4.63 (1.632)	.005		
Political Chat Room Discussion (Predicted Probability)*					9.75 (3.241)	.003
Traditional Media						
Newspaper	.36 (.138)	.009	.36 (.138)	.009	.36 (.139)	.010
Television	.55 (.111)	.000	.54 (.111)	.000	.54 (.111)	.000
Environmental Variables						
Number of Initiatives on State Ballot	−.01 (.019)	.448	−.01 (.019)	.472	−.01 (.019)	.446
State Racial Diversity	−.76 (.352)	.032	−.76 (.352)	.030	−.75 (.352)	.033
Demographic Controls						
Democrat	.28 (.123)	.023	.36 (.124)	.033	.28 (.124)	.026
Republican	.54 (.133)	.000	.44 (.143)	.002	.54 (.133)	.000
Log Age	1.61 (.147)	.000	1.55 (.140)	.000	1.63 (.150)	.000
Female	−.03 (.105)	.747	−.01 (.106)	.931	.04 (.111)	.729

Table 4.A.1
(continued)

Covariates	Voting					
	b (s.e.)	p > z	b (s.e.)	p > z	b (s.e.)	p > z
Latino	.10 (.183)	.594	.11 (.183)	.563	−.001 (.183)	.993
African American	.21 (.171)	.216	.21 (.170)	.220	.04 (.175)	.826
Asian American	−1.45 (.340)	.000	−1.22 (.343)	.000	−1.66 (.350)	.000
Education	.29 (.043)	.000	.30 (.043)	.000	.34 (.038)	.000
Income	.15 (.029)	.000	.16 (.028)	.000	.16 (.028)	.000
Constant	−7.31 (.570)	.000	−7.09 (.550)	.000	−7.54 (.535)	.000
N	2440		2440		2440	
Pseudo R²	.17		.17		.17	
LR Chi²	471.34	.000	470.58	.000	471.72	.000

Note: Unstandardized logistic regression estimates with robust standard errors in parentheses. Reported probabilities are based on two-tailed tests. *The Internet and American Life Daily Tracking Survey, September–December 2000,* Pew Internet and American Life Project.

* Predicted probabilities from first-stage binary logistic regressions where the independent variables are urban, suburban, income, education, Latino, female, African American, Asian American, Democrat, Republican, age, and Internet access.

Table 4.A.2
The Impact of Internet Activities on the Probability of Voting, Pew Internet and American Life 2002 (Second-Stage Estimates)

Covariates	Voting b (s.e.)	$p > z$	b (s.e.)	$p > z$	b (s.e.)	$p > z$
Reading Online News (Predicted Probability)*	**1.09 (.669)**	.103				
E-mail Mobilization (Predicted Probability)*			1.71 (1.300)	.185		
Political Chat Room Discussion (Predicted Probability)*					3.14 (4.126)	.447
Traditional Media						
Newspaper	.43 (.140)	.002	.42 (.140)	.003	.42 (.140)	.003
Television	-.07 (.136)	.620	-.07 (.140)	.606	-.08 (.135)	.581
Environmental Variables						
Number of Initiatives on State Ballot	.02 (.038)	.582	.02 (.038)	.612	.02 (.038)	.610
State Racial Diversity	-.82 (.415)	.047	-.80 (.415)	.053	-.81 (.415)	.052
Demographic Controls						
Democrat	.29 (.156)	.061	.31 (.156)	.048	.32 (.156)	.040
Republican	.58 (.153)	.000	.64 (.149)	.000	.66 (.151)	.000
Log Age	1.70 (.182)	.000	1.66 (.178)	.000	1.66 (.201)	.000
Female	.14 (.124)	.259	.11 (.122)	.366	.15 (.138)	.269

Table 4.A.2
(continued)

Covariates	Voting					
	b (s.e.)	p > z	b (s.e.)	p > z	b (s.e.)	p > z
Latino	−.16 (.244)	.513	−.13 (.251)	.617	−.19 (.245)	.445
African American	.17 (.221)	.449	.15 (.221)	.490	.17 (.223)	.453
Asian American	−1.68 (.549)	.002	−1.70 (.550)	.002	−1.72 (.550)	.002
Education	.15 (.050)	.002	.17 (.048)	.000	.19 (.044)	.000
Income	.13 (.036)	.000	.15 (.033)	.003	.16 (.033)	.000
Political Interest	.58 (.070)	.000	.58 (.070)	.000	.59 (.070)	.000
Constant	−9.79 (.718)	.000	−9.76 (.721)	.000	−9.87 (.847)	.000
N	1520		1520		1520	
Pseudo R²	.21		.21		.21	
LR Chi²	444.93	.000	444.05	.000	442.87	.000

Note: Unstandardized logistic regression estimates with robust standard errors in parentheses. Reported probabilities are based on two-tailed tests. *The Internet and American Life Daily Tracking Survey, October–November 2002,* Pew Internet and American Life Project.

* Predicted probabilities from first-stage binary logistic regressions where the independent variables are urban, suburban, income, education, Latino, female, African American, Asian American, political interest, Democrat, Republican, age, and Internet access.

Table 4.A.3.
The Impact of Internet Activities on the Probability of Voting, Pew Internet and American Life 2004 (Second-Stage Estimates)

Covariates	Voting					
	b (s.e.)	p > z	b (s.e.)	p > z	b (s.e.)	p > z
Reading Online News (Predicted Probability)*	1.54 (.400)	.000				
E-mail Mobilization (Predicted Probability)*			1.92 (.533)	.000		
Political Chat Room Discussion (Predicted Probability)*					4.78 (2.01)	.017
Traditional Media						
Newspaper	.14 (.104)	.187	.14 (.104)	.180	.13 (.104)	.229
Television (Local)	.278 (.140)	.048	.27 (.140)	.050	.26 (.140)	.064
Television (National)	−.15 (.146)	.294	−.15 (.142)	.308	−.14 (.146)	.332
Environmental Variables						
Number of Initiatives on State Ballot	.003 (.026)	.922	.004 (.026)	.892	.001 (.026)	.965
State Racial Diversity	−.39 (.571)	.495	−.59 (.578)	.309	−.41 (.566)	.467
Demographic Controls						
Democrat	.35 (.184)	.058	.36 (.184)	.049	.38 (.184)	.041
Republican	.68 (.197)	.001	.74 (.197)	.000	.74 (.197)	.000
Log Age	1.10 (.236)	.000	.83 (.205)	.000	.88 (.226)	.000

Table 4.A.3
(continued)

Covariates	Voting					
	b (s.e.)	p > z	b (s.e.)	p > z	b (s.e.)	p > z
Female	.14 (.155)	.378	.09 (.155)	.572	.25 (.163)	.128
Latino	−.43 (.271)	.110	−.46 (.268)	.090	−.44 (.270)	.102
African American	.29 (.250)	.249	.26 (.247)	.290	.06 (.247)	.822
Asian American	−1.79 (.505)	.000	−1.67 (.505)	.001	−1.81 (.499)	.000
Education	.12 (.061)	.050	.12 (.061)	.051	.20 (.055)	.000
Income	.07 (.042)	.104	.07 (.042)	.101	.11 (.041)	.008
Political Interest	.39 (.083)	.000	.40 (.083)	.000	.42 (.085)	.000
Mobilization (Phone)	.66 (.175)	.000	.66 (.175)	.000	.67 (.174)	.000
Mobilization (Mail)	.71 (.165)	.000	.69 (.165)	.000	.72 (.164)	.000
Constant	−6.32 (.888)	.000	−5.19 (.806)	.000	−5.85 (.887)	.000
N	1504		1504		1504	
Pseudo R²	.23		.23		.23	
LR Chi²	339.31	.000	337.68	.000	331.06	.000

Note: Unstandardized logistic regression estimates with standard errors in parentheses. Reported probabilities are based on two-tailed tests. *The 2004 Postelection Survey*, Pew Internet and American Life Project.

* Predicted probabilities from first-stage binary logistic regressions where the independent variables are urban, suburban, income, education, Latino, female, African American, Asian American, Democrat, Republican, age, Internet access, and political interest.

Table 5.A.1
Predicting Who Has Home Internet Access (General Population versus Disadvantaged Subgroups), Current Population Survey 2003

Covariates	General Population b (s.e.)	p < z	African American Subsample b (s.e.)	p < z	Latino Subsample b (s.e.)	p < z	Less-Educated Subsample b (s.e.)	p < z	Poor Subsample b (s.e.)	p < z
Female	−.03 (.01)	.035	−.02 (.06)	.687	.03 (.05)	.555	−.01 (.02)	.679	−.07 (.02)	.000
Latino	−.82 (.02)	.000					−1.03 (.03)	.000	−.90 (.03)	.000
African American	−.66 (.02)	.000					−.73 (.04)	.000	−.78 (.03)	.000
Asian American	−.03 (.04)	.384					.01 (.06)	.990	−.08 (.04)	.061
White (Reference Category)										
Age	−.02 (.001)	.000	−.01 (.002)	.000	−.003 (.18-2)	.112	−.01 (.001)	.000	−.02 (.001)	.000
Education	.34 (.01)	.000	.37 (.02)	.000	.46 (.02)	.000			.33 (.01)	.000
Urban	.02 (.02)	.211	−.02 (.06)	.700	−.01 (.06)	.882	.07 (.03)	.030	$.18^{-2}$ (.02)	.944
Suburban	.14 (.01)	.000	.19 (.07)	.014	.05 (.06)	.411	.14 (.02)	.000	.22 (.02)	.000
Rural (Reference Category)										
Professional	.21 (.03)	.000	.19 (.10)	.073	.58 (.11)	.000	.47 (.07)	.000	.46 (.03)	.000
Management	.30 (.03)	.000	.19 (13)	.146	.72 (.13)	.000	.41 (.06)	.000	.54 (.03)	.000
Service	−.01 (.02)	.873	−.08 (.08)	.303	.04 (.07)	.520	.03 (.03)	.360	.17 (.03)	.000
Sales	.29 (.03)	.000	.13 (.12)	.302	.68 (.10)	.000	.34 (.05)	.000	.41 (.03)	.000
Secretary	.21 (.03)	.000	.10 (.09)	.278	.39 (.09)	.000	.31 (.04)	.000	.38 (.03)	.000
Farming	−.37 (.10)	.000	−1.10 (.71)	.126	−.16 (.20)	.414	−.39 (.11)	.001	−.17 (.12)	.179

Table 5.A.1
(continued)

Covariates	General Population b (s.e.)	p < z	African American Subsample b (s.e.)	p < z	Latino Subsample b (s.e.)	p < z	Less-Educated Subsample b (s.e.)	p < z	Poor Subsample b (s.e.)	p < z
Construction	−.29 (.04)	.000	−33 (.16)	.037	−.17 (.10)	.112	−.27 (.05)	.000	−.11 (.04)	.010
Repair	.09 (.05)	.076	.18 (.19)	.336	.34 (.15)	.023	.15 (.06)	.021	.29 (.05)	.000
Transportation	−.12 (.04)	.004	−.12 (.12)	.313	−.07 (.11)	.486	−.05 (.05)	.271	−.06 (.04)	.153
Production (Reference Category)										
Child	.22 (.02)	.000	.19 (.06)	.003	.23 (.06)	.000	.30 (.03)	.000	.30 (.02)	.000
Married	36 (.02)	.000	.25 (.06)	.000	.01 (.06)	.794	.28 (.02)	.000	.61 (.02)	.000
Annual Income	.19 (.003)	.000	.22 (.009)	.000	.18 (.008)	.000	.23 (.004)	.000		
Constant	−1.71 (.04)	.000	−2.79 (.14)	.000	−3.28 (.13)	.000	−1.65 (.06)	.000	.38 (.04)	.000
N	84107		7652		8438		38481		65743	
Wald Chi^2	18055.76	.000	1696.35	.000	1485.31	.000	7431.40	.000	8039.11	.000

Note: Unstandardized logistic regression coefficients with robust standard errors in parentheses to control for heteroskedasticity. Probabilities based on two-tailed tests. Dependent variable is binary, coded 1 for home Internet access and 0 for no access. 2003 CPS data, October Supplement on Information Technology.

Table 5.A.2
Predicting Digital Citizenship/Daily Internet Use (General Population versus Disadvantaged Subgroups), Current Population Survey 2003

Covariates	General Population b (s.e.)	p < z	African American Subsample b (s.e.)	p < z	Latino Subsample b (s.e.)	p < z	Low-Educated Subsample b (s.e.)	p < z	Poor Subsample b (s.e.)	p < z
Female	−.05 (.01)	.000	.12 (.05)	.022	.04 (.05)	.417	.16 (.02)	.000	−.12 (.01)	.000
Latino	−.85 (.02)	.000					−1.19 (.03)	.000	−.89 (.03)	.000
African American	−.63 (.02)	.000					−.70 (.04)	.000	−.68 (.02)	.000
Asian American	−.25 (.03)	.000					−.39 (.05)	.000	−.29 (.03)	.000
White (Reference Category)										
Age	$-.03\ (.53^{-3})$	.000	$-.04\ (.19^{-2})$	.000	$-.03\ (.20^{-2})$	.000	$-.03\ (.78^{-3})$	.000	$-.03\ (.61^{-3})$	.000
Education	.44 (.01)	.000	.48 (.02)	.000	.61 (.02)	.000			.44 (.01)	.000
Urban	.05 (.01)	.005	.15 (.06)	.011	−.14 (.06)	.027	.05 (.03)	.071	.06 (.02)	.002
Suburban	.08 (.01)	.000	.27 (.06)	.000	.03 (.06)	.567	.09 (.02)	.000	.17 (.01)	.000
Rural (Reference Category)										
Professional	.71 (.02)	.000	.74 (.08)	.000	1.09 (.09)	.000	1.01 (.05)	.000	.84 (.02)	.000
Management	.90 (.02)	.000	.99 (.11)	.000	1.27 (.11)	.000	.93 (.04)	.000	1.07 (.02)	.000
Service	.08 (.02)	.001	.07 (.07)	.314	.04 (.07)	.559	.08 (.03)	.015	.24 (.02)	.000
Sales	.67 (.02)	.000	.53 (.11)	.000	1.02 (.09)	.000	.68 (.04)	.000	.76 (.03)	.000
Secretary	.92 (.02)	.000	.99 (.08)	.000	1.06 (.08)	.000	1.08 (.03)	.000	.94 (.02)	.000
Farming	−.57 (.09)	.000	−.46 (.63)	.459	−.96 (.26)	.000	−.69 (.11)	.000	−.51 (.11)	.000

Table 5.A.2
(continued)

Covariates	General Population		African American Subsample		Latino Subsample		Low-Educated Subsample		Poor Subsample	
	b (s.e.)	p < z	b (s.e.)	p < z	b (s.e.)	p < z	b (s.e.)	p < z	b (s.e.)	p < z
Construction	−.42 (.03)	.000	−.54 (.16)	.001	−.35 (.11)	.002	−.29 (.04)	.000	−.32 (.04)	.000
Repair	.16 (.04)	.000	.29 (.16)	.075	.55 (.15)	.000	.30 (.05)	.000	.27 (.04)	.000
Transportation	−.11 (.03)	.003	−.02 (.11)	.800	.14 (.11)	.212	.01 (.04)	.875	−.06 (.04)	.123
Child	−.10 (.01)	.000	−.01 (.05)	.818	−.09 (.05)	.121	−.02 (.02)	.278	−.05 (.01)	.003
Married	.04 (.01)	.019	.04 (.05)	.411	−.12 (.06)	.035	.15 (.02)	.000	.25 (.01)	.000
Not Married (Reference Category)										
Annual Income	.12 ($.22^{-2}$)	.000	.14 ($.76^{-2}$)	.000	.11 ($.75^{-2}$)	.000	.15 ($.33^{-2}$)	.000		
N	84107		7652		8438		38481		65743	
Wald Chi²	29579.41	.000	2626.64	.000	2593.30	.000	9612.57	.000	17937.36	.000

Note: Unstandardized ordered logistic regression coefficient with robust standard errors in parentheses to correct for heteroskedasticity. Probabilities based on two-tailed tests. Dependent variable ("Internet use, access over the last year") coded 4 ("at least once a day"), 3 ("at least once a week but not every day"), 2 ("at least once a month but not every week"), 1 ("less than once a month"), and 0 ("no Internet access"). 2003 CPS data, October Supplement on Information Technology.

Table 5.A.3
Predicting Access and Digital Citizenship: Young versus Old Old Subgroups, Current Population Survey 2003

Covariates	Home Internet Access				Frequency of Internet Use			
	Young (32 Years of Age and Less)		Old (59 Years of Age and Older)		Young (32 Years of Age and Less)		Old (59 Years of Age and Older)	
	b (s.e.)	p < z	b (s.e.)	p < z	b (s.e.)	p < z	b (s.e.)	p < z
Female	−.09 (.03)	.006	.04 (.03)	.217	−.08 (.03)	.004	.09 (.03)	.005
Latino	−.87 (.04)	.000	−.48 (.08)	.000	−.89 (.04)	.000	−.69 (.08)	.000
African American	−.64 (.05)	.000	−.48 (.08)	.000	−.65 (.04)	.000	−.58 (.07)	.000
Asian American	.06 (.07)	.377	−.02 (.09)	.813	−.01 (.06)	.000	−.55 (.09)	.000
White (*Reference Category*)								
Education	.37 (.01)	.000	.32 (.01)	.000	.46 (.01)	.000	.46 (.01)	.000
Urban	.01 (.04)	.675	−.03 (.04)	.437	.06 (.03)	.078	−.07 (.04)	.118
Suburban	.13 (.03)	.000	.10 (.03)	.004	.10 (.03)	.001	.07 (.03)	.043
Rural (*Reference Category*)								
Professional	$-.71^{-2}$ (.06)	.908	.40 (.08)	.000	.36 (.04)	.000	1.04 (.06)	.000
Management	.01 (.08)	.853	.37 (.07)	.000	.46 (.06)	.000	1.06 (.06)	.000
Service	−.11 (.04)	.419	.16 (.07)	.041	−.12 (.04)	.003	.38 (.07)	.000
Sales	.15 (.06)	.011	.35 (.09)	.000	.32 (.05)	.000	.98 (.07)	.000
Secretary	.04 (.05)	.419	.37 (.07)	.170	.50 (.04)	.000	1.36 (.06)	.000
Farming	−.34 (.16)	.039	−.40 (.29)	.170	−.79 (.13)	.000	−.98 (.36)	.008

Table 5.A.3
(continued)

| | Home Internet Access | | | | Frequency of Internet Use | | | |
| | Young (32 Years of Age and Less) | | Old (59 Years of Age and Older) | | Young (32 Years of Age and Less) | | Old (59 Years of Age and Older) | |
Covariates	b (s.e.)	p < z	b (s.e.)	p < z	b (s.e.)	p < z	b (s.e.)	p < z
Construction	−.65 (.07)	.000	−.13 (.14)	.347	−.87 (.06)	.000	.25 (.13)	.061
Repair	−.19 (.09)	.041	.19 (17)	.259	−.42 (.08)	.000	.61 (.14)	.000
Transportation	−.31 (.07)	.000	.10 (.10)	.335	−.40 (.06)	.000	.28 (.11)	.012
Production (Reference Category)								
Child	−.21 (.04)	.000	.90 (.14)	.000	−.33 (.03)	.000	.35 (.11)	.002
Married	.02 (.04)	.497	.45 (.03)	.000	−.22 (.03)	.000	.31 (.03)	.000
Annual Income	.17 $(.43^{-2})$	.000	.23 $(.56^{-2})$	.000	.09 $(.37^{-2})$	.000	.14 (.01)	.000
Constant	−1.81 (.06)	.000	−3.63 (.06)	.000				
N	21601		20307		21601		20307	
Wald Chi^2	3926.55	.000	4310.03	.000	5877.11	.000	5935.34	.000

Note: Unstandardized ordered logistic regression coefficient with robust standard errors in parentheses to correct for heteroskedasticity. Probabilities based on two-tailed tests. 2003 CPS data, October Supplement on Information Technology.

Table 6.A.1
Who Has Internet Access (Broadband or Dial-up) at Home? Pew Internet and American Life 2003 and 2005

Covariates	2003 Models: Compared to No Access				2005 Models: Compared to No Access			
	Dial-up		Broadband		Dial-up		Broadband	
	b (s.e.)	p > z	b (s.e.)	p > z	b (s.e.)	p > z	b (s.e.)	p > z
Urban	.22(.15)	.16	.76(.21)	.00	−.18(.17)	.27	.58(.18)	.00
Suburban	.31(.13)	.02	.65(.19)	.00	−.15(.15)	.33	.66(.16)	.00
Rural (Reference Category)								
Married	.48(.12)	.00	.50(.16)	.00	.21(.14)	.14	.24(.14)	.09
Income	.26(.03)	.00	.46(.04)	.00	.19(.04)	.00	.41(.04)	.00
Education	.34(.04)	.00	.46(.05)	.00	.31(.04)	.00	.45(.04)	.00
African American	−.50(.20)	.01	−.74(.28)	.00	−.83(.23)	.00	−.92(.22)	.00
Asian American	.28(.55)	.60	.58(.58)	.31	−.82(.55)	.14	−.87(.48)	.07
Latino	−.51(.21)	.01	−.87(.29)	.00	−.48(.26)	.07	−.21(.23)	.37
White (Reference Category)								
Age	−.04(.00)	.00	−.07(.00)	.00	−.03(.00)	.00	−.05(.00)	.00
Male	−.11(.11)	.28	.19(.14)	.17	−.13(.13)	.30	−.06(.12)	.59
Children Ages (11 and Under)	−.14(.14)	.33	−.32(.17)	.06	−.08(.17)	.62	−.37(.16)	.03
Children Ages (12 to 17)	−.04(.15)	.78	.32(.18)	.09	.43(.18)	.02	.59(.17)	.00
Employed	−.11(.13)	.36	−.27(.17)	.12	.07(.15)	.63	.04(.15)	.70

Table 6.A.1
(continued)

Covariates	2003 Models: Compared to No Access				2005 Models: Compared to No Access			
	Dial-up		Broadband		Dial-up		Broadband	
	b (s.e.)	p > z	b (s.e.)	p > z	b (s.e.)	p > z	b (s.e.)	p > z
Unemployed (Reference Category)								
Government Employee	−.00(.17)	.99	−.08(.20)	.69				
Constant	−.81(.29)	.00	−2.31(.39)	.00	−1.06(.34)	.00	−2.08(.15)	.00
N	2284		2284		2139		2139	
Pseudo R²	.1830		.1830		.1878		.1878	
LR Chi²	877.52	.00	877.52	.00	861.94	.00	861.94	.00

Note: Unstandardized multinomial logistic regression coefficients with robust standard errors in parentheses. Probabilities based on two-tailed tests. In each model, either dial-up or broadband are being compared with no home Internet access. Pew Internet and American Life Project, national random digit-dialed telephone surveys. The first (August 2003) was focused on e-government, and the second (December 2005) was focused on broadband.

Table 6.A.2
Who Has Digital Citizenship and Digital Experience?

Covariates	Digital Citizenship/ Frequency Internet Use b (s.e.)	p > z	Digital Experience/ Proxy Skills b (s.e.)	p > z|
Home Broadband Access	**.14 (.06)**	**.011**	**.64 (.11)**	**.000**
Age	−.01 (.001)	.000	−.01 (.002)	.000
Male	.03 (.04)	.328	.17 (.06)	.004
Latino	−.12 (.07)	.082	−.31 (.11)	.006
African American	−.19 (.05)	.000	−.24 (.08)	.002
Asian American	−.15 (.20)	.440	.36 (.35)	.308
Education	.14 (.02)	.000	.21 (.03)	.000
Income/Poor	−.20 (.04)	.000	−.23 (.07)	.000
Democrat	−.08 (.04)	.070	−.02 (.08)	.783
Republican	.003 (.05)	.942	.09 (.08)	.244
Unemployed	−.17 (.05)	.000	−.32 (.08)	.000
Constant	1.61 (.09)	.000	1.81 (.14)	.000
N	925		903	
Pseudo R^2	.12		.31	
Wald Chi^2	516.55	.000	36.49	.000

Note: Unstandardized Poisson regression coefficients, with standard errors in parentheses. Probabilities based on two-tailed tests. Survey data (conducted in August 2001) from Karen Mossberger, Caroline Tolbert, and Mary Stansbury, *Virtual Inequality: Beyond the Digital Divide* (Washington, DC: Georgetown University Press, 2003).

Notes

Chapter 1

1. Analyses using multivariate regression give us the ability to take overlapping influences into account and ascertain which factors underlie these disparities. We can examine the impact of race or ethnicity, for example, while holding constant or "controlling for" factors such as education and income, which might really be driving what seem like racial differences at first. For all years between 1995 and 2000 in the Katz and Rice (2002) study, race and ethnicity were not statistically significant for predicting Internet use anywhere. But their sample sizes of approximately one thousand to sixteen hundred did not include an oversample for minorities and the poor, as did the Mossberger, Tolbert, and Stansbury study (2003). A small sample of African Americans and Latinos in the Katz and Rice study may have accounted for the difference in results, and may not have been representative of the population of African Americans and Latinos (see Katz and Rice 2002, 52–54).

2. The data reported by the NTIA are drawn from survey questions from the U.S. Census Bureau's Current Population Survey (CPS), administered to a large sample of households. In this study, the 2003 CPS that we use includes over a hundred thousand households.

3. Updated July 19, 2006.

4. A somewhat different question available in some Pew surveys asks respondents "How often do you use the Internet at home?" or "How often do you use the Internet at work?" This question introduces more potential recall bias or social bias than simply asking whether the respondent used the Internet yesterday in these places. Additionally, the "used yesterday" question allows us to compare use at both home and work, while the other questions do not.

Chapter 2

1. See, for example, the results from the 1991 International Social Justice Project surveys (cited in Jencks and Tach 2006). See also (Jacobs and Skocpol 2005, 8).

2. Electronic commerce is "the online transaction of business, featuring linked computer systems of the vendor, host, and buyer (U.S. Department of Commerce [n.d.]), and its emergence created the dot-com boom of the 1990s.

3. These include: management, business, and financial; professional and related; service; sales and related; office and administrative support; farming, fishing, and forestry; construction and extraction; installation, maintenance, and repair; production; transportation and material moving; and armed forces.

4. Because of the low number of responses, a separate binary variable for the armed forces was not included, with respondents whose occupation was armed forces coded 0.

5. In the 2003 CPS, 9,695 respondents reported being black only. Also, the multiple race categories (with only two races) that included black were included in the construction of the variable for a total of 9,920 black respondents.

Chapter 3

1. That the media has been found to increase political knowledge does not negate other important predictors of political sophistication. What an individual receives can also be determined by their background level of knowledge and mediated by education. Vincent Price and John Zaller (1993) suggest that background political knowledge, not media use, is the strongest and most consistent predictor of current news story recall across a wide range of topics.

2. Of course, online political information is transmitted to consumers through a combination of means—not merely through print. As with television and/or radio, individuals can consume news on the Internet through audio-streamed speeches, streaming video, and Web cam images. Nevertheless, Internet news is largely a print-driven format, and at any rate, all forms of media can increase political knowledge (Delli Carpini and Keeter 1996).

3. Although Freedman, Franz, and Goldstein (2004) conceptualize knowledge separately from engagement, the literature on social capital and engagement considers knowledge as a form of civic engagement (Putnam 2000; Delli Carpini and Keeter 1996).

4. We are not using the 2002 and 2004 NES because it did not ask the respondents about Internet use for political information.

5. In the 2000 NES, the respondents were asked: (1) "What position does Trent Lott hold?" (2) "What position does William Rehnquist hold?" (3) "What position does Tony Blair hold?" (4) "What position does Janet Reno hold?" (5) "Which party had a majority in the House before the election?" and (6) "Which party held a majority in the Senate before the election?" In the 2004 Pew survey, the respondents were asked: "Do you happen to know which of the Democratic presidential candidates" (1) "served as an army general?" and (2) "served as the majority leader in the House of Representatives?"

6. 1 for "not at all closely," 2 for "not too closely," 3 for "fairly closely," and 4 for "very closely."

7. The survey questions used in this analysis measure obtaining news online, rather than participating in an e-mail, chat, blog, or online forum. The analysis is constrained by the availability of the data in the 2000 NES. While more detailed questions regarding online news are available for the Pew surveys, we focus on the consumption of online news for consistency between the 2000 NES and 2002 and 2004 Pew surveys. Establishing a general pattern of the impact of the Internet on civic engagement is the aim of this research. We also acknowledge the significant diversity in online news content, such as the *New York Times* versus the *Drudge Report*. The national survey instruments are not refined enough to measure this type of variation. In future research, we hope to use a more refined measure of online news consumption.

8. As with any two-stage model, we made some identification assumptions in the structural models. We hypothesized that demographic factors—such as gender, race, age, education, and income—would affect the online consumption of election news as well as home Internet access, given the research on the digital divide (Norris 2001; Bimber 2003; Mossberger, Tolbert, and Stansbury 2003). We hypothesized that traditional media use (television national news and newspapers) would be an important predictor of the use of online news as well as political interest. We further hypothesized that political efficacy would affect the consumption of online news. In second-stage models predicting political interest, political interest is omitted from the creation of the instrumental variable. Table 3.A.5 presents the first-stage models for the 2000 NES, 2002 Pew, and 2004 Pew surveys.

9. We created this variable from the NES's 7-point measure of partisanship.

10. In straightforward one-stage models, reading online news was a positive and statistically significant predictor of all three forms of civic engagement (knowledge, interest, and discussion) using both the NES and Pew surveys.

11. Since our hypothesis is directional, the lower threshold of a one-tailed t-test used to test this hypothesis for the NES data is appropriate.

Chapter 4

1. The first was conducted from September 15 through December 22, 2000, and has a sample size of 8,378. The second was conducted from October 30 through November 24, 2002, and has a sample size of 2,745. Those surveyed before the November elections were asked if they planned to vote, while those interviewed after the election were asked if they had voted. To better establish the time order and remain consistent with previous research, this study will restrict itself to the 3,416 individuals interviewed in the survey after the 2000 presidential election took place and the 1,884 interviewed after the 2002 midterm election. All interviews from the 2004 survey were conducted immediately after the presidential election.

2. Individuals who had Internet access for less than one year at the time of the survey were grouped with those who did not have Internet access. This was done because individuals with less than one year of access would not have had

access during the entire election season. In addition, there is a learning curve associated with the Internet. It takes individuals time to become acquainted with features such as chat rooms and e-mails.

Chapter 5

1. Some of the fluctuation from year to year is due to sampling, especially for subgroups such as African Americans or Hispanics. With overall sample sizes of one or two thousand, it is not always possible to obtain a truly representative sample of the population of all African Americans or Latinos without oversampling. Internet use may not have actually dropped from 51 to 43 percent of African Americans in 2004. So it may be a mistake to dwell too closely on the exact percentages for each year, particularly for smaller groups within the sample. The overall trends are clear, however.

2. In the upper quartile of the sample.

3. See ⟨http://www.pewinternet.org/trends/UsageOverTime.xls⟩.

4. In the 2003 CPS 9,695 respondents reported being black only. Also, the multiple race categories (with only two races) that included black were included in the construction of the variable for a total of 9,920 black respondents.

5. These include: management, business, and financial; professional and related; service; sales and related; office and administrative support; farming, fishing, and forestry; construction and extraction; installation, maintenance, and repair; production; transportation and material moving; and armed forces. A series of binary variables was created for each occupation, with production as the reference (left-out category). Because of the low number of responses, a separate binary variable for the armed forces was not included, with the respondents whose occupation was the armed forces coded 0.

6. In contrast to the Mossberger, Tolbert, and Gilbert 2006 study, we could only control for urban residence and not for concentrated poverty.

7. For an exception, see Fox and Livingston (2007).

Chapter 6

1. High-poverty census tracts were defined as those with 50 percent or more of the households living at or below 150 percent of the federal poverty level. With multiple callbacks, the average response rate was 42 percent.

2. Multinomial logistic regression is a method that is useful in cases where there can be more than two possible nominal outcomes. The statistical method assumes that no other possible alternative nominal outcomes exist that are statistically correlated with those in the dependent variable (Long 1997). A multinomial logistic model allows us to assess the effects that independent variables have on the risk of individuals falling into one of three mutually exclusive nominal outcomes. Covariate effects are interpreted in comparison to a reference cate-

gory (no access), where a unit change in x affects the log odds of access (either dial-up or broadband) versus a reference category (Aldrich and Nelson 1984; Long 1997). Another interpretation is that a unit of x_j increases the odds of being in category m versus being in the reference category by a multiplicative factor of $\exp(\beta_{mj})$, controlling for all other covariates.

3. Even when we control for dial-up modem Internet access in the same model, broadband access remains a statistically significant predictor of digital experience or the use of the Internet for a variety of activities (data not shown).

References

Abbott, P. 1991. *Political Thought in America: Conversations and Debates.* Itasca, IL: F. E. Peacock Publishers.

Abramson, P., and J. Aldrich. 1982. The Decline of Electoral Participation in America. *American Political Science Review* 76:502–521.

Acemoglu, D. 2002. Technical Change, Inequality, and the Labor Market. *Journal of Economic Literature* 40 (1): 7–72.

Aldrich, J. H., and F. D. Nelson. 1984. *Linear Probability, Probit, and Logit Models.* Thousand Oaks, CA: Sage Publications.

Allen, S. 2001. Technology and the Wage Structure. *Journal of Labor Economics* 19 (2): 440–483.

Alliance for Public Technology and the Benton Foundation. 2003. A Broadband World: The Promise of Advanced Services. Available at ⟨http://www.benton.org/ publibrary/broadband/broadband-world.html⟩ (accessed July 21, 2004).

Alvarez, M. 1998. *Information and Elections.* Ann Arbor: University of Michigan Press.

Alvarez, M., and G. Glasgow. 2000. Two-Stage Estimation of Nonrecursive Choice Models. *Political Analysis* 8:147–165.

Arabsheibani, G. R., J. M. Emami, and A. Marin. 2004. The Impact of Computer Use on Earnings in the U.K. *Scottish Journal of Political Economy* 51 (1): 82–94.

Arnal, E., W. Ok, and R. Torres. 2003. Knowledge, Work Organisation, and Economic Growth. In *Internet, Economic Growth, and Globalization*, ed. C. E. Barfield, G. Heiduk, and P. J. J. Welfens, 327–376. Berlin: Springer-Verlag.

Aspden, P., and J. E. Katz. 1997. A Nation of Strangers? *Communications of the ACM* 40:81–86.

Atkinson, R. D. 2004. *The Past and Future of America's Economy: Long Waves of Innovation That Power Cycles of Growth.* Northampton, MA: Edward Elgar.

Autor, D. H. 2001. Wiring the Labor Market. *Journal of Economic Perspectives* 15 (1): 25–40.

Autor, D. H., L. Katz, and A. Krueger. 1998. Computing Inequality: Have Computers Changed the Labor Market? *Quarterly Journal of Economics* 113 (4): 1169–1213.

Autor, D. H., F. Levy, and R. J. Murnane. 2003. The Skill Content of Recent Technological Change: An Empirical Exploration. *Quarterly Journal of Economics* 118 (4): 1279–1333.

Ayres, R. U., and E. Williams. 2003. The Digital Economy: Where Do We Stand? *Technological Forecasting and Social Change* 71 (4): 315–339.

Barber, B. 1984. *Strong Democracy: Participatory Politics for a New Age.* Berkeley: University of California Press.

Barrington, L. 2000. Does a Rising Tide Lift All Boats? America's Full-Time Working Poor Reap Limited Gains in the New Economy. Conference Board report 1271–00–RR. Washington, DC: Conference Board.

Beck, P. A. 1991. Voters' Intermediation Environments in the 1988 President Contest. *Public Opinion Quarterly* 55:371–394.

Bellah, R., R. Madsen, W. Sullivan, A. Swidler, and S. Tipton. 1985. *Habits of the Heart: Individualism and Commitment in American Life.* New York: Perennial Library.

Bertot, J. C., C. R. McClure, and P. T. Jaeger. 2005. Public Libraries and the Internet 2004: Survey Results and Findings. Information Use Management and Policy Institute, Florida State University. Available at ⟨http://www.ii.fsu.edu/projectFiles/plinternet/2004.plinternet.study.pdf⟩ (accessed February 15, 2007).

Bimber, B. 1999. The Internet and Citizen Communication with Government: Does the Medium Matter? *Political Communication* 16 (4): 409–428.

Bimber, B. 2000. Measuring the Gender Gap on the Internet. *Social Science Quarterly* 81 (3): 868–876.

Bimber, B. 2001. Information and Political Engagement in America: The Search for Effects of Information Technology at the Individual Level. *Political Research Quarterly* 54:53–67.

Bimber, B. 2003. *Information and American Democracy: Technology in the Evolution of Political Power.* Cambridge: Cambridge University Press.

Blau, F. D., and L. M. Kahn. 2002. *At Home and Abroad: U.S. Labor-Market Performance in International Perspective.* New York: Russell Sage Foundation.

Blinder, A. 2000. The Internet and the New Economy. Brookings Institution policy brief no. 60.

Boneva, B., R. Kraut, and D. Frohlich. 2001. Using E-mail for Personal Relationships: The Difference Gender Makes. *American Behavioral Scientist* 45 (3): 530–549.

Bound, J., and H. J. Holzer. 2000. Demand Shifts, Population Adjustments, and Labor Market Outcomes during the 1980s. *Journal of Labor Economics* 18 (1): 20–54.

Bowler, S., and T. Donovan. 1998. *Demanding Choices: Opinion, Voting, and Direct Democracy.* Ann Arbor: University of Michigan Press.

Bowler, S., T. Donovan, and C. Tolbert, eds. 1998. *Citizens as Legislators: Direct Democracy in the United States*. Columbus: Ohio State University Press.

Brauer, D., and S. Hickok. 1995. Explaining the Growing Inequality in Wages across Skill Levels. *Economic Policy Review* 1 (1): 61.

Bresnahan, T. 1999. Computerisation and Wage Dispersion: An Analytical Reinterpretation. *Economic Journal* 109:F390–F415.

Brians, C., and M. Wattenberg. 1996. Campaign Issue Knowledge and Salience: Comparing Reception from TV Commercials, TV News, and Newspapers. *American Journal of Political Science* 40:172–193.

Bryce, J. 1888. *The American Commonwealth (Vol. 3)*. Repr., London: Macmillan, 1973.

Bucy, E. 2000. Social Access to the Internet. *Harvard International Journal of Press Politics* 5 (1): 50–61.

Burke, C. 2001. Women, Guilt, and Home Computers. *Cyberspsychology and Behavior* 4 (5): 609–615.

Burnham, W. D. 1982. *The Current Crisis in American Politics*. New York: W. W. Norton.

Cain, B. E., and K. McCue. 1985. The Efficacy of Registration Drives. *Journal of Politics* 47 (11): 1221–1230.

Caldeira, G. A., A. R. Clausen, and S. C. Patterson. 1990. Partisan Mobilization and Electoral Participation. *Electoral Studies* 9 (3): 191–204.

Campbell, A. 1966. Surge and Decline: A Study of Electoral Change. In *Elections and the Political Order*, ed. A. Campbell, P. E. Converse, W. E. Miller, and D. E. Stokes, 40–62. New York: Wiley.

Campbell, A., P. E. Converse, W. E. Miller, and D. E. Stokes. 1960. *The American Voter*. Chicago: University of Chicago Press.

Capelli, P. 1996. Technology and Skill Requirements: Implications for Establishment Wage Structures. *New England Economic Review* (May–June): 139–154.

Card, D. F., F. Kramarz, and T. Lemieux. 1996. Changes in the Relative Structure of Wages and Employment: A Comparison of the United States, Canada, and France. Working paper no. 5487. Cambridge, MA: National Bureau of Economic Research.

Carvin, A., C. Conte, and A. Gilbert. 2001. The E-Rate in America: A Tale of Four Cities. In *The Digital Divide: Facing a Crisis or Creating a Myth?* ed. B. M. Compaine, 223–242. Cambridge, MA: MIT Press.

Center for Responsive Politics. 2005. Moveon.org, 2004 Election Cycle. Available at ⟨http://www.opensecrets.org/527s/527events.asp?orgid=41⟩ (accessed December 7, 2006).

Chaffee, S., and J. McLeod. 1973. Individual vs. Social Predictors of Information-Seeking. *Journalism Quarterly* 50:95–120.

Chaffee, S., and S. Kanihan. 1997. Learning about Politics from the Media. *Political Communication* 14:421–430.

Cialdini R. B. 1990. *Influence and Manipulation*. Paris: First.

Coleman, J. 2001. The Distribution of Campaign Spending Benefits across Groups. *Journal of Politics* 63:916–934.

Coleman, J., and P. Manna. 2000. Congressional Campaign Spending and the Quality of Democracy. *Journal of Politics* 62:757–789.

Cornfield, M. 2004. Bush vs. Kerry on the Web. *Campaign and Elections* 25 (5): 33–35.

Crandall, R., and C. Jackson. 2001. The $500 Billion Opportunity: The Potential Economic Benefit of Widespread Diffusion of Broadband Internet Access. Washington, DC: Criterion Economics, L.L.C.

Crepon, B., and T. Heckel. 2002. Computerization in France: An Evaluation Based on Individual Company Data. *Review of Income and Wealth* 48 (1): 77–98.

Croteau, D., and W. Hoynes. 2000. *Media Society: Industries, Images, and Audiences*, 2nd ed. Thousand Oaks, CA: Pine Forge Press.

CTCNet. 2006. 2005 Member Survey Summary. Available at ⟨http://ctcnet.org/what/resources/2005survey.htm⟩ (accessed March 23, 2006).

Dataquest, Inc. 2002. Gartner Dataquest Says Implementation of "True" Broadband Could Bolster U.S. GDP by $500 Billion a Year. Available at ⟨http://www4.gartner.com/5_about/press_releases/2002_08/pr20020826a.jsp⟩ (accessed July 30, 2004).

Davis, R., ed. 1994. *Politics and the Media*. Englewood Cliffs, NJ: Prentice Hall.

Davis, R., and D. Owen. 1998. *New Media and American Politics*. New York: Oxford University Press.

DeFleur, M. L., and S. J. Ball-Rokeach. 1989. *Theories of Mass Communication*, 5th ed. New York: Longman.

Delli Carpini, M., and S. Keeter. 1996. *What Americans Know about Politics and Why It Matters*. New Haven, CT: Yale University Press.

Dewey, J. 1927. *The Public and Its Problems*. New York: Holt.

Dickard, N. 2003. Edtech 2002: Budget Challenges, Policy Shifts, and Digital Opportunity. In *The Sustainability Challenge: Taking Edtech to the Next Level* Available at ⟨http://www.benton.org/publibrary/sustainability/sus_challenge.html⟩ (accessed December 7, 2006).

DiMaggio, P., and C. Celeste. 2004. Technological Careers: Adoption, Deepening, and Dropping Out in a Panel of Internet Users. Available at ⟨http://www.russellsage.org/publications/workingpapers⟩ (accessed February 15, 2006).

DiMaggio, P., and J. Cohen. 2004. Network Externalities: A Comparative Study of the Diffusion of Television and the Internet. Available at ⟨http://www.russellsage.org/publications/workingpapers⟩ (accessed February 15, 2006).

DiMaggio, P., E. Hargittai, W. Neuman, and J. Robinson. 2001. Social Implications of the Internet. *Annual Review of Sociology* 27:307–336.

DiNardo, J. C., and J. S. Pischke. 1997. The Returns to Computer Use Revisited: Have Pencils Changed the Wage Structure Too? *Quarterly Journal of Economics* 112:291–303.

Donovan, T., and S. Bowler. 2003. *Reforming the Republic: Democratic Institutions for the New America*. Upper Saddle River, NJ: Pearson Prentice Hall.

Dryzek, J. 1990. *Discursive Democracy: Politics, Policy, and Political Science*. Cambridge: Cambridge University Press.

Dryzek, J. 2000. *Deliberative Democracy and Beyond: Liberals, Critics, and Contestations*. Cambridge: Cambridge University Press.

Dunne, T., J. C. Haltiwanger, and K. Troske. 1997. Technology and Jobs: Secular Change and Cyclical Dynamics. *Carnegie-Rochester Series on Public Policy*, 1–7–78.

Eccles, J. 2005. Studying Gender and Ethnic Differences in Participation in Math, Physical Science, and Information Technology. *New Direction for Child and Adolescent Development* 110:7–14.

Edutopia News. 2004. Ed-Tech Funding Reduced for 2005. December 1. Available at ⟨http://www.edutopia.org/products/changeformat.php⟩ (accessed December 7, 2006).

eGovernment News. 2005. UK Government Launches New Digital Strategy. April 5. Available at ⟨http://europa.eu.int/idabc/en/document/4077/345⟩ (accessed December 7, 2006).

Elazar, D. 1984. *Federalism: A View from the American Federalist States*. 3rd ed. New York: Harper and Row.

Elster, J., ed. 1998. *Deliberative Democracy*. Cambridge: Cambridge University Press.

Engardio, P., R. S. Dunham, H. Dawley, I. Kunii, and E. Malkin. 1999. Activists without Borders. *Business Week* 3649:144–149.

Entorf, H., M. Gollac, and F. Kramarz. 1999. New Technologies, Wages, and Worker Selection. *Journal of Labor Economics* 17 (3): 464–491.

European Commission. 2004. eEurope 2005 Broadband. Available at ⟨http://europa.eu.int/information_society/eeurope/2005/all_about/broadband/index_en.htm⟩ (accessed July 30, 2004).

Fairlie, R. 2004. Race and the Digital Divide. *Contributions of Economic Analysis and Policy* 3 (1): 1–35. Available at ⟨http://www.bepress.com/bejeap⟩ (accessed August 10, 2005).

Fallows, D. 2005. How Women and Men Use the Internet. Pew Internet and American Life Project. December 28. Available at ⟨http://www.pewinternet.org/PPF/r/1717/report_display.asp⟩ (accessed March 15, 2006).

Ferguson, C. 2002. The United States Broadband Problem: Analysis and Policy Recommendations. Working paper. May 31. Washington, DC: Brookings Institution. Available at ⟨http://www.brookings.org/view.papers/ferguson/working_paper_20020531.pdf⟩ (accessed December 7, 2006).

Ferguson, C. 2004. *The Broadband Problem: Anatomy of a Market Failure and a Policy Dilemma*. Washington, DC: Brookings Institution Press.

Fishkin, J. 1993. *Democracy and Deliberation*. New Haven, CT: Yale University Press.

Fishkin, J. 1995. *The Voice of the People*. New Haven, CT: Yale University Press.

Ford, G., and T. Koutsky. 2005. Broadband and Economic Development: A Municipal Case Study from Florida. Available at ⟨http://www.publicpower.com/telecom_study/municipal_broadband_&economic_development.pdf⟩ (accessed December 15, 2005).

Fountain, J. E. 2001. *Building the Virtual State: Information Technology and Institutional Change*. Washington, DC: Brookings Institution Press.

Fox, S. 2005. Digital Divisions. Pew Internet and American Life Project. Available at ⟨http://www.pewinternet.org⟩ (accessed December 7, 2006).

Fox, S., and G. Livingston. 2007. Latinos Online: Hispanics with Lower Levels of Education and English Proficiency Remain Largely Disconnected from the Internet. Pew Internet and American Life Project and Pew Hispanic Center. Available at ⟨http://www.pewinternet.org⟩ (accessed June 6, 2007).

Freedman, P., M. Franz, and K. Goldstein. 2004. Campaign Advertising and Democratic Citizenship. *American Journal of Political Science* 48:723–741.

Freepress. 2006. Community Internet. Available at ⟨http://www.freepress.net/docs/comminternetbrochurefinal.pdf⟩ (accessed February 15, 2007).

Friedberg, L. 2003. The Impact of Technological Change on Older Workers: Evidence from Data on Computer Use. *Industrial and Labor Relations Review* 56 (3): 511–529.

Friedman, B. M. 2003. Introd. to *Inequality in America: What Role for Human Capital Policies?* by J. J. Heckman and A. B. Krueger, ix–xiv. Cambridge, MA: MIT Press.

Gallagher, M. D. 2005. ISD December 2005 EU-U.S. Plenary Session: Focus on Broadband. U.S. Department of Commerce, National Telecommunication and Information Administration. Available at ⟨http://www.ntia.doc.gov/ntiahome/speeches/2005/gallagher_ISD2005_broadband_files/frame.htm⟩ (accessed March 25, 2006).

Gandy, O. H. 1982. *Beyond Agenda Setting: Information Subsidies and Public Policy*. Norwood, NJ: Ablex Publishing Co.

Gates Foundation, Bill and Melinda. 2004. U.S. Library Program: Summary of Research Reports. Available at ⟨http://www.gatesfoundation.org/Libraries/USLibraryProgram/Evaluation/default.htm⟩ (accessed March 23, 2006).

Gates Foundation, Bill and Melinda. 2005. U.S. Public Libraries Providing Unprecedented Access to Computers, the Internet, and Technology Training. Available at ⟨http://www.gatesfoundation.org/Libraries/USLibraryProgram/Announcements/Announce-050623.htm⟩ (accessed March 23, 2006).

Gerber, A. S., and D. P. Green. 2000. The Effects of Canvassing, Telephone Calls, and Direct Mail on Voter Turnout: A Field Experiment. *American Political Science Review* 94 (3): 653–663.

Gillett, S. E. 2006. Municipal Wireless Broadband: Hype or Harbinger? *Southern California Law Review* 79:561–593.

Gorski, P., and M. Brimhall-Vargas. 2000. Bridges and Discussion: Online Dialogues toward Educational Change. *Multicultural Perspectives* 2 (1): 41–45.

Goss, E., and J. Phillips. 2002. How Information Technology Affects Wages: Evidence Using Internet Usage as a Proxy for IT Skills. *Journal of Labor Research* 23 (3): 463–474.

Graf, J., and C. Darr. 2004. Political Influentials Online in the 2004 Presidential Election. February 5. Available at ⟨http://www.ipdi.org⟩ (accessed December 7, 2006).

Grofman, B., ed. 1995. *Information, Participation, and Choice: An Economic Theory of Democracy in Perspective.* Ann Arbor: University of Michigan Press.

Gutmann, A., and D. Thompson. 1996. *Democracy and Disagreement.* Cambridge, MA: Belknap Press.

Habermas, J. 1996. *Between Facts and Norms: Contribution to a Discourse Theory of Law and Democracy.* Trans. W. Rehg. Cambridge, MA: MIT Press.

Hacker, J. S., S. Mettler, and D. Pinderhughes. 2005. Inequality and Public Policy. In *Inequality and American Democracy: What We Know and What We Need to Learn*, ed. L. R. Jacobs and T. Skocpol, 89–155. New York: Russell Sage Foundation.

Hamblen, M. 2006. Municipal Wireless Networks Are Growing. *Computer World*, October 25. Available at ⟨http://www.freepress.net/news/18666⟩ (accessed December 6, 2006).

Hargittai, E., and S. Shafer. 2006. Differences in Actual and Perceived Online Skills: The Role of Gender. *Social Science Quarterly* 87 (2): 432–448.

Hartz, L. 1955. *The Liberal Tradition in America.* New York: Harvest.

Hauge, J. A., M. A. Jamison, and R. J. Gentry. 2005. Bureaucrats as Entrepreneurs: Do Municipal Telecom Providers Hinder Private Entrepreneurs? Paper presented at the Telecommunications Policy Research Conference, Arlington, VA. Available at ⟨http://www.tprc.org⟩ (accessed July 20, 2006).

Healy, A., and D. McNamara. 1996. Verbal Learning and Memory: Does the Modal Model Still Work? In *Annual Review of Psychology*, ed. J. Spense, J. Darley, and D. Foss, 47:143–172. Palo Alto, CA: Annual Reviews.

Hero, R. 1992. *Latinos and the U.S. Political System: Two-Tiered Pluralism.* Philadelphia, PA: Temple University Press.

Hero, R. 1998. *Faces of Inequality: Social Diversity in American Politics.* New York: Oxford University Press.

Hero, R. 2007. *Racially Contingent Community: Racial Diversity, Social Capital, and American Politics.* Cambridge: Cambridge University Press.

Hero, R., and C. Tolbert. 1996. A Racial/Ethnic Diversity Interpretation of Politics and Policy in the States of the U.S. *American Journal of Political Science* 40:851–871.

Hill, K., and J. Leighley. 1999. Racial Diversity, Voter Turnout, and Mobilizing Institutions in the United States. *American Politics Quarterly* 27:275–295.

Hochschild, J. 1995. *Facing Up to the American Dream: Race, Class, and the Soul of the Nation.* Princeton, NJ: Princeton University Press.

Hochschild, J., and N. Scovronick. 2000. Democratic Education and the American Dream. In *Rediscovering the Democratic Purposes of Education*, ed. L. M. McConnell, P. M. Timpane, and R. Benjamin, 209–242. Lawrence: University Press of Kansas.

Holzer, H. J. 1996. *What Employers Want: Job Prospects for Less-Educated Workers.* New York: Russell Sage Foundation.

Horrigan, J. 2004. Broadband Penetration on the Upswing. Washington, DC: Pew Internet and American Life Project. Available at ⟨http://www.pewinternet .org⟩ (accessed December 7, 2006).

Horrigan, J. 2005. Broadband Adoption in the United States: Growing but Slowing. Pew Internet and American Life Project, September 21. Available at ⟨http:// www.pewinternet.org/PPF/r/164/report_display.asp⟩ (accessed March 15, 2006).

Horrigan, J. 2006. Home Broadband Adoption 2006: Home Broadband Adoption Is Going Mainstream and That Means User-Generated Content Is Coming from All Kinds of Internet Users. Available at ⟨http://www.pewinternet.org/pdfs/ PIP_Broadband_trends2006.pdf⟩ (accessed February 16, 2007).

Horrigan, J., K. Garrett, and P. Resnick. 2004. The Internet and Democratic Debate: Wired Americans Hear More Points of View about Candidates and Key Issues Than Other Citizens; They Are Not Using the Internet to Screen out Ideas with Which They Disagree. Available at ⟨http://www.pewinternet.org⟩ (accessed December 7, 2006).

Howard, P., L. Rainie, and S. Jones. 2001. Days and Nights on the Internet: The Impact of Diffusing Technology. *American Behavioral Scientist* 45:383–404.

Huckfeldt, R., and J. Sprague. 1991. Discussant Effects on Vote Choice: Intimacy, Structure, and Interdependence. *Journal of Politics* 53:122–158.

Institute for Politics, Democracy, and the Internet. 2003. The Net and the Nomination: Spring 2003. Available at ⟨http://www.ipdi.org/⟩ (accessed December 7, 2006).

Introna, L., and H. Nissenbaum. 2000. Shaping the Web: Why the Politics of Search Engines Matters. *Information Society* 16 (3): 169–185

Jackson, L. A., K. Ervin, P. Gardner, and N. Schmitt. 2001. Gender and the Internet: Women Communicating and Men Searching. *Sex Roles* 44:363–379.

Jackson, R. 1997. The Mobilization of U.S. State Electorates in the 1998 and 1990 Elections. *Journal of Politics* 59:520–537.

Jacobs, L. R., and T. Skocpol. 2005. American Democracy in an Era of Rising Inequality. In *Inequality and American Democracy: What We Know and What*

We Need to Learn, ed. L. R. Jacobs and T. Skocpol, 1–18. New York: Russell Sage Foundation.

Jason, L. A., T. Rose, J. R. Ferrari, and R. Barone. 1984. Personal versus Impersonal: Methods for Recruiting Blood Donations. *Journal of Social Psychology* 123:139–140.

Jefferson, T. 1810. To John Tyler, ME 12:393. Available at ⟨http://etext.virginia.edu/jefferson/quotations/jeff1370.htm⟩ (accessed December 7, 2006).

Jencks, C., and L. Tach. 2006. Would Equal Opportunity Mean More Mobility? In *Mobility and Inequality: Frontiers of Research in Sociology and Economics*, ed. S. L. Morgan, D. B. Grusky, and G. S. Fields, 23–58. Stanford, CA: Stanford University Press.

Jennings, M., and V. Zeitner. 2003. Internet Use and Civic Engagement. *Public Opinion Quarterly* 67 (3): 311–334.

Kaestle, D. F., A. Campbell, J. D. Finn, S. T. Johnson, and L. J. Mickulecky. 2001. *Adult Literacy and Education in America: Four Studies Based on the National Adult Literacy Survey*. NCES publication number 2001534. Washington, DC: U.S. Department of Education, National Center for Education Statistics. Available at ⟨http://nces.ed.gov/pubsearch/pubsinfo.asp?pubid=2001534⟩ (accessed December 7, 2006).

Kahn, K., and P. Kenney. 2001. The Importance of Issues in Senate Campaigns: Citizens' Reception of Issue Messages. *Legislative Studies Quarterly* 26:573–597.

Katz, E. 1992. On Parenting a Paradigm: Gabriel Tarde's Agenda for Opinion and Communication Research. *International Journal of Public Opinion Research* 4:80–85.

Katz, J. E., and R. E. Rice. 2002. *Social Consequences of Internet Use: Access, Involvement, and Interaction*. Cambridge, MA: MIT Press.

Katz, L. F. 2000. Technological Change, Computerization, and the Wage Structure. In *Understanding the Digital Economy: Data Tools, and Research*, ed. E. Brynjolfsson and B. Kahin, 217–244. Cambridge, MA: MIT Press.

Kelley, D. J. 2003. A Study of the Economic and Community Benefits of Cedar Falls, Iowa's Municipal Telecommunications Network. Available at ⟨http://www.iprovo.net/projectInfoDocs/economcAndCommunityBenefitsStudy.pdf⟩ (accessed December 15, 2005).

Kerbel, M. R. 1995. *Remote and Controlled: Media Politics in a Cynical Age*. Boulder, CO: Westview Press.

Kim, Y.-C., J. Jung, E. L. Cohen, and S. J. Ball-Rokeach. 2004. Internet Connectedness before and after September 11, 2001. *New Media and Society* 6 (5): 611–631.

Kim, Y.-H. 2002. A State of the Art Review on the Impact of Technology on Skill Demand in the OECD Countries. *Journal of Education and Work* 15 (1): 89–109.

Kinder, D. R., and L. M. Sanders. 1996. *Divided by Color: Racial Politics and Democratic Ideals*. Chicago: University of Chicago Press.

King, G., M. Tomz, and J. Wittenberg. 2000. Making the Most of Statistical Analysis: Improving Interpretation and Presentation. *American Journal of Political Science* 44:341–355.

Kleiner, A., and L. Lewis. 2003. *Internet Access in U.S. Public Schools and Classrooms: 1994–2002* (NCES 2004–011). U.S. Department of Education. Washington, DC: National Center for Education Statistics.

Kramer, G. H. 1970. The Effects of Precinct-Level Canvassing on Voter Behavior. *Public Opinion Quarterly* 34 (4): 560–572.

Kretchmer, S., and R. Carveth. 2001. The Color of the Net: African-Americans, Race, and Cyberspace. *Computers and Society* 34:9–14.

Krueger, A. B. 1993. How Computers Have Changed the Wage Structure: Evidence from Microdata, 1984–1989. *Quarterly Journal of Economics* 109 (1): 57–68.

Krueger, A. B. 2002. Assessing the Potential of Internet Political Participation in the United States. *American Politics Research* 30:476–498.

Krueger, A. B. 2003. Inequality, Too Much of a Good Thing. In *Inequality in America: What Role for Human Capital Policies?* ed. J. J. Heckman and A. B. Krueger, 1–76. Cambridge, MA: MIT Press.

Krueger, A. B., and Robert M. Solow, eds. 2001. *The Roaring Nineties: Can Full Employment Be Sustained?* New York: Russell Sage Foundation.

Kyllonen, P., and R. Christal. 1990. Reasoning Ability Is (Little More Than) Working-Memory Capacity? *Intelligence* 14:389–433.

Larsen, E., and L. Rainie. 2002. The Rise of the E-citizen: How People Use Government Agencies' Web Sites. Pew Internet and American Life Project. Available at ⟨http://www.pewinternet.org⟩ (accessed December 7, 2006).

Lassen, D. 2005. The Effect of Information on Voter Turnout: Evidence from a Natural Experiment. *American Journal of Political Science* 49 (1): 103–118.

Lazarsfeld, P. F., B. Berelson, and H. Gaudet. 1948. *The People's Choice.* New York: Columbia University Press.

Lehr, W. H., C. A. Osorio, S. E. Gillett, and M. A. Sirbu. 2005. Measuring Broadband's Economic Impact. Paper presented at the Telecommunications Policy Research Conference, Arlington, VA. Available at ⟨http://www.tprc.org⟩ (see also Broadband Properties, December 2005, available at ⟨http://www.broadbandproperties.com⟩) (accessed December 6, 2006).

Lenhart, A. 2003. The Ever-Shifting Internet Population: A New Look at Internet Access and the Digital Divide. Pew Internet and American Life Project. Available at ⟨http://www.pewinternet.org/⟩ (accessed December 7, 2006).

Levy, F., and R. Murnane. 1996. With What Skills Are Computers a Complement? *American Economic Review* 86 (2): 258–262.

Lewis-Beck, M. S., and T. W. Rice. 1992. *Forecasting Elections.* Washington, DC: CQ Press.

Litan, R. E., and A. M. Rivlin, eds. 2002. *The Economic Payoff from the Internet Revolution.* Washington, DC: Brookings Institution Press.

Long, J. S. 1997. *Regression Models for Categorical and Limited Dependent Variables. Advanced Quantitative Techniques in Social Sciences*, Vol. 7. Thousand Oaks: Sage Publications.

Long, J. S., and J. Freese. 2001. *Regression Models for Categorical Dependent Variables Using Stata.* College Station, TX: Stata.

Lupia, A. 1994. Shortcuts versus Encyclopedias: Information and Voting Behavior in California Insurance Reform Elections. *American Political Science Review* 88:63–76.

Lupia, A., and Z. Baird. 2003. Can Web Sites Change Citizens? Implications of Web, White, and Blue 2000. *PS: Political Science and Politics* 37:77–82.

Lupia, A., and M. McCubbins. 1998. *The Democratic Dilemma: Can Citizens Learn What They Need to Know?* New York: Cambridge University Press.

Lupia, A., and T. S. Philpot. 2002. More Than Kids Stuff: Can News and Information Web Sites Mobilize Young Adults? Paper presented at the annual meeting of the American Political Science Association, August 31–September 2, Boston.

Luskin, R. 1987. Measuring Political Sophistication. *American Journal of Political Science* 31:856–899.

Luskin, R. 1990. Explaining Political Sophistication. *Political Behavior* 12:331–361.

MacPherson, K. 2004. Critics Call for Overhaul of No Child Left Behind. *Pittsburgh Post Gazette*, March 21, A1.

Madden, M. 2006. Data Memo: Internet Penetration and Impact—April 2006. Available at ⟨http://www.pewinternet.org⟩ (see also Demographics of Internet Users, available at ⟨http://www.pewinternet.org/trends/User_Demo_4.26.06 .htm⟩) (accessed August 12, 2006).

Manzo, K. 2001. Academic Record. *Education Week on the Web.* Available at ⟨http://www.edweek.org/sreports/tc01/tc01article.cfm?slug=35academic.h20⟩ (accessed December 7, 2006).

Margolis, M., and D. Resnick. 2000. *Politics as Usual: The Cyberspace "Revolution."* Thousand Oaks, CA: Sage.

Marshall, T. H. 1992. The Problem Stated with the Assistance of Alfred Marshall [originally delivered in 1949]. In *Citizenship and Social Class*, T. H. Marshall and T. Bottomore, 3–51. London: Pluto Perspectives.

Massey, D. S., and N. A. Denton. 1993. *American Apartheid: Segregation and the Making of the Underclass.* Cambridge, MA: Harvard University Press.

McChesney, R. W. 1999. *Rich Media, Poor Democracy: Communication Politics in Dubious Times.* Urbana: University of Illinois Press.

McClure, C. R., and C. J. Bertot. 2002. Public Library Internet Services: Impact of the Digital Divide. Available at ⟨http://slis-two.lis.fsu.edu/~jcbertot/ DDFinal03_01_02.pdf⟩ (accessed December 7, 2006).

McDermott, K. 2000. The Web Snares More Candidates Than Ever This Year. *St. Louis Dispatch*, July 7, A1.

McGuckin, R., and B. Van Ark. 2001. *Making the Most of the Information Age: Productivity and Structural Reform in the New Economy.* New York: Conference Board.

McKenna, K. Y. A., and J. A. Bargh. 2000. Plan 9 from Cyberspace: The Implications of the Internet for Personality and Social Psychology. *Personality and Social Psychology Review* 4:57–75.

McLeod, J., and D. McDonald. 1985. Beyond Simple Exposure: Media Orientations and Their Impact on the Political Process. *Communication Research* 12:3–34.

Miller, P., and C. Mulvey. 1997. Computer Skills and Wages. *Australian Economic Papers* 36:106–113.

Mishel, L., J. Bernstein, and J. Schmitt. 2001. *The State of Working America:* 2000–2001. Ithaca, NY: Cornell University Press.

Mondak, J. 1995. Media Exposure and Political Discussion in U.S. Elections. *Journal of Politics* 57:62–85.

Morgan, S. L., and Y.-M. Kim. 2006. Inequality of Conditions and Intergenerational Mobility: Changing Patterns of Educational Attainment in the United States. In *Mobility and Inequality: Frontiers of Research in Sociology and Economics,* ed. S. L. Morgan, D. B. Grusky, and G. S. Fields, 165–194. Stanford, CA: Stanford University Press.

Morissette, R., and M. Drolet. 1998. Computers, Fax Machines, and Wages in Canada: What Really Matters? Working paper no. 126. Ottawa: Statistics Canada.

Moss, P., and C. Tilly. 2001. *Stories Employers Tell: Race, Skill, and Hiring in America.* New York: Russell Sage Foundation.

Mossberger, K., D. Kaplan, and M. Gilbert. 2006. How Concentrated Poverty Matters for the "Digital Divide": Motivation, Social Networks, and Resources. Paper presented at the American Political Science Association Meeting, August 31–September 3, Philadelphia.

Mossberger, K., C. Tolbert, and M. Gilbert. 2006. Race, Concentrated Poverty, and Information Technology. *Urban Affairs Review* 41 (5): 583–620.

Mossberger, K., C. Tolbert, and M. Stansbury. 2003. *Virtual Inequality: Beyond the Digital Divide.* Washington, DC: Georgetown University Press.

Mueller, M. L., and J. Schement. 2001. Universal Service From the Bottom UP: A Study of Telephone Penetration in Camden, NJ. In *The Digital Divide: Facing a Crisis or Creating a Myth?* ed. B. M. Compaine, 119–146. Cambridge, MA: MIT Press.

National Academy of Sciences. 2002. *Broadband: Bringing Home the Bits.* Washington, DC: National Academy Press.

National Conference of State Legislatures. 2004. Initiative, Referendum, and Recall. Available at ⟨http://www.ncsl.org/programs/legman/elect/initiat.htm⟩ (accessed December 7, 2006).

National School Boards Foundation. 2002. Are We There Yet? Available at ⟨http://www.ncsl.org/programs/legman/elect/initiat.htm⟩ (accessed December 7, 2006).

NetImpact. 2002. Study Overview and Key Findings. Available at ⟨http://www.netimpactusdy.com/nis_2002.html⟩ (accessed July 30, 2004).

Nie, N., and L. Erbring. 2000. *Internet and Society: A Preliminary Report*. Stanford, CA: Stanford Institute for the Qualitative Study of Society.

Norris, D. F., P. D. Fletcher, and S. Holden. 2001. Is Your Local Government Plugged In? Highlights of the 2000 Electronic Government Survey. Prepared for the International City/County Management Association and Public Technology, Inc. Available at ⟨http://www.umbc.edu.mipar/final_draft/PDFs/e-gover.icma.final-4-25-01.pdf⟩ (accessed June 10, 2002).

Norris, P. 2001. *Digital Divide: Civic Engagement, Information Poverty, and the Internet Worldwide*. Cambridge: Cambridge University Press.

Nye, J. S., Jr., P. D. Zelikow, and D. C. King, eds. 1997. *Why People Don't Trust Government*. Cambridge, MA: Harvard University Press.

Oosterbeek, H. 1997. Returns from Computer Use: A Simple Test on Productivity Interpretations. *Economic Review* 55:273–277.

Orfield, G., and C. Lee. 2005. *Why Segregation Matters: Poverty and Educational Inequality*. Cambridge, MA: Civil Rights Project, Harvard University. Available at ⟨http://www.civilrightsproject.harvard.edu⟩ (accessed August 10, 2005).

Organization for Economic Cooperation and Development (OECD). 2003. Seizing the Benefits of ICT in a Digital Economy: Meeting of the OECD Council at Ministerial Level 2003. Available at ⟨http://www.eldis.org/static/DOC12670.htm⟩ (accessed February 15, 2007).

Organization for Economic Cooperation and Development (OECD). 2004. The Development of Broadband Access in Rural and Remote Areas. Working Party on Telecommunication and Information Services Policies. Available at ⟨http://www.oecd.or/document/43/0,2340,en_2649_34225_31718315_1_1_1_1,00.html⟩ (accessed December 7, 2006).

Organization for Economic Cooperation and Development (OECD). 2005a. OECD Broadband Statistics, June 2005. Available at ⟨http://www.oecd.org/document/16/0,2340,en_2649_34225_35526608_1_1_1_1,00.html⟩ (accessed March 10, 2006).

Organization for Economic Cooperation and Development (OECD). 2005b. OECD Science, Technology, and Industry Scoreboard 2005: Briefing Note for the United States. Available at ⟨http://www.oecd.org/sti/scoreboard⟩ (accessed February 15, 2007).

Page, B. 1996. *Who Deliberates? Mass Media in Modern Democracy*. Chicago: University of Chicago Press.

Peris, R., M. A. Gimeno, D. Pinazo, G. Ortet, V. Carrero, M. Sanchiz, and I. Ibanez. 2002. Online Chat Rooms: Virtual Spaces of Interaction for Socially Oriented People. *CyberPsychology and Behavior* 5 (1): 43–51.

Pew Internet and American Life Project. 2006. February–April 2006 Data for Internet Usage over Time. Available at ⟨http://pewinternet.org/trends/UsageOverTime.xls⟩ (accessed February 16, 2007).

Pew Research Center for the People and the Press. 1998. Internet Takes off: Biennial News Consumption Survey. Available at ⟨http://www.people-press.org/med98rpt.htm⟩ (accessed December 7, 2006).

Pew Research Center for the People and the Press. 2004a. Cable and Internet Loom Large in Fragmented Political News Universe. January 11. Available at ⟨http://www.people-press.org⟩ (accessed December 7, 2006).

Pew Research Center for the People and the Press. 2004b. News Audiences Increasingly Politicized: Online News Audiences Larger, More Diverse. June 8. Available at ⟨http://www.people-press.org⟩ (accessed December 7, 2006).

Piven, F. F., and R. A. Cloward. 1988. *Why Americans Don't Vote*. New York: Pantheon.

Popkin, S. 1991. *The Reasoning Voter*. Chicago: University of Chicago Press.

Price, V., and J. N. Cappella. 2001. Online Deliberation and Its Influence: The Electronic Dialogue Project in Campaign 2000. Paper presented at the annual meeting of the American Association of Public Opinion Researcher, Montreal.

Price, V., and J. Zaller. 1993. Who Gets the News? Alternative Measures of News Reception and Their Implications for Research. *Public Opinion Quarterly* 57:133–164.

Prieger, J. E. 2003. The Supply Side of the Digital Divide: Is There Equal Availability in the Broadband Internet Access Market? *Economic Inquiry* 41 (2): 346–363.

Prime Minister's Strategy Unit and Department of Trade and Industry. 2005. Connecting the UK: The Digital Strategy. March 2005. London: Cabinet Office. Available at ⟨http://www.strategy.gov.uk⟩ (accessed March 26, 2006).

Progressive Policy Institute. 2002. State New Economy Index. Available at ⟨http://www.neweconomyindex.org/states/2002/index.html⟩ (accessed February 16, 2007).

Putnam, R. 2000. *Bowling Alone: The Collapse and Revival of American Community*. New York: Simon and Schuster.

Rae, D., D. Yates, J. Hochschild, J. Morone, and C. Fessler. 1981. *Equalities*. Cambridge, MA: Harvard University Press.

Rainie, L. 2005. Shifting Worlds. October 24. Pew Internet and American Life Project. Available at ⟨http://www.pewinternet.org/207.21.232.103/PPF/r/47/presentation_display.asp⟩ (accessed March 15, 2006).

Rappoport, P. N., D. J. Kridel, and L. D. Taylor. 2002. The Demand for Broadband: Access, Content, and the Value of Time. In *Broadband: Should We Regulate High-Speed Internet Access?* ed. R. W. Crandall and J. H. Alleman, 57–82. Washington, DC: AEI-Brookings Joint Center for Regulatory Studies.

Rawls, J. 1971. *A Theory of Justice*. Cambridge, MA: Belknap Press.

Reams, M. A., and B. H. Ray. 1993. The Effects of Three Prompting Methods on Recycling Participation Rates: A Field Study. *Journal of Environmental Systems* 22 (4): 371–379.

Reilly, K. T. 1995. Human Capital and Information: Employer Size-Wage Effect. *Journal of Human Resources* 30 (1): 1–18.

Rheingold, H. 2000. *The Virtual Community: Homesteading on the Electronic Frontier*. Cambridge, MA: MIT Press.

Riva, G., and C. Galimberti. 1998. Interbrain Frame: Interaction and Cognation in Computer-Mediated Communication. *CyberPsychology and Behavior* 1:295–309.

Robinson, M. J. 1976. Public Affairs Television and the Growth of Political Malaise. *American Political Science Review* 70:409–432.

Rosenstone, S. J., and M. Hansen. 1993. *Mobilization, Participation, and Democracy in America*. New York: Macmillan.

Schattschneider, E. E. 1960. *The Semisovereign People*. New York: Holt, Rinehart and Winston.

Sen, A. 1993. Capability and Well-Being. In *The Quality of Life*, ed. M. Nussbaum and A. Sen, 30–53. Oxford: Clarendon Press.

Shah, D., N. Kwak, and R. Holbert. 2001. "Connecting" and "Disconnecting" with Civic Life: Patterns of Internet Use and the Production of Social Capital. *Political Communication* 18:141–162.

Skocpol, T. 1992. *Protecting Soldiers and Mothers: The Political Origins of Social Policy in the United States*. Cambridge, MA: Belknap Press.

Smeeding, T. M., and L. Rainwater. 2001. *Comparing Living Standards across Nations: Real Income at the Top, Bottom, and in the Middle*. Luxembourg Income Studies Series No. 266. Available at ⟨http://www.lisproject.org/publications/liswps/266.pdf⟩ (accessed February 16, 2007).

Smith, D., and C. Tolbert. 2004. *Educated by Initiative: The Effects of Direct Democracy on Citizens and Political Organizations in the American States*. Ann Arbor: University of Michigan Press.

Smith, E. 1989. *The Unchanging American Voter*. Berkeley: University of California Press.

Smith, M. 2002. Ballot Initiatives and the Democratic Citizen. *Journal of Politics* 64:892–903.

Smith, R. M. 1993. Beyond Tocqueville, Myrdal, and Hartz: The Multiple Traditions in America. *American Political Science Review* 87 (3): 549–566.

Sniderman, P., R. Brody, and P. Tetlock. 1991. *Reasoning and Choice: Explorations in Political Psychology*. New York: Cambridge University Press.

Sommers, P., and D. Carlson. 2003. What the Information Technology Revolution Means for Regional Economic Development. A discussion paper prepared for the Brookings Institution Center on Urban and Metropolitan Policy. February. Washington, DC: Brookings Institution. Available at ⟨http://www.brookings.edu/es/urban/publication/sommers.pdf⟩ (accessed March 25, 2006).

Spooner, T., and L. Rainie. 2000. African-Americans and the Internet. October 22. Available at ⟨http://www.pewinternet.org/reports_archive.asp⟩ (accessed December 7, 2006).

Sproul, L., and S. Kiesler. 1991. *Connections: New Ways of Working in the Networked Organization.* Cambridge, MA: MIT Press.

Stack, C. B. 1974. *All Our Kin: Strategies for Survival in a Black Community.* New York: Harper and Row.

Stanley, L. 2001. *Beyond Access.* Report from the UCSD Digital Divide Project University of California, San Diego: UCSD Civic Collaborative. Available at ⟨http://www.mediamanage.net/Beyond_Access.pdf⟩ (accessed February 16, 2007).

Stiroh, K. 2001. Investing in Information Technology: Productivity Payoffs for U.S. Industries. *Current Issues in Economics and Finance* 7 (6): 1–6. Available at ⟨http://www.newyorkfed.org/research/current_issues/ci7-6.pdf⟩ (accessed February 15, 2007).

Stone, D. 2002. *Policy Paradox: The Art of Political Decision Making.* New York: W. W. Norton.

Strategic Networks Group. 2003. Economic Impact Study of the South Dundas Township Fibre Network. Paper prepared for the Department of Trade and Industry, United Kingdom. Available at ⟨http://www.ta.doc.gov/reports/TechPolicy/Broadband_02921.pdf⟩ (accessed December 15, 2005).

Strover, S. 1999. Rural Internet Connectivity. Rural Policy Research Institute. Available at ⟨http://www.rupi.org/⟩ (accessed December 7, 2006).

Sunstein, C. 2001. Freedom of Expression in the United States: The Future. In *The Boundaries of Freedom of Expression and Order in American Democracy,* ed. T. Hensley, 391–448. Kent, OH: Kent State University Press.

Tan, A. S. 1980. Mass Media Use, Issue Knowledge, and Political Involvement. *Public Opinion Quarterly* 44:241–248.

Tanaka, G. Y. 2004. *Digital Deflation: The Productivity Revolution and How It Will Ignite the Economy.* New York: McGraw-Hill.

Tapia, A., M. Stone, and C. Maitland. 2005. Public-Private Partnerships and the Role of State and Federal Legislation in Wireless Municipal Networks. Paper presented at the Telecommunications Policy Research Conference, Arlington, VA. Available at ⟨http://www.tprc.org⟩ (accessed July 20, 2006).

Tapscott, D., D. Ticoll, and A. Lowy. 2000. *Digital Capital: Harnessing the Power of Business Webs.* Boston: Harvard Business School Press.

Tarde, G. 1899. *Opinion and Conversation.* Unpublished translation of "L'opinion et la conversation," in G. Tarde, *L'opinion et la foule.* Repr., Paris: Presses Universitaires de France, 1989.

Teixeira, R. 1992. *The Disappearing American Voter.* Washington, DC: Brookings Institution Press.

Telecommunications Industry Association. 2003. The Economic and Social Benefits of Broadband Deployment. Available at ⟨http://www.tiaonline.org⟩ (accessed July 21, 2004).

Thomas, J., and G. Streib. 2003. The New Face of Government: Citizen-Initiated Contacts in the Era of E-government. *Journal of Public Administration Research and Theory* 13 (1): 83–102.

Thompson, N. 2002. How the Internet Is Really, Truly—Seriously!—Going to Change Elections. *Washington Monthly* (May). Available at ⟨http://www.washingtonmonthly.com/features/2001/0205.thompson.html⟩ (accessed December 7, 2006).

Tocqueville, A. d. 1835. *Democracy in America*. In *Political Thought in America: An Anthology*, ed. M. B. Levy. 2nd ed. Chicago: Dorsey Press, 1988.

Tolbert, C., and R. McNeal. 2003. Unraveling the Effects of the Internet on Political Participation. *Political Research Quarterly* 56 (2): 175–185.

Tolbert, C. J., R. S. McNeal, and D. A. Smith. 2003. Enhancing Civic Engagement: The Effects of Direct Democracy on Political Participation and Knowledge. *State Politics and Policy Quarterly* 3 (1): 23–41.

Tolbert, C., and K. Mossberger. 2006. The Effects of E-government on Trust and Confidence in Government. *Public Administration Review* 66 (3): 354–369.

Trotter, A. 2001. Closing the Digital Divide. *Education Week on the Web*. Available at ⟨http://www.edweek.org/sreports/tc01article.cfm?slug=35solutions.h20⟩ (accessed December 7, 2006).

U.S. Department of Commerce. n.d. E-Commerce Tool Box. Available at ⟨http://www.export.gov/sellingonline/whatisecommerce.asp⟩ (accessed February 16, 2007).

U.S. Department of Commerce. 2007. *U.S. Census Bureau News*. Quarterly Retail E-Commerce Sales, 4th Quarter 2006. Available at ⟨http://www.census.gov/mrts/www/data/pdf/06Q4.pdf⟩ (accessed February 16, 2007).

U.S. Department of Commerce, National Telecommunications and Information Administration. 1995. *Falling through the Net: A Survey of the "Have Nots" in Rural and Urban America*. Available at ⟨http://www.ntia.doc.gov/ntiahome/fallingthru.html⟩ (accessed December 7, 2006).

U.S. Department of Commerce, National Telecommunications and Information Administration. 1998. *Falling through the Net II: New Data on the Digital Divide*. Available at ⟨http://www.ntia.doc.gov/ntiahome/net2falling.html⟩ (accessed February 16, 2007).

U.S. Department of Commerce, National Telecommunications and Information Administration. 1999. *Falling through the Net: Defining the Digital Divide*. Available at ⟨http://www.ntia.doc.gov/ntiahome/fttn99/FTTN_I-1.html⟩ (accessed February 16, 2007).

U.S. Department of Commerce, National Telecommunications and Information Administration. 2002. *A Nation Online: How Americans Are Expanding Their Use of the Internet*. Available at ⟨http://www.ntia.doc.gov/ntiahome/dn/anationonline2.pdf/⟩ (accessed December 7, 2006).

U.S. Department of Commerce, National Telecommunications and Information Administration, and Economics and Statistics Administration. 2004. *A Nation Online: Entering the Broadband Age*. Available at ⟨http://www.ntia.doc.gov/reports/anol/NationOnlineBroadband04.htm⟩ (accessed February 26, 2005).

Uslander, E. 2004. Trust, Civic Engagement, and the Internet. *Political Communications* 21 (2): 223–242.

Van Dijk, Jan A. G. M. 2005. *The Deepening Divide: Inequality in the Information Society*. London: Sage Publications.

Verba, S., K. Schlozman, and H. Brady. 1995. *Voice and Equality: Civic Voluntarism in American Politics*. Cambridge, MA: Harvard University Press.

Von Hipple, E. 2005. *Democratizing Innovation*. Cambridge, MA: MIT Press.

Walsh, E. O. 2001. The Truth about the Digital Divide. In *The Digital Divide: Facing a Crisis or Creating a Myth?* ed. B. M. Compaine, 279–284. Cambridge, MA: MIT Press.

Warschauer, M. 2003. *Technology and Social Inclusion: Rethinking the Digital Divide*. Cambridge, MA: MIT Press.

Weaver, D. H. 1996. What Voters Learn from Media. *Annual of the AAPSS* (July): 34–47.

Weaver, D. H., and D. Drew. 1993. Voter Learning in the 1990 Off-Year Election: Did the Media Matter? *Journalism Quarterly* 70:356–368.

Welch, E. W., C. Hinnant, and M. J. Moon. 2005. Linking Citizen Satisfaction with E-government with Trust in Government. *Journal of Public Administration Research and Theory* 15 (1): 271–291.

Welfens, P., and A. Jungmittag. 2003. Telecommunications, Internet, Innovation, and Growth in Europe. In *Internet, Economic Growth, and Globalization*, ed. C. E. Barfield, G. Heiduk, and P. J. J. Welfens, 9–65. Berlin: Springer-Verlag.

Wellman, B. 2001. Physical Place and Cyberplace: Changing Portals and the Rise of Networked Individualism. *International Journal of Regional Research* 25 (2): 227–252.

Wentling, T., C. Waight, and R. King. 2002. The Foundation of HRD in a Networked World. In *Human Resource Development and Information Technology: Making Global Connections*, ed. C. M. Sleezer, T. L. Wentling, and R. L. Cude, 1–20. Boston: Kluwer Academic Publishers.

West, D. M. 2004. E-government and the Transformation of Service Delivery and Citizen Attitudes. *Public Administration Review* 64 (1): 15–27.

West, D. M. 2005. *Digital Government: Technology and Public Sector Performance*. Princeton, NJ: Princeton University Press.

Wolfinger, R., and S. J. Rosenstone. 1980. *Who Votes?* New Haven, CT: Yale University Press.

Yankee Group. 2001. The Collaborative Commerce Value Statement: A $223 Billion Cost Savings Opportunity over Six Years. *Module B-to-B Commerce and Applications* 6 (6).

Index